SACRED COSMIC MARRIAGE
Revealing Sacred Scientific Knowledge
Of the
Egyptian Mystery School Teachings
Written By
Willy Gaspar

ADAM & EVA
Publishing
Holman, N.M.

Sacred Cosmic Marriage

Published in the year 2006 in the United States by

ADAM & EVA Publishing
P.O. Box 241, Holman, N.M. 87723

Visit our website at **www.celestialclock.com**
Or email us at celclock@swpc.net

Library of Congress Cataloging– in –Publication Data
Gaspar , W.A. , 1957 –
Sacred Cosmic Marriage

p. cm.
Includes bibliographical references and index.
ISBN 0-9678936-1-5

Printed in the United States of America

Previous work from this same author: 'The Celestial Clock' ISBN 0967893607

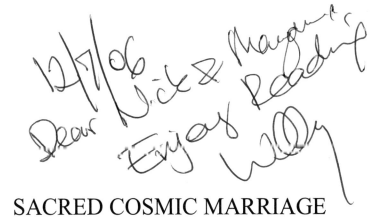

SACRED COSMIC MARRIAGE

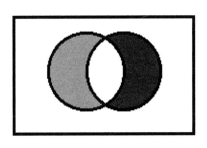

" For My Family , Eva , Rubina , and Austin,

Whose Love Helped Me Be Inspired...

And Also,

For All My Relations...

Past , Present , and Future . "

CONTENTS

Introduction

The Sacred Cosmic Marriage ceremony of the Egyptians was one of their most ancient and revered celebrations. The living and ruling Pharaoh and his Queen were active participants in this Mardi gras like festivity. What was so important about this 'cosmic union' that peaked the interest of the well-educated and enigmatic order of the Egyptian Ra Priests? Did the secret of the Cosmic Marriage reach the early Europeans? Is there evidence that its astronomical meaning is deposited in the Holy Books of seemingly unrelated cultures? And if it was such an important concept in the religious lives of so many different nations that what is the incredible scientific knowledge that was hidden behind the soap opera like depictions of these old tales?

Is it possible that the Ancients recorded down the last major cosmic disaster that happened to human kind as a kingly marriage and the subsequent birth of the 'divine Child'? Why the highly educated scientific minded Ra Priests of Egypt decided to present their 'gods' as having human bodies and animal heads? Was there a specific reason behind that? If those Ra Priests were so intelligent then their message had to be easily decipherable and scientifically universal comparative ideas. What did those Ancients know that needed to be carved thousands of times on the walls of the tombs of those huge pyramids? Was the intended message about superstitious religious beliefs or did it contain superb 'cosmic' secrets as the word in the sacred marriage ceremony suggests? Well, the latter is what I shall demonstrate. One might ask why is it important for our times all of a sudden? Well, the birth of the Prince, the Son of the Sun hides very important scientific concepts for our era. The Sun is acting up lately out of its season. In the years of a sunspot minimum the Sun is behaving as if it was in a worst solar maximum.

As we examine the Egyptian legends and the closely related Babylonian, Hindu, Greco-Roman and Biblical tales we shall uncover unified scientific secrets behind seemingly innocent animal symbols, such as the golden-colored Easter chick, the Owl, and the Stork who brings the 'Baby'. The astronomical tales of the Crab, Dragon, Jackal, Chariot of the Sun, Bee Hive, Wild Donkey and the She-Goat will reveal a perfect tale of an ancient cosmic tragedy that soon will repeat itself in our age.

Therefore, one might ask –Why would it be important for anyone to know about some oblivious superstitious Egyptian ceremony in today's advanced western society? The answer is that the carefully manufactured scientific messages contained in those ancient legends were specifically intended and targeted for our changing modern times. I am hoping by my work to enrich our understanding of the scientific knowledge base the Semitic Ra Priests of Egypt possessed and transmitted to us in innocent appearing geometric and animal hieroglyphs. The astronomical secrets of the Holy Grail, the meaning of the medieval War of the Roses and thus, the 'Rose Line' enigma of Dan Brown's book titled The Da Vinci Code shall be revealed. All previous historical explanations to these age-old enigmas will be useless after we learn the Universal Cosmic Truths about these tales. The face and the mouth of God along with the Evil Serpent will be explained.

I can promise you this much. No membership of any science club or secret organizations will teach you about ancient enigmas as much as you may learn from this book. Enjoy the reading!

Willy Gaspar
December 2005
Chacon, N.M.

Chapter 1.
The Egyptian Legacy.

The ancient and mysterious Egyptians who erected the Great Pyramids of Giza several thousands of years ago undoubtedly possessed high level of technological skills and they were superb scientists. After the Deluge and the sinking of the continent of Atlantis and the destruction of their advanced civilization they had to understand that science would be ignored for thousands of years. Therefore, the mainly Semitic Priesthood of Ra had to develop a simple system to preserve their advanced scientific knowledge for future generations. It required a common sense universality to be understood by the scientists of today and it also had to display the unreal aspects, such as animal headed human gods. This is to bluntly imply that the tales are not real or even historical, not about people, animals or gods. The very carefully chosen animal characters represented unique scientific concepts each animal would stand for and nothing else. I can promise you that after reading this work you may pick up any sacred book and be able to understand and interpret the scientific meanings behind the clever animal symbols and the astronomical tales.

For example, on the coming pages we will decipher the cosmic meaning for the name of **the well-known biblical pharaoh, 'Ramsess'.** Interpreting the hieroglyphic pictures behind the **name translates to 'Ra, the Sun gave birth to Him'.** Just wait until we find out who is this mysterious pharaoh king and why a male entity gave birth to another male offspring without a female involvement. This **'virgin birth'** is an important aspect of world mythology. Later we will also learn about what crucial function the old king and the harlot represent? Equally interesting will be to know what purpose the young prince and the virgin mother was supposed to accomplish in the name of cosmic science?

Before we unravel that enigma, let me begin with the simple concept of the horns of the **'ram'** or the **'lamb'.** The spiral animal horns of the ram secretly represent the unseen creative **spiral electro-magnetic forces** governing our galaxy. Some would argue that the 'ram' represented the 'soul' of the deity, but it is not contradictory to what I state. The word 'SPIR-it' spells with the same four first letters as what constitutes 'SPIR-al', thus our everlasting spirit is derived from the indestructible spiral origin of the electro-magnetic forces. I shall clearly demonstrate that scientifically in Chapter 4. **Creation works as a spiral that breaks into five parts (4+1).** That is most easily visualized as our four fingers and a thumb. **Both the human heartbeat and earth's heartbeat display that same graphic pattern, four small waves and a beat.** (See Figures 4-9 and 4-10) We do live in a spiral galaxy and according to the 12th century's Christian monk, Fibonacci - everything seems to be growing and happily reproducing in a spiral fashion. Even our critically important 'Tree- North Pole' progressively tilts due to the spiral movement of the Chandler Wobble. Spiral forces control most everything.

The main **Egyptian god Amun** is commonly shown as **ram-headed**. The Son of God, Jesus is said to be the **'Lamb of God'.** The Roman Catholic Pope carries a ceremonial shepherd's crook that ends in a spiral. The Jewish Rabbi blowing into the ram horn during religious festivities similarly means that the sacred music of the spheres is spiral in nature. Even the ancient Greco-Roman philosophers including **Pythagoras** were the followers of the **Orphean mysteries. The Golden Fleece of the Ram and the Lyre of Orpheus** was part of their secrets. The magical 'harp' is the only musical instrument in the sky amongst 88 constellations. It will be revealed that the director of the harmonic cosmic source of this sacred tune is the Black Hole of the Galactic Center. This one 'eye' of our hundred-eyed god controls the movement of the stars. In Native lore He is probably our Grandfather. But who is the Father and Son? Are they the Sun king and his erupted Son?

4

FIGURE 1-1: The Horns of the Ram is Spiral Force
(Used by the permission of the Trustees of the
University Museum, Philadelphia, Pennsylvania)

The priceless Babylonian Ram statue shown in Figure 1-1 was
unearthed from the King's Chamber of a Babylonian Temple.
The Ram stands by the Sacred Tree (Earth's Axis) with flowers.
These flowers demonstrate 'eight' petals, an important reference
to the **eight years of the path of the planet Venus**. As we will
learn later, the Venus Calendar is an important secret of the ages.

This Ram is wearing eagle or hawk feathers. This is a very important clue. The falcon / hawk / eagle are all majestic birds that can provide a common imagery to mythology. The star Vega – that is part of the Lyre /Harp constellation of Magnetic North - in the Arabic astronomy is called the **'swooping hawk / eagle'.** The dare devilish diving down action of a hunting hawk / eagle eloquently represents a sudden axis shift or a downwardly motion. In the astronomical sense this animal trait mimicked the **axis shift** of the Magnetic North. This 'swooping hawk / eagle' star Vega marks **the Solar Apex and the Magnetic North.** Now it starts making sense why the Egyptian Horus, Falcon-headed god carried a Sun on his head. For the religiously minded readers, this concept is hidden in Chapter 9 of the biblical Book of Job following the declaration that; ... **'He (the Lord) made the <u>Bear, Orion and the Pleiades</u> and the <u>chambers of the south</u>'** and then a few paragraphs later mentions the **<u>swooping eagle.</u>** These three constellations tell us about an important ancient disaster. Amongst them, initially Orion is the less obvious as far as an exact cosmic scientific meaning is concerned. This is how Prof. Barbara S. Lesko in her book titled 'The Great Goddesses of Egypt' writes about the god Osiris and the above Orion:

> "I have pointed out that probably very early, in the predynastic period, a segment of the population was engaged in closely watching the heavens. Orion was seen to disappear (or die) for a time and then reappear (or be resurrected). Whether this gave rise to the myth of **Osiris** being **killed by Seth** or whether the myth predated and was affixed to the recognition of the celestial activities we cannot know. Egypt ended up with two Osirises: the god of vegetation (resurrected after the dry season by the receding waters of the Nile) and the sky god, identified with **Orion** and part of a more elaborate "sky religion". As Osiris was believed to be the father of the reigning king, identified with **Horus**, this placed the goal of the deceased in the heavens as well."

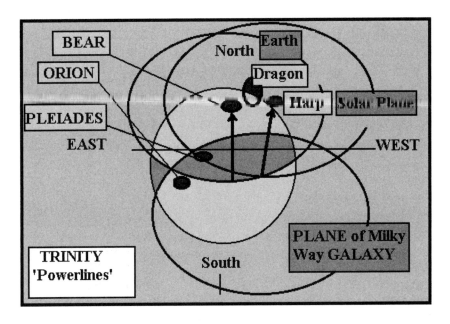

FIGURE 1-1a: Trinity Power Lines

Figure 1-1a is depicting the Egyptian 'secret fish' that is also **the biblical 'Fish'.** This 'Fish' is transposed on the Sun by the **three 'equatorial' planes; the Galactic, Solar and Earth lines**. The East and West are reversed on the Sun. One can observe on it the **Bear, Orion and the Pleiades from 'the Book of Job'** along with the **Dragon and the Harp**. This enigmatic quote about the 'Bear, Orion, and Pleiades' is found three times in the Bible. The blind religious scholars currently translate the animal symbols as a designation for a country. They take the Dragon as a symbol of China in a Third World War scenario. Why China, why not the UK since the patron saint of England is Saint George who slays the Dragon? The answer is that none of these animals symbolize a country. Once someone is made familiar with Cosmic, Solar, and Earth mechanics in the context of current astronomy it will become easy to decipher the secrets of these animal symbols.

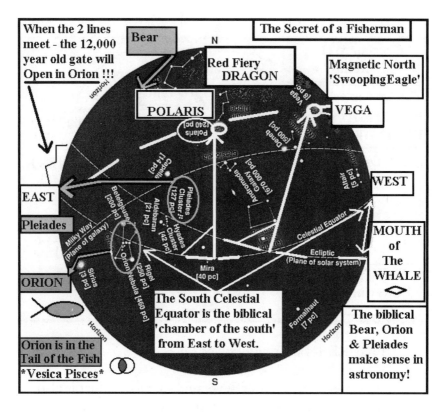

FIGURE 1-1b. The Bear, Orion and Pleiades in Astronomy
(Modified from *Astronomy*, 5th. Edition by Hartman / Impey)

East and West are appropriately reversed on this Sun shaped celestial map of Figure 1-1b. The **Bear** stands for **Polaris**, the north axis and was designated the **Upper Kingdom.** It became associated with the **'south'**. This was for two main reasons. First, East and West were marked by the Sun's path and North was defined by Magnetic North, thus seemingly the Polar North received the designation of 'south'. The reason was that the 'hawk' swoops toward south when the Magnetic North shifts.

> "26 'Does the **hawk fly by your wisdom**, and spread
> its wings **toward the south?"** (Author's heavyset)
> (Bible, Book of Job, Chapter 39, Vs.26)

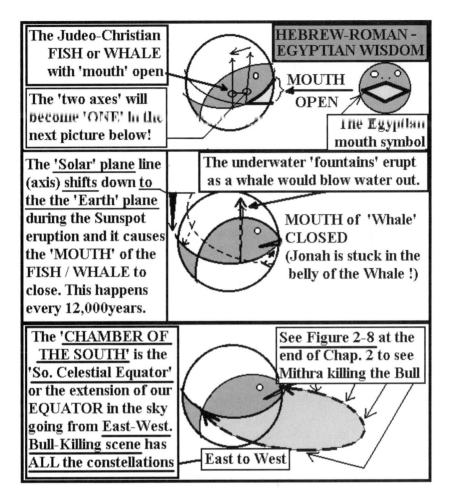

FIGURE 1-1c: The Fish, Whale and the Chamber of the South

The Solar Plane moves to the Earth Equatorial Plane by the shifting action of Vega, the 'Swooping Eagle/Hawk' dives down and closes the 'mouth' of the 'Fish / Whale', thereby closing the 'Celestial Womb' and tying the 'Vulva' shut. Ankh!!! When the **Magnetic North** shifted toward the **Polar North - the 'Two Kingdoms of Egypt united'.** This war and then the 'unification' are present in several religious tales, none of which is historical!

The Polar North was the **'Upper' Kingdom** since it was on the **surface of Earth and it bore the white color of snow**. The **deep Core** of the Earth was designated by the **'Lower Kingdom'** and was represented by the **red color** of lava and a **Magnetic North**. This is shown in details in Figure 4-3. The constellation **Orion** is the 'crossroads' **where the three celestial 'power lines' meet.** These three lines are the **Galactic, Solar and Earth celestial planes**. Thus, few pages from here the **'mesi'**- (ah) hieroglyphic sign will tell us about a sacred cosmic birth. That is why the old Egyptians tied the constellation Orion to Osiris and to the concept of 'rebirth'. It was a cosmic rebirth every 12,000years. The **Pleiades** marked the **East direction where the Sun rises and erupts from!** The educated Semitic Ra Priesthood was certainly not just amazed by the daily rising of the Sun, rather they were interested ONLY in **ONE DAY** out of the about 4,234,000days in 11,600years when the Sun rose. Biblically, it was the **DAY OF THE LORD, when 'the Lord sent fire from Heaven'**. On this day Prometheus also stole the fire from the gods for mankind. Following that ancient Sunspot eruption that scorched the Earth, the axis shifted and the Sun was 'risen twice' and it 'born again'. I will demonstrate that from the Hindu Myths later in this book.

The polar 'Bear' was chosen because it could climb the 'sacred tree / earth axis', but was there any 'bee hives' with bees and honey on top of that magical tree? We will know by the end. The Seven Sisters of the Pleiades marked the East direction of the Sun – the mythological **'shoulder blade'** of the Bull. In the **Mithraic bull-killing scene** at the end of Chapter 2 in Figure 2-8 one can see that the group of constellations **define the South Celestial Equator.** Therefore, the sacred Latino and biblical ritual of the Bull Sacrifice represents the South Celestial Equatorial Plane. This celestial secret of the Mithraic Bull-killing statue of the pre-Christian Rome explains why successive Catholic Popes kept that non-Christian and seemingly brutal depiction of a bull sacrifice in the basement of St. Clemens Church in the Holy Vatican City.

In my previous book, 'The Celestial Clock' I spend a whole chapter on this concept. In the bull-killing scene, the animal constellations that sit on the south celestial equator are all present. These are the **Scorpio, Raven, Grail, Hydra the Water Serpent and the Bull.** Figure 2-8 depicts those constellations.

Revisiting the concept of the harp, let me demonstrate with a Bible quote the fact that the sacred celestial 'Harp' (Magnetic North – Earth Core) is implying a connection to the mysterious 'voice of god' (resonation) and the subsequent Flood of Noah:

> "2 And I heard a **voice from heaven**, like the **voice of many waters**, and like the voice of loud thunder. And I **heard the sound of harpists** playing their harps.
> (Bible, Revelation, Chapter 14)

Also, the source of the 'Fire' is clearly given as the 'Sun':

> "8 Then the **fourth angel poured out his bowl on the sun**, and power was given to him **to scorch men with fire**." (Bible, Revelation, Chapter 16)

Hopefully, now we start grasping the cosmic secrets behind the seemingly animalist and superstitious sounding depictions of the Ancients. By using these timeless animal symbols of astronomy I will explain how the Black Hole from the Galactic Center exerts a controlling force on our tiny planet Earth. These few stars and constellations along with the planets will be extremely important in our developing cosmic story. The biblical Bear is the magical **polar bear (Polaris-North Pole)** sitting on top of a mythological **sacred tree -earth's polar axis- that is also the Tree of Life.** This polar region is where the Christmas tree grows, that is why old Santa took up residence there. In some secret scientifically spiritual ways - believing in old Santa Claus may be a rewarding endeavor after all. Then the magic Lyre of Orpheus tells about the harmony and the occasional periodic disharmony of the sky.

Sacred Cosmic Marriage

When the major super wave explosion from the powerful Galactic Center's Black Hole erupts, in turn causing the Sun to blow, it is the **Magnetic North** – represented by the '**Harp**'- that **tilts and begins the demonic angelic music** of the spheres.

The beautifully carved bull-headed harp from the Babylonian Temple is shown with the Bear and other astronomical animal symbols (See Figure 4-7). In Chapter 4 we will analyze that prize Babylonian Harp, which was unearthed by a pioneer American archeologist from the King's Chamber in the 1800's and is now kept at the University Museum in Pennsylvania. This 4,600year old piece shown in Art History texts - alone tells volumes about cosmic order and the timing of the switches in astronomy. Just as the '**shooting of an arrow' resonates**, similarly the '**vocal cord of God'**, the '**cords' of the harp** or any **stringed instruments** give out **sound by resonation.** This Galactic Center-Sun eruption concept was utilized by the old bards to equate the striking of the cord to the resonating word coming from the mouth of god. The striking of the cord and the subsequent playing of the music of the gods or the flying arrow symbolized this natural disaster. This harp of mythology is called 'Benet' in the Egyptian hieroglyphic language (Figure 4-8). This classic angelic lyre-harp of the Egyptian and Greco-Roman goddesses shines above the constellation Hercules - exactly to the Magnetic North – defining the heat generating iron 'Core' of the Earth. The bowstring tied to the fire of Doomsday is demonstrated in the Hindu Myths:

"For the lord Rudra is <u>Time and Death,</u> and the <u>year is his bow,</u> and therefore the **<u>Night of Doomsday</u>** for men was **<u>made the unwithering string of that bow</u>**. ... The lord cast onto that arrow his unbearable, sharp anger, **the fire of** anger, born of the anger of Bhrgu and Angiras, which is very hard to bear. The red and blue one, the smoky one, the Wearer of Skins, the Terrifier blazed forth enveloped in **flames of energy like ten thousand suns.**"
(Author's heavyset, underlining) (Hindu Myths, pg.133)

12

Returning to Egyptian disasters, we learn about the death of Osiris from the Egyptian Pyramid Texts of the Old Kingdom, although the complete version of the myth is contained in the writings of the second-century Greek writer, Plutarch. In the ancient Legend of Osiris - talking about the first pharaoh King of Egypt, who married his sister, the goddess Isis - we learn about the chief features of the Egyptian religion.

There were **five special days** in the year of the Egyptians and the Mayans when the main gods were born. Adding these five days to the 360 degrees of the circle made up the simplified solar year of 365 days. The Mayans recognized these five unlucky days in early August when the hurricane season is in full force. On these same five 'unlucky' days the gods were born in Egypt. Osiris was born on the first day, Horus on the second, Set on the third, Isis on the fourth, and Nephthys ('Hathor') on the fifth day. Osiris was the Lord of Creation. He devoted his time to civilize different nations. While he was gone from home, his wife Isis ruled the kingdom with great pride. Then evil Set (Seth/Typhon) who is the brother of Osiris was overcome with malice and envy. He was jealous of his brother's popularity and started plotting against him with seventy-two of his comrades. Set decided to kill Osiris, his brother to take his place as king.

The evil brother needed a plan to murder Osiris and to be able to unseat him on the throne. Set secretly obtained the exact measurements of the body of his brother and resolved to make a fair chest, a funerary sarcophagus. It would be tailored exactly to the body size of Osiris. When that royal coffin was completed he promised the beautifully carved and painted chest as a gift to the person who would exactly fit this 'divine' sarcophagus. Several adventurous souls attempted to win the prize to no avail by trying to fit their differing sized bodies into that enigmatic and specifically manufactured sacred coffin. Nobody matched that special chest since it was strictly made for Osiris.

Finally, Set was able to convince Osiris, his brother to try to fit into the sacred chest. These things happened on the seventeenth day of the month of Hathor, the first month of the Egyptian Year. Furthermore, this occurred in the 28th year of his age or reign. Trying out the coffin seemed as an innocent joke between the two brothers, so Osiris unsuspectedly climbed into the sarcophagus that was manufactured to house his body. Not sooner he perfectly filled the box with his body, Set jumped over and shut the top of the coffin and closed it tight, so Osiris could not get out. The evil one was satisfied that his brother is buried alive thus he rushed the coffin to the Nile and thrown it into the waters of the river.

Isis, the faithful wife who was determined to find the body of Osiris was also aided by Anubis, the Jackal / Dog deity. The two retrieved the body of Osiris, which floated ashore near the sacred town of **Byblos** (Biblia / Bible). A magical **tamarisk tree** sprung out of his body to protect him. As Isis succeeded recovering her find, she managed to conceal the body of Osiris in the depth of the forest. The evil brother Set received news of the location and rushed there to find the body of his slain brother Osiris, which now he proceeded to cut into fourteen pieces and scattered the body parts all over Egypt so the goddess would not been able to recover it. But Isis, being the loving and devoted wife went on a mad search and found thirteen out of the fourteen pieces of her husband's body. A fish apparently consumed the last piece that was Osiris penis, thus Isis had to replace it by a piece of wood. She was still able to get pregnant from the stiff corpse of the resurrected Osiris and had her son **Horus**, the young prince, the God of Time (**'Heru / Hora / Hour'**) who helped her revenge the great King's death, just as it happened with **Odyssey**. In loose comparison - in Greek mythology, it is **Saturn** who overtakes **Jupiter** and castrates **Ouranus**. Reading the story of Isis and Osiris from Plutarch, one can conclude that the Greco-Roman mythology is closely tied and may be even derived from the Egyptian and Hindu tales, which are clearly cosmic events.

The intense interest **Plutarch, Plato** and others showed in the Egyptian myths, astronomy and the **Precession of Equinoxes** are proof that these early scientists understood that these stories were about cosmic tragedy and a **sky calendar to record the events.**

Continuing on with our Isis and Osiris story, according to the Greek sources, after Isis buried the body of Osiris near **Philae** a tomb was erected in his honor. You may have already noticed that our Freemasonic Founding Fathers carefully named some of our American cities with Egyptian and Greek names in honor of these ancient cosmic tales to turn our attention to the old wisdom buried in the myths of these heroes. Some of these old cities are **Philadelphia, Memphis, Alexandria** and others.

I will demonstrate how this vast amount of cosmic scientific knowledge was cleverly preserved and transmitted to us through simple **hieroglyphic pictures** in a very effective common sense way. This **visual method** allowed the common concepts to still remain unaltered while the lost unknown science was kept a deep secret in full sight from both initiated and uninitiated. The great difference between the two groups – initiated and uninitiated - was merely a question of the spiritual openness for carrying the keys that would open the gates of 'illumination' in the distant future. Here I have to emphasize that when I say 'I would like to see more light' or simply want more '**illumination**' - I do not only mean **spiritual open-mindedness.** I also imply that I need to know the secret of this **'huge bright light'** connected to the immense flare of that ancient **sunspot eruption!** Even for the initiates, these secret doors were distantly positioned thousands of years away at the end of an era when science reached the level of comprehension. Only the recent emergence of our space age scientific knowledge sheds light onto **the genius of the Ra Priesthood of ancient Egypt.** The simple enigmatic knowledge that is hidden in those hieroglyphic pictures is much more advanced than what we were prepared to believe until recently.

The chants and hymns they recited suggest a spiritual openness to the possibility of communications with the other side. The utilization of magical spells and elaborate rituals to influence the decisions of the gods were seemingly common practice amongst the Ancients. They left behind a large volume of hieroglyphs on the walls of those enormous size tombs and pyramids. Attempts at translating the messages became the basis of the **Egyptian Mystery School Teachings** and provided the foundation for the large volumes of Egyptian Hebrew Wisdom and also the widely available Judeo-Christian religious teachings. A discernable connection of the secret mythological arts of the Egyptians to the Greco-Romans, Babylonians, Hindus and even Native Aboriginal cultures throughout the different continents exists. Most of what is preserved in oral traditions and written down in the sacred books imply cosmic, astronomical and scientific knowledge.

This ancient way of picture art preserved old scientific wisdom that is currently falsely interpreted as mere historical tales. The message left for our generation is at least multi layered, but it is certainly not a depiction of idyllic country living with half human half animal genetic mistakes. It would be ludicrous to assume that simple shepherds 5,000years ago built these huge complex pyramids, which even by today's advanced technology would be a difficult undertaking. I am certain that the Egyptians did not erect those enormous sized structures to paint on them their simple way of life. To assemble a **very complex** tomb **to show a very simple** life would be a great **oxymoron.** It would not make any logical sense to create several thousands of stone structures and then carve millions of pictures inside and out to state; - *'Hey future scholars, we just wanted you to know that we are simple half-naked sheepherders and we harvest the wheat by hand, and we also wanted you to know that the people wearing hawk or dog heads were so ugly in real life that we could only depict them as half human half animal genetic rejects'.*

Understandably, it is difficult for most of us to assume that those ancient Egyptians were scientifically more advanced than we are today. So how did we solve the hieroglyphic alphabet?

The deciphering of the hieroglyphic pictures received an early boost with an important archeological find. The discovery of the **Rosetta stone** by the French military engineers, who were brought over by Napoleon Bonaparte's expedition in 1798, helped create a new enthusiasm about Egypt and the real alphabetic translation of those picture recordings. The Rosetta stone, which contained three different version of the same text written first in Egyptian Hieroglyphics, then Demotic cursive, and also in ancient Greek. This tri-language combination allowed a comparative deciphering of the picture writings. At least four prominent scientists and linguists began the tedious task of deciphering the enigma of the Rosetta stone. The English scientist, Dr. Thomas **Young** rightfully concluded that the symbols of the hieroglyphs conveyed a sense of the whole world, but he failed to recognize that the picture symbols also stood for letters. It was the young Frenchman linguist, Jean-Francois **Champollion** with a working knowledge of Hebrew, Greek, and Latin and later Coptic and Arabic who was able to lay the initial foundations for the **Egyptian Hieroglyphic Alphabet**. Historical sounding stories of ancient divine kings ruling a mysterious land emerged, although the names of the pharaoh kings and the major holidays seemed to carry distinctive cosmic significance.

The Egyptians seemed to have several major holidays and of one of the greatest celebrations amongst them was the **Sacred Cosmic Marriage** ceremony. Besides the carnival mood of singing, dancing and drinking on the streets, the celebrating crowd from the shores of the Nile had to tow the heavy boat of the goddess toward her fiancée. The boat **of Hathor (Het-heru) the goddess** of fertility and sexuality thus slowly progressed up the river Nile to her future **husband and lover Horus (Heru).**

What had to be the cosmic secret, which moved the masses of people to commit this physical sacrifice and make the festivities unravel in a very specific way?

The Temple of Hathor was located at Dendera where the festivities began in the **last week of July**, when the **Dog Star, Sirius** was **highest in the sky**. This was about two weeks before the **August New Moon.** The celebrations then shifted to the waterway of the Nile. Horus, the amorous god lived up stream on the river Nile. The goddess was transported there for the Cosmic Marriage Ceremony to begin. She traveled from her hometown of Dendera in a boat on the Nile going south against the current to reach his town. There in Edfu, the sacred couple spent two weeks honey mooning and love making starting from the New Moon until the Full Moon of the third summer month of the Egyptians. During the ceremonies **the living Pharaoh and his wife took the symbolic role for the god and the goddess.** The festivities also resembled a harvest celebration along with the marriage of the deities. It was **early time for the harvest** festivities in mid-August, but as our cosmic story unfolds, these hieroglyphic animals, tools, and offerings may provide the important pieces of information to the etiologies of these untimely harvest season. The most spectacular festivity in Hungary is also the Harvest Celebration and it is conventionally held on August 20th.

To visit **Horus**, her lover, the goddess **Hathor** had to be towed against the current in her golden vessel requiring a large number of her followers to lend some muscles to drag the boat by ropes from the shore. The towns bordering the Nile between the two locations also became focal points on the way in the great celebration. In a **Mardi gras fashion**, the local town people greeted the goddess and his large entourage with loud music and hearty merrymaking. Flower petals were covering the main streets to set the mood for the fertility rites of this sacred couple.

The early mythmakers understood the necessary elements for a successful festival. The famous sistrum rattles were shaken in the hands of the dancers creating the rattling sound reminiscent of a *snake*. The **'sesheshet' sistrum** was closely associated with the **goddess Hathor** and was mainly used by the priestesses of the cult. Sounding it off was thought to represent good blessings and to honor the *concept of rebirth*. But what a rattlesnake has to do with a beautiful goddess and her cosmic marriage? Does then our biblical goddess, Eve and the evil Serpent has anything to do with this ancient cosmic scientific mystery? They sure do, but for now let us remain with our celebrating Egyptian couple.

Thus, it was the role of the living Pharaoh and his Queen to fulfill the sacred human representations of the gods and goddesses here on earth during the early celebrations. Food offerings were displayed and animal sacrifices performed to appease the gods. <u>Cutting the head off of certain animals was a common ritual. The beheading of Hydra at the end of this book will explain this strange ceremony</u>. The prayers then asked the gods for protection and the people believed that the negative things would transfer into the heads of the sacrificial animals. Then the heads and the carcasses would be burnt and the sins of the people would be released to the sky via the smoke. Also an ancient tradition of releasing the geese toward the four corners of the earth was replayed during these festivities. The goose that lays the golden egg would also have a very important scientific explanation unfolding on the coming pages.

According to Maureen Gallery Kovacs' statement in her book of 'The Epic of Gilgamesh' the following is said:

> "In the Ur III and early Old Babylonian periods the **cosmic Sacred Marriage** of Inanna / **Ishtar** to Dumuzi / **Tammuz** was reenacted by their human representative, a priestess and the king." (Author's heavyset)

Therefore, even the **Babylonians had this Sacred Cosmic Marriage ceremony**. This marital / sexual reenactment of the ancient secrets was **an important element of** Dan Brown's book titled **'The DaVinci Code'** even though 'they' decided on a safe smoke screen ending. He still opened up a few important doors.

Returning to the Egyptian goddesses, in a sense the three main feminine deities may have represented the same woman divinity in a different stage of maturity. There were certainly obvious overlaps between the characteristics shared by these different goddesses at varying dynasties. Thus after her marriage, **Hathor** may have become **Isis**, the good wife and mother thereby having shed the promiscuous harlot image. Then later on she became the widow, the Mother Goddess **Mut**. Interestingly, 'Mom' is called 'Muti' in the German language. Through these family ties the greater cosmic concepts survived. Figure 1-1A depicts Hathor, the goddess - in a vignette of the Egyptian Book of the Dead in spell 186 - as an actual sacred cow with the sun between her horns. At her shoulder blade ran a mountain of water, which she appeared to emerge from. The crocodile was leading her to the Royal Couple. In between them, there were tables full of rich food offerings. The Royal Pair lifted their arms toward the Sacred Cow and the Crocodile Deity in adoration. **The name of the Divine Cow** was Hesat or Mekhweret, which literary **meant the 'Great Flood'.** Astronomically the 'Bull' is the constellation Taurus, and the 'Crocodile' is the constellation Draco the Dragon. The 'Bull' marked the East of the horizon and the 'Dragon' occupied the North, between the Magnetic North and the Polar North. These two 'Norths' – that is the 'two olive trees', which 'have power over heaven to shut down' according to the biblical Revelations - are the 'two hotwires of the Earth's Geo-Dynamo'. The Sacred Cow represented the bountiful nature of the Milky Way. Even the name for the galaxy is derived from the sacred cow that is the ancient Greek word **'Gala'**, meaning **'milk'** is what named our nourishing celestial neighborhood.

The Crocodile – being the well-known predator that emerges from the depth of the Nile to take human lives - naturally became the scientific synonym to the deadly watery disaster of the major flood of Noah. Then this Egyptian crocodile god was transformed into the fiery red Dragon in the north. Even in Greek mythology – in the famous story of Jason and the Argonauts – the Dragon is very central. It is the giant Hercules who is able to retrieve the Golden Fleece of the Ram from the Old Tree only when Orpheus plays his Harp that charms the Dragon. It is exciting to re-watch the movie about Jason and the Argonauts and for the first time discover its sacred astronomical meaning. This Greek myth is a perfect example of the advanced astronomical knowledge of the Ancients. To see the red fiery Dragon in its cosmically important position in the sky - please see Figure 1-2A and also Figure 3-17.

FIGURE 1-1A Adoring the Crocodile and the Sacred Cow
(Book of the Dead. Spell 186.)

Another wall carving shows the **cow horned Hathor** standing with **Sebek, the Crocodile Deity**. (Figure 1-1 B) Sebek is similar to the mythical beast, **Ammit** – a terrifying mixture of crocodile, hippopotamus and a lion - who fearsomely stood by the scale at the **Judgment Hall of the Afterlife** and viciously **devoured the hearts** of those who failed the test. The cults of the Crocodile Deity, Sebek believed that he had the ability to grant power and life to his followers. He was closely tied to the 'Son of the Sun'. **But how are cows, crocodiles and dragons connected to the Son of the Sun and to the promiscuous beautiful Goddess?**

FIGURE 1-1B. Hathor and Sebek.
(Picture taken by Szekely)

22

In pictures of their astronomical constellations the hero spears the crocodile, just as St. George did with the Dragon. A secret universal meaning of the evil fiery dragon permeates the sacred literature of the whole world. Long ago the dragon became the mascot of the Chinese New Year and also appeared as the enigmatic 'beast' for the Book of Revelation in the Bible. But for thousands of years stories of this infamous beast did not yield a common sense scientific explanation - until now.

In Figure 1-1B, Sebek, the Crocodile God is depicted with a headdress showing two fountain-like protrusions, which stands for the Unifying Of The Two Kingdoms. That is **the Magnetic North** (Core of the Earth) **and the Polar North, the two poles of the inner heat producing earth geo-dynamo. The Dragon is the only constellation with seventeen named stars that sits in-between the 'two Norths'.** Thus, the Dragon is the 'unifier'.

The Crocodile's headdress is resting on the Ram horns, the symbol for the 'spiral force of the Milky Way Galactic Center'. The **'serpents'** are wrapped around the sun and ready to strike. These serpents are the scientific **'resonating'** representatives of the **solar eruptions**, and the **'Ankh'** symbols that each of them carries in their hands ties these Earth changing events to the **Venus Calendar**. More specifically to the **Venus Transit Pairs**, whose members came seven years apart transiting in front of the Sun when it was passing in between the astronomical horns of the Bull. That is the real astronomical reason for the goddess with cow horns. On the next graph in Figure 1-2A I demonstrate how the fiery Dragon constellation is in between the hot wires of the Geo-Dynamo. The Roberts-Glatzmaier Geo-Dynamo, named after the two scientists from the Los Alamos National Laboratory is the currently accepted scientific theory. The Dragon is a truly brilliant way to preserve this basic scientific concept as he sits North to South between 'two norths' while the Sun cuts through the sky from East to West to complete the sacred four direction.

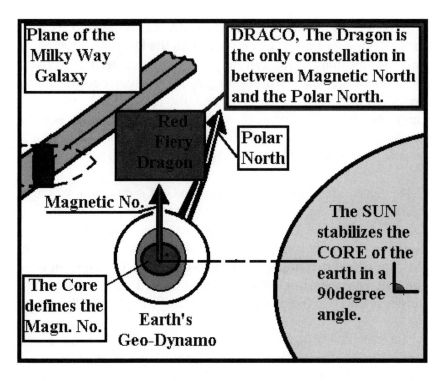

FIGURE 1-2A. The Crocodile-Dragon Sits Between The
Magnetic North and the Polar North

Slowly as we progress to a unifying astronomical calendar of these creatures, one will be able to tell the hidden Egyptian Mystery School Teachings that were clearly translated into the Bible. The major Earth destruction, which happened about 11,500years ago, is discussed in the scholarly book 'Cataclysm!' written by Professors D.S. Allan and J.B. Delair. It coincides with Plato's Timaeus that mentions a 9,600 B.C. mark that is 11,600years B.P to the era of the deluge, around the time when the famous continent of Atlantis submerged into the ocean.

One of the main researchers of the Greenland Ice Core Project in the early 1990's determined from the ice samples with quite accuracy that the latest cataclysm happened 11,650years ago.

Even my favorite astrophysicist, Dr. Paul LaViolette recognizes this period in his excellent book titled *Earth Under Fire:* "The most recent subdivision (Stage 1) marks the warm interglacial period that has presided during the past 11,600 years and which is termed the *Holocene.*"

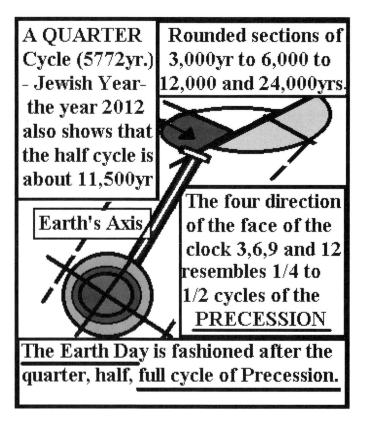

A QUARTER Cycle (5772yr.) - Jewish Year- the year 2012 also shows that the half cycle is about 11,500yr

Rounded sections of 3,000yr to 6,000 to 12,000 and 24,000yrs.

Earth's Axis

The four direction of the face of the clock 3,6,9 and 12 resembles 1/4 to 1/2 cycles of the PRECESSION

The Earth Day is fashioned after the quarter, half, full cycle of Precession.

FIGURE 1-2B. The 24 Hour Day Tied To The
Calendars and the Precession.

Thus, the Sacred Tree (Earth Axis) rotated 12,000+12,000= 24,000years – that was symbolized in a **12/12=24 Hour Day**. That is why our **HeRo**, HoRus (HeRu), HeRackles, HeRcules carry the same consonants as the **HouR** (HoRa), that is **H+R**.

Multiplying the 1/2 cycle measure of the Jewish calendar year of 2012 by 2, which would read 5,772 at the end of the Mayan Calendar, it yields us the same ballpark figure, namely 5,772 x 2 = 11,544. Thus it is safe to say that the major Deluge of Noah's Flood must happened around a little more than 11,500years ago. The Ancients rounded it up to the 12,000year half cycle of the **Precession of the Equinoxes. The full cycle is 24,000years! The Galactic Core is 23-24,000light years away** from us and it erupts **periodically. This is most likely what determines this dominant Precessional cycle of the Ice ages.** A quote from Kersey Graves book of 'The World's Sixteen Crucified Saviors' resurrected by Adventure Unlimited Press verify these cycles:

"The Egyptians marked their houses with red, to indicate that the world would be destroyed by fire. Some nations held that the alternate destruction of the world by water and fire had already occurred, and would occur again. Theopompus informs us that some of the orientalists believed that **'the God of light and the God of darkness reigned by turn every six thousand years** (commencing with an astronomical Cycle of course), and that during this period the other was held in subjection, which finally resulted in **'a war in heaven;'** a counterpart to St. John's story. (See Rev. chap. Xii.)

This accords with Volney's statement, that **'it was recorded in the sacred books of the Persians and Chaldeans that the world, composed of a total revolution of twelve thousand periods, was divided into two partial revolutions of six thousands years each ..."** (Author's heavyset)

So my question is: Why are we keep talking about a very hypothetical 13,000 and 26,000years Precessional cycles when the Ancients correctly recorded down a rounded 6,000 - 12,000 and 24,000year dominant cycles and that is also what we find in the scientifically correct Ice Age cycles of Milankovitch?

In my theory the catastrophic events, which led up to the Flood of Noah, including the Sunspot eruption (fire from heaven) and the following Seven Years of Famine are the sacred cosmic tales wrapped into the human tragedy of the gods. Therefore the old stories of the God Osiris, the Goddess Isis, King Tut, Anubis the Jackal, the fiery Serpent, Crocodile king and Sacred Bull are the astronomical cosmic events of this Flood. By examining creation legends of different cultures and compare the sacred religious writings, one can decipher the chain of events of this old disaster that happened about 11,600years ago and was rounded up to 12,000year cycles by the myth makers. In their myths and calendar makings the Ancients utilized the four directions, and the four brightest objects in the sky. The clever constellations of the so named animals and tools represented a very specifically coded and universally acceptable scientific chain of events bringing us the timing of the progressively worsening catastrophe that happened about 11,600years ago.

The genius way of constructing interrelated words and basic symbols was clearly an amazing achievement of the ancient Egyptians. This form of primary picture language creation prevented the so commonly seen mistranslations, which would happen between different cultures and generations. There is no slang in animal pictures. The symbols were carefully selected and to the point. For example, if *darkness* or death had to be depicted then the wise Ancients would pick the **owl,** an animal, which is widely recognized as a ***nocturnal hunter.*** Words constructed with connotations to *darkness*, such as *evening* or *death* would start with the **letter *'m'*, that corresponds to the *'owl'* in the Egyptian Hieroglyphic Alphabet.** Besides having individual letters, there were also biliterals and triliterals in the complex Egyptian Alphabet. The biliterals and the triliterals contained more than one letter corresponding to a particular hieroglyphic symbol. In the back under the heading of 'The Alphabet of Hieroglyphic Symbols' these depictions are organized.

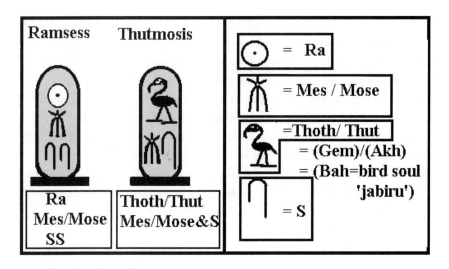

FIGURE 1-2C. Ramsess and Thutmosis.

According to the great book titled 'Illustrated Hieroglyphics Handbook' - by Ruth Schumann-Antelme and Stephane Rossini - the pioneer French linguist Francois Champollion found a parallel between the sign of 'Mes/Mesi/Mose' and the Coptic word 'mose', meaning "to give birth to". By deciphering the hieroglyphic letters from the cartouche of king 'Ptolemy', Cleopatra's Macedonian Greek lineage, which also contained the symbol for the 'mes/mose/mesi', Champollion began the arduous task of assembling the initial Egyptian Letter Alphabet. The concepts **'Mesi' (Mesi-ah)** and **'Mose' (Moses)** both have hidden biblical connotations to the promise of a **'Divine Birth'**.

The name of the biblical Pharaoh 'Ra-mes-ss' in its traditional interpretation means 'Ra gave birth to him'. But let us begin with analysis of the names of Ramesses and Thutmosis in Fig.1-2C. The symbols for **'Ra-Mess/Ra-Mose-ss'** would mean to me that **'Ra, the Sun'** - with the **son dot** in the middle that **means Venus Transit and Sunspot eruption – gives divine 'birth' when the 'three cosmic lines meet in Orion' and the two axes will unify**.

We already explored the Biblical Bear, Orion and Pleiades and demonstrated that it is derived from Egypt and also present in Babylonia. As we suggested earlier, it was the Greco-Romans and the Hebrews who transmitted this knowledge from Egypt to Europe and were responsible for depositing it into our Bible. Therefore, it behooves us to investigate the possibility to see if Orion is tied to the Pleiades in 'The Myths of Greece and Rome' written by H.A. Guerber: "Endymion was not, however, the
> only mortal loved by **Diana**, for it is also related that her affections were bestowed upon a young hunter by the name of **Orion**. All day long this youth scoured the forest, his faithful **dog Sirius** at his heels. One day, in the dense shade of the forest, he met a group of Diana's nymphs, the seven **Pleiades**, daughters of Atlas. These fair maidens needed but to be seen to be passionately loved, and Orion's heart burned as he sought to approach them; " (Author's heavyset)

A number of hidden connotations are contained in the above quote besides tying Orion to the Pleiades. The bright star Sirius, the dog and Orion's burning heart will gain further understanding in the coming chapters, but for now back to the pharaohs.

The hieroglyphic symbols for the name 'Thutmosis' introduce the 'ibis' or the **stork** to our understanding. It is the 'ba', which is a kind of spirit of the person ready to pass to the other-side. Since we know that these events are connected to the earth changes, we need to consider that the 'ba-spirit' may relate to the 'Holy Spirit', which came to visit us on that special 'Day of the Lord'.

The mythological stork/crane/ibis/heron type of water bird to me means scientifically an animal that is **known to stand in water,** and also implies an animal, which commonly seen **standing on 'one leg'**. Interestingly, Hun-rakan (hurricane) in the Mayan language means the 'one-legged'. If the Magnetic North undergoes an axis shifts then the underwater fountains would erupt from the ground. These underwater volcanoes would help heat the oceans and thus generate increasingly larger hurricanes. Not only the hurricane is 'one-legged', but also at the same time the Earth would be standing on one leg as the Magnetic North Pole would go and join the Polar North. All right, but how is that tied to the stork and the birth? We know that **the stork nests on smoky chimneys and the stork also bring the 'Baby'.** All of these clues refer to the Cosmic Divine Birth of the princely Sunspot to the old king Sun. The English language cleverly maintained a similar sounding and spelling to the words 'Sun' and 'Son'. The 'Son of the Sun' and the Venus Calendar is the 'Big Secrets' of the ages. This is how Wilkinson writes about the heron:

> " Like the ibis, the heron was also considered a manifestation of the resurrected Osiris, ... In astronomical paintings the heron may represent Dja: "the Crosser" – the Egyptian name for the planet Venus, ... "

One of the questions naturally arises in my mind when looking at the names of those supposed 'pharaohs'. – If there were actual human bodies behind those 'cartouches' or were they ever even meant to represent human rulers at all? Were they rather just simply clever hieroglyphic messages of natural cosmic forces exerted on Earth trying to tell us about the last time the globe suffered a major change? The rulers in these tales were not humans rather they represented the cosmic forces of the Galactic Center, the erupting Sun, the 'two trees/pillars', the Magnetic North and the Polar North. Those two 'hot wires' of the geo-dynamo are the so-called positive and negative charges of the globe's battery. This is one of the main factors that allow us to experience life on this beautiful planet. The sad but true story is that about every 12,000years or so, the Creator Force needs to recharge and at times even change the polarity on the earth's poles to re-power the diminishing magnetic field.

If that recharging did not happen regularly, then the life maintaining magnetic shield – such as the Gaspar de Corioles forces - around the earth and the inner-heat producing dynamo would fade away. A life taking big re-creation has to take place for new life to go on this amazing fertile planet.

Those stories are not about history such as the so commonly publicized 'religion and rural life style' of the ancient Egyptians. If it would have been the idyllic rural pictures of simple life of agricultural existence then the intelligent Ra Priest of Egypt would have not insisted on drawing human bodies with falcon heads and other unrealistic scenes, which are not commonly part of a farming community. The traditional interpretations of the Egyptologists of the falcon-headed deities of Egypt would not account for or make the obvious connections of the 'swooping eagle' from the Bible that is the Arabic name of the star Vega. Several different angles left to us by the Egyptian legacies.

Returning back to the Egyptian 'word pictures', as a very important reminder, let me explain here that the Egyptians or ancient Semitic Tribes did not use *soft vowels* in their writings. Therefore the letters 'o' or 'e' or any other soft vowels are either assumptions from the languages of the Coptics, the Arabs or the other neighboring Semitic languages or even just pure guesses. At times, they are only assumption on the part of the linguists to what would sound easier to pronounce.

A definitely more proper designation for the picture symbols named 'mes / mose or mesi' should be written as **'m( )s(?)'**, using only consonants. I will try to follow the examples of the most commonly applied spellings, but at times I will show the few alternative words and names used by scholars. The above Figure 1-2C depicts two of the initial cartouches Champollion started working with. The Old Testament mentions the Pharaoh Ramsses of Egypt who may have never existed in flesh.

31

The old pharaohs are not historical, rather these hieroglyphic symbols contain utterly important cosmic concepts. That is why the hieroglyphs are so essential. **The name of the pharaoh 'Ramsses' simply translates as 'Ra, the Sun gave birth to'.** Yes, the Sun gave birth to His son. The traditional Egyptologist explain this concept that - the ancient primitive Egyptians had to be so amazed by the Sun coming up and going down that they compulsively made tens of thousands of depictions on the walls of the pyramids. Do you honestly think that they built all of those enormous size structures just to say the 'Sun is reborn everyday'? Do you - in your right mind - honestly believe that? I don't! What I believe is that they knew the calendar to calculate the return of those awful end days and they made their best effort to record down what happened to them and to warn us over and over again with those sacred carvings on the walls. That's what so amazing!

So many millions of 'wasted' hours of manpower were poured into the making of the wall paintings to warn future generations. These ancient teachers were true altruistically minded souls who understood spiritual eternity and thus, they did not worry about their king or their own death. Their noble concerns were for the future of the human race. **The mummification of the ruler in different contexts implied a state of the old sun or the earth when it could not move as a dynamo.** It clearly was not about earthly rulers! I believe that the ancient spirits from 12,000years ago, who wrote down the early hieroglyphic pictures, are now reincarnating to Earth in large numbers and are taking refuge in our bodies to rediscover the old secrets we / they planted then.

The hieroglyphic symbols begin to take on new biblical and folklore connotations with names such as Ramsses, and Moses along with the oldwives' tales of the 'stork who is bringing the baby'. Now we just have to solve the mystery of the Egyptian Child and see if that 'child' is similar or even the same sibling, which is so often mentioned in the Old Testament.

The word 'Child' is written as 'Keredj' in Egyptian. Knowing that some of the Semitic tribes read backwards, it is interesting to me to see that 'Djerek' is very similar to 'Gyerek' (means 'child' in Hungarian and is pronounced as 'Djerek'). I will periodically demonstrate other word origin examples from Hungarian (H), Latin (L) or Spanish (S), Hindu (HD), Hebrew (J) and English (E). For example, the name of the Sun King ' **Ra / Re**' are found in important scientific concepts and word connotations all around the world.

'**Ra**-z' (H) means 'electrical shock' and '**Ra**-ngat' translates to 'shaking' in Hungarian. The English '**Ra**-ys' and '**Re**-sonation' implies a similar '**re**-petitious' movement or pulsed rhythm. The name **Ra**-khel (ewe in Hebrew), Ba-**Ra**-ny (lamb in Hungarian), A-**Ra**-ny (gold in Hungarian), Ki-**Ra**-ly (king in Hungarian), **Ra**-jan (prince / king in Hindu) and El **Re**y (king in Spanish) all show derivation from the Egyptian Ra /Re or Hindu Raj. The numerous examples in any languages are truly countless. So many names that seem to relate to these astronomical secrets of the Egyptians obviously derived from the basic hieroglyphic symbols of a wide variety of languages. There are not enough pages in this book for me to demonstrate the numerous examples, but it is worthwhile for someone to investigate the picture roots of the basis of our languages. I will show a few examples.

A truly marvelous way is how the ancient Egyptian Ra Priests began to assemble the spellings of basic words. The clever story of the very important total 'Darkness' (Owl) created by the tilting of the 'Axis' (Candy Cane) shaped Magnetic North at the time when the 'three cosmic lines met in Orion' (Mesi sign) is very beautifully demonstrated in the simple word of 'Mesi', that is 'Give Birth To'. And as you guessed already the Sun gives birth to the Son of the Sun. Figure 1-2D will demonstrate the 'Birth'. The male king gave birth to a male son while the harlot and the virgin felt sexually ignored in this twisted cosmic soap opera.

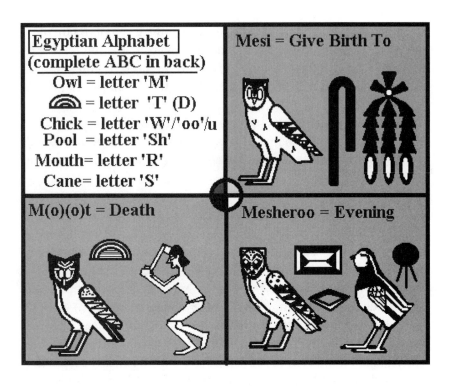

FIGURE 1-2D. The Owl Is Not Just Darkness.
(Modified from IHH by Schumann-Antelme & Rossini)

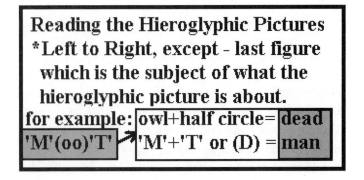

FIGURE 1- 2E. How To Read Hieroglyphic Words

On Figure 1-2D we can observe the words M(oo)T /(Mut) referring to 'death' or 'murdering, that is causing death'. It is also a cognate of the Goddess Mut (is she the old dark witch or the mythological widow?). The next picture on the bottom right hand section is 'Mesheroo', meaning 'Evening'. These two words, 'death' or 'evening' generally make sense with these pictures. Although, still early in this game of deciphering, we would have trouble seeing the relevance of a pool of water (flood), a mouth (God speaks), and a one-day-old quail chick (birth of a New Sun /Age), but soon it will all make sense. But even more intriguing is the word 'Mesi' in the upper right hand corner of Figure 1-2D. With the Hebrew 'HA' or 'AH', meaning 'the' when correctly reading it backwards, the word 'Mesi-ah' or 'A(h) Mesi-Birth' truly does connect to a divine cosmic birth.

For a short moment, let us stop and analyze the individual hieroglyphic signs in the Egyptian word 'Mesi'. As one can read the word above **'Mesi'** in Egyptian means **'Giving Birth To'** or 'the **Child'**. The 'owl' symbol does not make much sense unless we think of the birth canal as 'dark', but still the 'giving birth to' a Child should actually arrive 'into the light'. Also, the strange cane or 'shepherd's crook ' appearing hieroglyph does not make sense to me right away. Egyptologists translated it as a towel or a 'folded cover thrown over the back of a chair'. It might make sense to have a 'folded towel' to wipe the child off after a birthing process. Certainly the 'crook' shaped cane would be more difficult to interpret as we would have to use that tool to 'twist' the child out of there, unless, it is about a cosmic birth. But even more perplexing is the last symbol, which should stand for the actual subject of the 'Childbirth'. It reads as 'mes / mesi' and it shows three lines or three 'something', which meet in one point. Would it stand for the enigmatic celestial constellation **'ORION'**, in which we will soon learn that the three celestial lines, the Milky Way Galactic, the Solar, and Earthly celestial equators rendezvous every about 12,000years?

35

The traditional Egyptologists offer a different and naturally faulty meaning for 'mesi'. The depiction to them means either the 'three fox or jackal skins attached together' or a loincloth, but apparently there is no consensus on it. They might be right, but I strongly doubt it. I will quote from the book titled the 'Illustrated Hieroglyphics Handbook' by Ruth Schuman-Antelme a great Egyptologist who was a member of the Egyptian Department of the Louvre Museum, and Stephane Rossini a professional designer in the science and drawings of the hieroglyphs. Their book is an exceptional storehouse of richly illustrated knowledge for the students of Egyptian writings. I will question a few of their interpretation, understanding that it is not their own, but the widely accepted traditional interpretations of the Egyptologist science community. In their 'Semantics' section for the 'mose' or **'mes / mesi'** word of the '**three fox skins attached together**' (Orion crossroads) symbol they write the following:

> "<u>This biliteral is contained in most terms related to **birth, descendants, childhood,**</u> and produce. ... Neither the divine nor the celestial escape the semantic poetry inherent in becoming : **Meskhenet is the goddess of childbirth**. At the opposite extreme of life is found the catafalque. The same term is also related to the naos used in the procession of divinities. **Mesekhtyoo is the Big Dipper**; **meseket is the Milky Way**. What about the ear?"
>
> (Author's heavy set and underlining.)

I think they made my argument with their own semantics section. The **'mes'** biliteral hieroglyphic **symbol is involved in a 'cosmic childbirth'** as in the constellation **Orion**. And since the question arose about the ear above, I will venture to guess that the 'ear' is a reference to the 'cow ears' of Hathor (Venus) as she was often depicted. When the Earth changes happened in the past, the noise was loud that accompanied those events. One needs 'an ear to hear it'! So have ears to hear the ancient secrets.

FIGURE 1-2F. Hathor with Cow Ears.
(Picture by Szekely)

Kersey Graves acclaims the following in his 1875 classic book titled 'The World's Sixteen Crucified Saviors':

> **"The whole thing, then, is evidently an astronomical legend.** Albert the Great, in his "Book on the Universe," tells us, 'The sign of the **celestial virgin** rises above the horizon, at the moment we find fixed for the birth of our Lord Jesus Christ.' To which we will add the declaration of Sir William Drummond, who, in his 'Oedipus Judaicus,' p. 27, most significantly remarks, 'The **anointed of *El*, the male infant**, who rises in the arms of Virgo, was **called Jesus** by the Hebrews, … and was hailed as the **anointed king or Messiah'** – still further proof of the astrological origin of the story."

Not only our ancient creation stories find their beginning in the starry sky, but also it seems likely that the origin of modern languages is clearly tied to the Egyptian hieroglyphic writings. The Latin 'eres' (being from), the English 'are' (being) and the Hungarian words 'ered' (originating from) or the 'er' (artery/origin) and the 'v-er' (blood) are most likely remnants of the ancient efforts of language making to incorporate these concepts with the crucial astronomical and cosmological calendar secrets. The letter 'E' shows us three parallel lines that are connected together. The letter 'V' is unquestionably represents the female deity, the upside down pyramid and the goddess Venus. The **letter 'R'** in the Egyptian Hieroglyphic pictures is represented as an **open 'mouth'**. That mouth is none others, but the mouth of god - that is where the sacred word is *'R'esonating* out of.

I think, I am the first scholar who demonstrates clear interconnectedness to the Venus Calendar's astronomy; the Egyptian hieroglyphic pictures, sacred geometry all tied to the last major Earth change and to the developing new language base of 'Noah'. The basic words, the mythological stories, the folklore designs, the decorations, ritual tools, in essence every of their efforts seems to be related to that beginning of their New Age nearly 12,000years ago.

In our attempt to decipher a number of biblical names, we have to understand that the Ra Priests brought us the Egyptian wisdom by applying their Semitic language rules in the process of reading, translating and recording. By reading from right to left the Jews placed 'the' at the end (for them the beginning) of the word. This 'THE' was their 'HA/AH', that is why so many biblical names end in –AH, such as Mari-ah, No-ah, Jeremi-ah. In the combined wisdom of Egyptian hieroglyphics written and translated to our alphabet by Hebrew scribes, let me demonstrate the secret letters behind the name of Noah.

Making sense out of the translated word for NO-AH in view of the Flood and the knowledge that Moses' writings were done in Egyptian hieroglyphic symbols and only hundreds of years later translated to the ancient Hebrew and then later to Greek, Latin and English. Thus, the clever Hebrew interpretation from Egyptian maintained a scientific meaning to the name, rather then using an assumed name for NOAH. Let me demonstrate this concept with NO-AH's name.

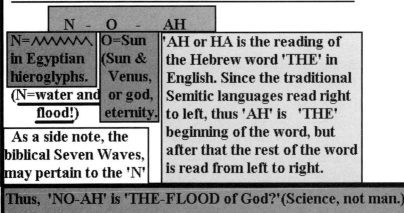

N -	O -	AH
N=ᗺᗺᗺᗺ in Egyptian hieroglyphs. (N=water and flood!)	O=Sun (Sun & Venus, or god, eternity.	'AH or HA is the reading of the Hebrew word 'THE' in English. Since the traditional Semitic languages read right to left, thus 'AH' is 'THE' beginning of the word, but after that the rest of the word is read from left to right.
As a side note, the biblical Seven Waves, may pertain to the 'N'		

Thus, 'NO-AH' is 'THE-FLOOD of God?'(Science, not man.)

Therefore, names such as Mari-AH, Isai-AH, and other 'AH' endings should be reconsidered when interpreting for real meaning with the above rule in mind.

FIGURE 1-2G.   The Meaning Of The Name NOAH.

The name of Noah was not meant to represent a single person. We know from other flood legends from India, Babylonia, and the Americas that the name of the surviving person usually meant something like the 'cleverest'. The Old Testament teachers decided to record the name as a translation of the 'seven wave' symbol of the **letter 'N'** from the hieroglyphic alphabet. Not only it **represents '*water*'**, but it also can stand for the '*resonation*', that is the biblical **serpent.**

The resonation would be translated to the Bible as the 'word' of God. What a clever symbol. Just as the sound is unseen, but it is meaningful as it received by the ear, similarly the **'word of god'** would come from the sky as '**an increasing resonation'** that in the past apparently caused the earth changes and the Flood of the biblical Noah. This resonation was cleverly depicted by an evil **'serpent'** (Figure 4-4), which slowly increased in height or was shown as a cobra standing up and ready to strike.

Therefore, the Ancients must have understood that the only way they had a chance for meaningful scientific recording of their messages for future generations, if they would leave us animal symbols and simple tools of scientific significance instead of only the meaningless letters for a sound. An innocent appearing animal character, which would be missed by the uninitiated eye, could easily contain cosmic scientific ideas without arousing the suspicions of the uneducated masses. The Semitic Ra Priests then later taken the message to Europe and other parts of the world.

A simple sentence from mythology could suggest the power of *electromagnetic forces*, such as 'his hair was standing up on edges', but the clever Egyptians needed to be more certain that their sacred message was clear and not ambiguous. They picked an animal, which was common and operated on the principles of **electromagnetic forces**. It was the **goose** that lays the golden egg. Not only it uses the electromagnetism to navigate, it has even a **North to South direction in its flight plan**, which for their purposes was an important distinction. Thus, the goose commonly shows up on the heads of a few important gods, such as Geb and Osiris.

Allow me to start with an example early on to demonstrate the incredible wisdom and scientific knowledge they had to possess for the kind of hieroglyphs they employed.

In the next few diagrams I will delineate the incredible cosmic and astronomical knowledge they had to possess for the symbols to provide good sense. Unfortunately, even today in the higher scientific circles, the knowledge of astronomy and geology only reached to an acceptable level of complexity in the last few decades. Amongst average high school graduates today it is still difficult to find a few amongst the thousands who would even understand the celestial mechanics of the Earth's geo-dynamo in the solar system and the Milky Way Galaxy. Thus, in order to fully comprehend the enormous geniality of the Egyptian hieroglyphs we need to first review some basic information on how the earth works and what are the calendar rounds for the ages.

In the recent ice age record of the Antarctic Ice sheet and later in the Greenland ice core we can observe a rounded up period of the 12,000year half cycle and a 24,000year long full cycle. Besides the calendar measures, and the ice age records our scientists improved our understandings of how we believe the earth operates today. I will give a simplified version.

The earth generates inner heat through the **friction** of the two moving parts of the **geo-dynamo**. The two hot wires are pointing to the Polar North in the star **Polaris** and then **Vega**, which would stand for the Magnetic North. It is assumed that the **Black Hole or the surrounding Super Sun controls both hot wires of the geo-dynamo, but the Sun is the one, which is responsible for the stabilization of the iron core of the earth**. Knowing this scientific concept allows the reader to discover the astronomical tales hidden in the Egyptian hieroglyphics, and the related sacred writings, which include the Babylonian, Hebrew and Judeo-Christian, also Nordic, Eastern and Native wisdom. There is no culture without the basic knowledge of that above.

The Milky Way Galaxy contains a Super Sun, which is about 2.6 million times the Sun's Mass. In the center of it there spins the Black Hole. It only takes a quick glance at the map of the Milky Way Galaxy to note that all the stars and solar systems rotate around this center. NASA finally officially admitted about two years ago that it is the Galactic Center of each galaxy, which controls the movement of the stars. Prior to that I argued this same point with astronomers and teachers of astronomy and geology and the consensus was that the Galactic Center is so far away that it would not exert significant power over our Earth. Obviously those assumptions turned out to be faulty.

Another confusion is still alive today amongst the scholars is the length of the Precession of the Equinoxes being 26,000year. It is actually a little more than 23,000years and ended up to be the rounded up 24,000year cycle. Those who doubt it can see the 'footprints' of that main 'ice volume collapse' cycle in the Antarctic and Greenland ice core finding. The fatal mistakes of calculating 26,000year Precession come from scholars who are accepting the rudimentary estimates of the ancient Greeks who made this prediction based on the full and perfect cycle of the Earth's path in the sky. The actual path of the Precession of the Equinoxes is closer to the elliptical shape, and most likely two half spirals, thus it is the rounded cycles of 12K & 12K= 24K.

In this book we will not spend much time with that discussion, rather we shall provide only a crude basic graphic understanding of the 'Trinity Forces' operating in our galaxy and then we could quickly progress to the Egyptian Mysteries. The ice age graphs put out by well-respected international scientists clearly show patterns, which reverse. These reversals come regularly about every 11,500 – 12,000years. Certainly, there are other cyclical patterns, such as an 18,000year, a dominant 23,000year, 41,000 and 115,000year ice age cycles. The question anymore is not whether those climate changes happen on the regular basis, the question becomes – how, when and by what process?

Thinking of the Egyptian religion as primitive and animist the 19th century historian W. Max Muller writes in his book titled the **Egyptian Mythology** about worship of the Sun that ties the 'hawk' symbol to the solar deity and the 'serpent' uraeus is connected to the fire. Around the early 1900's we cannot expect him to understand the cosmic manifestations of these animal symbols. Thus, this is how he writes:

> "By their very contradictions the later attempts to **transform the old local spirits** and fetishes into personifications of **cosmic powers** prove that no such personification was acknowledged in the prehistoric period to which the majority of Egyptian cults are traceable, thus confirming the general absence of homage to cosmic powers. It is even doubtful whether the worship of the **sun-god** was originally important; "

> "**The first of all cosmic powers to find general worship was the sun,** whose rays dominate Egypt so strongly. The earliest efforts to personify it **identified it with an old hawk-god,** and thus sought to describe it as a hawk which flew daily across the sky. Therefore, the two most popular forms of **the solar deity, Re and Horus, have the form of a hawk or of a hawk-headed man** ...
> At the beginning of the dynastic period Horus seems to have been the sun-god who was most generally worshipped in Egypt. ...
> Then the sun may rest in the cabin as a disk in which the god himself may be enthroned, or as the **uraeus asp, the symbol of fire;** " (Author's heavyset)

The above quote equating the hawk flying across the sky to the sun is obviously wrong. The falcon, the hawk, or the swooping eagle represented the erupting Sun causing the Magnetic North to plummet toward the south and unify with the Polar North.

Therefore, in Figure 1-3A, I will demonstrate the cosmic powers and explain the connection of the hawk to the sun.

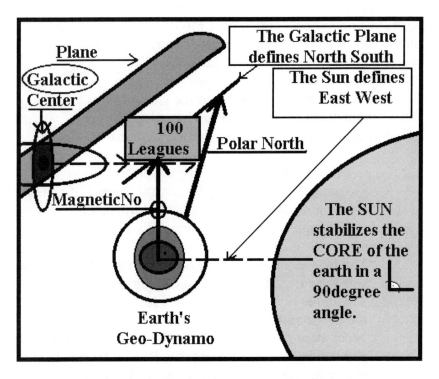

FIGURE 1-3A. Control Powers of the Earth's Geo-Dynamo

The 'core' of the Earth points to the Magnetic North, which is symbolized in astronomy as the bright star Vega in the Lyra constellation. Vega's Arabic name is 'the swooping hawk/eagle'. Imagining a 'spinning top', every planetary body that rotates around an axis also has to have a plane or equator. This equator is at a 90 degree angle to the axis. In the case of the Core's Magnetic North, this equatorial plane extends out toward the sun. This implies that the Sun is the controlling and stabilizing factor of the inner core of the Earth.

Thus, when the Sun erupts this controlling aspect is lost on the Core and the Magnetic North shifts to the Polar North, because the Galactic Center's Black Hole takes over sole control. This is the concept of 'unifying the two lands of Egypt'. Figure 1-1 earlier demonstrates the 'three cosmic lines' and one can easily observe that both Vega and Polaris are perfectly parallel to the Milky Way Galactic Plane, but Polaris is 90 degree angle to the Earth's Celestial Plane, while Vega is 90 degree angle to the Solar Plane. A beautiful power sharing in the sky of the 'trinity lines'. Another important mythological marker of cosmic significance was the distance between the Magnetic North and the Polar North. This was the sacred 100 league long 'Red Road' that the Magnetic North (red) Lower Kingdom of the North traveled in an axis shift toward the Polar North (white) Upper Kingdom of the South. Before I progress any further let me quote a few lines showing that different cultures, including the Hindu, the Babylonian, the Egyptian, and naturally even Judeo-Christian mythologically thought of **the distance between the earth's two axes as the 100 leagues distance.** This 100 leagues long perfect valley, the cosmic 'birth canal' is where the infamous DRAGON housed in the sky.

> "The demons agreed and brought the milk. She drank that demonic milk …Then she crossed back over the Rasa, which extended for a ***hundred leagues***, …"
>
> (pg.72, Hindu Myths.)

> "And the **embryo** which the **earth received when she was menstruating** – the **goddess earth** herself **will care for him** secretly for a long time after his birth, and when the proper time has come the **goddess, suffering under her extreme burden, will announce to you the time for his slaughter,** and **then you will kill him**. When the earth, suffering under the burden, has sunk down for a ***hundred leagues***, I will take the form of a tusked **boar** and raise her up."   (pg.196, Hindu Myths.)

The newborn 'embryo' causes extreme burden on Mother Earth and He will have to be killed. Is that not the faith of every hero? Besides the Egyptian Book of the Dead this **hundred leagues** measurement is emphasized in the Bible and is also present in the Babylonian Epic of Gilgamesh and the Hindu Myths. The above mentioned 'embryo' of the divine Child is introduced along with the **boar**. The word *embryo* seemed to be related to the word for 'man' or 'ethnic designation' in the related Hebrew, Spanish, and Hungarian languages. The Hebrew 'Hebber /Ebber', the Spanish 'Hombre' and the Hungarian 'Ember' sound similar to 'Embryo'.

The menstruating Mother Earth goddess - with the help of the newborn male embryo - is the one who will **turn the water to blood**. Actually, it is the underwater volcanism, which causes the ocean and sea waters to turn blood color. This is the biblical 'making of the Red Sea'. Again we see an example for presenting a real and meaningful scientific explanation to the strange mythological and religious tales. As an interesting comparison to the blood connection to the Hindu Lord Skanda and his Christian counter part - let me quote from the New Testament:

> "6 This is **He who came by water and blood – Jesus Christ**; not only by water, but **by water and blood**. And it is the Spirit who bears witness, because the Spirit is truth.
> 7 For there are three who bear witness in heaven: the **Father, the Word, and the Holy Spirit**; and these three **are one**.
> 8 And there are three that bear witness on earth: the **Spirit, the water, and the blood**; and **these three agree as one**." (Author's heavyset) (John I, Chapter 5, Verses 6-8.)

Interestingly, the 'WORD' is substituted for the 'SON' in this version of the Trinity and 'water' and 'blood' is added. These three agree as 'one' as happens during 'unification'. Because the Spiral-Spirit Force causes the Sun to have a Son, therefore, the Spirit Force, the King Sun and the Prince Son are all the same.

Since the **'word'** can be heard, but is truly invisible, to me it represents **'unseen resonation'**. Then the **'SON'** of the Sun logically is tied to the Sunspot eruption. In quiet times the whispered 'word' of God can sustain the harmony of the Universe, but when it is shouted out loud using the **vocal cords**, or the cord of a stringed musical instrument as if it was the **string of a bow** then problem follows. Regardless which cord we strike the result is still the **'resonation' (serpent)** that is rather deadly. Let us hear more from the Hindu Myths about fire, water, cosmic sex, embryo and the subsequent disaster.

> **"The earth**, in the water, is full of desire and **behaving like a woman**; she has been violated and has **conceived a cruel embryo from your fiery seed; she is menstruating**, …
> …But **the boar** went to his own mountain, named World-non-World, and he **made love with the earth…"**
>
> (pg. 188-189, Hindu Myths.)

Thus, it is obvious that the 'love-making' is in between Mother Earth and Father Sky. The cruel embryo is conceived by fire. The original 'sin' is in fact that Mother Earth is menstruating while she is having sex with this fiery eruption from above. Another quote from the Hindu Myths will give away the location from where the purifying 'fiery lord' comes from.

> "As the lord pondered in this way, … and he bowed to the Grandfather and said, 'Appoint a great hero to be the husband of this goddess' … All the gods, following the God of a Hundred Sacrifices, came to the sacrifice of those sages, … When the noble sages had performed the sacrifice in the proper way, they offered the oblation into the Oblation-devourer kindled with good fuel for all the dwellers in heaven. **The <u>marvelous fire</u>, the carrier of oblation, <u>the lord</u>, was summoned there; he <u>came out from the orb of the sun</u>**, restraining his <u>speech</u> according to the ritual." (Author's underlining and heavyset)

47

The above amazing quote identifies the *'lord'* as the **carrier of oblation**, that is the **marvelous fire** who *'came out of the orb of the sun'* and is also connected to the speech or **word**. Thus, at least from the Hindu mythology it is becoming clear that the **earth-purifying lord is a fire coming out of the orb of the sun as a command from the divine word of the cosmic resonation!** (As a personal note, the Schumann Resonance almost doubled from 7.8 Hertz to about 13 Hz from the 1950 to the early 2000's.)

The next few quotes will attach the Harlot, the Serpent and the Dragon from the Bible to these above fires and waters.

> "1 Now a great sign appeared in heaven: a **woman clothed with the sun**, with the moon under her feet, and on her head a garland of twelve stars.
> 2 Then **being with child**, she **cried out** in labor and **in pain to give birth**,
> 3 And another sign appeared in heaven: behold, a great, **fiery red dragon** having seven heads and ten horns, and seven diadems on his heads.
> 4 **His tail drew a third of the stars** of heaven and threw them to the earth. <u>And the dragon stood before the woman who was ready to give birth, to devour her Child as soon as it was born.</u>
> 5 **She bore a male Child who was to rule all** nations with **a rod of iron**. And her Child was caught up to God and His throne. (Bible, Revelation, Chapter 12, Verses 1-5.) (Author's heavy set and underlining.)

The 'Child' cannot be the peaceful Christ, as this male Child's demeanor above is depicted as harsh 'to rule all nations with a rod of iron'. It may be Attila the Hun, or King Arthur? And why cannot they just say the word 'sword', instead of referring to 'a rod of iron'? Unless, the 'rod of iron' refers to the Egyptian 'was' symbol that is the direction of the 'iron core of the earth', which shifts when the Sunspot erupts.

Well, those quotes certainly are not talking about warlords; this sounds more like a cosmic event for rulership. The above quotes amply illustrate that the 'Child' is tied to a woman who is 'clothed with the sun'. That woman is the planet Venus when transits in front of the Sun. It also ties this birthing event to the Dragon   the only constellation in the sky between the star Vega (Magnetic North) and Polaris (Earth's Axis). This is the beast and 'His tail drew a third of the stars of heaven'. These are 'Draco'-nian measures. In Figure 1-3B I illustrate the number 666 and also why 1/3 of the stars will be moved by the Dragon's tail.

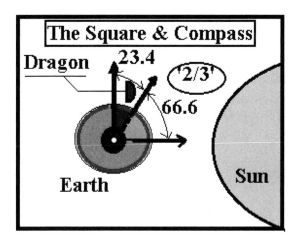

FIGURE 1-3B. Square and Compass

This is how Maureen Gallery Kovacs' book on the Babylonian hero, 'The Epic of Gilgamesh' brings us the Flood and the 1/3 measure of the axis tilt in Tablet I:

> "It was he ... who restored
> the sanctuaries that the **Flood** destroyed! ...
> **Two-thirds of him is god, one-third of him is human**.
> The Great Goddess (Aruru) designed (?) the model for
> his body, she prepared his form ..."

A 'third' of a 'hundred' (from Figure 1-3A) is about 33.3, that almost exactly what's left after we discount the 66.6degrees that is the number of the 'dragon beast'. We arrived at this number by subtracting 23.4degrees from the 90degree horizontal line and it gives 66.6degrees. Then take that away from a hundred and we are left with one third.

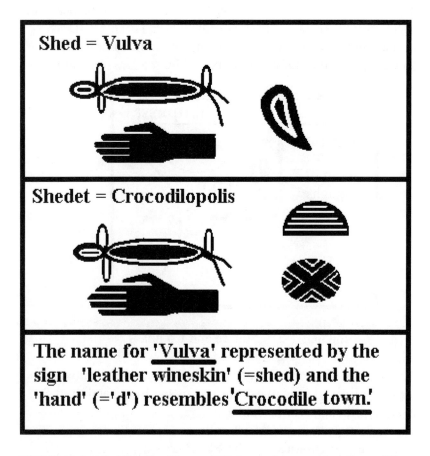

FIGURE 1-3C: The Spelling of Vulva relates to the Crocodile
(Modified from IHH by Schumann-Antelme & Rossini)

Actually the word 'Shed' for 'Vulva is spelled the same way as that of the 'town of the Crocodile' that is also 'Shed'- (eT). The

'-et' ending is incorrectly added to 'Shed' as the half-circle hieroglyphic sign for the letter 'T' is not in the spelling section of the word, but rather it is in the interpretive symbols on the right hand side.

The star constellation Draco, the Dragon has exactly seventeen named stars in the body of the dragon, thus our seven headed biblical dragon has 'seven heads and ten horns', adding up to seventeen in the above quote of the Book of Revelation. The Egyptians had the Crocodile in place of the Dragon. If my theory is correct than they would tie the Crocodile / Dragon to this 'Cosmic Birth Process' we are unrevealing. (Figure 1-3C).

By now we suspect that if the Dragon or Crocodile sits in between the two hot wires of the Earth's geo-dynamo, then it has to have some sort of semantic relation to the cosmic female birth canal. Sure enough, we find the word 'vulva' almost spelled the same as the 'town of the Crocodile, that is Crocodilopolis'. It seems obvious that the ancient Egyptians understood the cosmic birth processes well, and in their stories recorded down the celestial events. They were advanced scientists not 'incestuous' Pharaohs marrying their sisters and their daughters.

Those hieroglyphic carvings on the walls of the pyramids describe the Sun and his sisters, which is Mother Earth and planet Venus. They are 'planet sisters and brothers', not incest performing humans. Who ever interpreted those stories, as incest must had a double dose lecture on Oedipus complex by the psychologists. The Egyptians who erected the pyramids and left us those carvings on the walls would not waist their time to tell us that some humans had ugly looking animal heads (we know that!) or that some people develop incestuous relationships with their family members (we also know that!), but they left us invaluable scientific information about the periodic Earth changes, so we could be ready (we don't seem to know that!).

They certainly did understand the workings of the geo-dynamo with the dragon in charge of the wheel. Then in the next quote from the Bible again the great harlot is sitting on many waters. It exactly has seven waves and the corresponding hieroglyphic letter is drawn as **'seven waves' ='N' and means 'water/flood'.**

"1 … Come, I will show you the judgment of the **great harlot who sits on many waters**.

2 "With whom the **kings** of the earth committed fornication, and the inhabitants of the earth were made **drunk with the wine** of her fornication.

3 So he carried me away in the Spirit into the wilderness. And I saw a **woman sitting on a scarlet beast** which was full of names of blasphemy, **having seven heads and ten horns**.   (Bible, Revelation, Chapter 17, Verses 1-3.)

By now it seems clear that the Dragon (Crocodile) is the star constellation in between the Compass. That explains the opening of the Mouth of the Crocodile Ceremony. The two long jaws of the crocodile's mouth in this instance become the 'two pillars' or the 'two olive trees' that defines the Magnetic North and the Polar North. The opening of the two hot wires of the geo-dynamo resembles a compass as it is shown when the Grand Architect measures it in Figure 2-2C of the next chapter.

Therefore, any well read open-minded Freemason should be proud to find **the Square & Compass** on this graph. This ancient scientific knowledge of an about **24degree angle opening** of the compass, which also naturally corresponds to the **24hour day** and the **24,000year Precessional cycle** of the Earth's orbit coincidentally resonates with the **24 stars (17 and 7) who are the 24 biblical elders in Revelation.** It comes from the sum of the stars in the Dragon (17) and the Bear (7). That **is the hidden basics of the cosmic mechanics of the geo-dynamo.**

Only the study of astronomy and Earth mechanics will reveal that. A local Bible study group may not. That opening between the 'two north poles' also was divided into 100leagues to jointly correspond to the rounded number of the 100 Venus Transit Pairs that close the 'mouth of the Crocodile'. That is the time when those 'sister loving' Pharaohs are getting into trouble and have to devise a Ceremony of the Opening of the Mouth of the Crocodile'. In a cosmic moral sense it is an acceptable story.

In Figure 1-4 I illustrate the fact that the Goose / Cygnus constellation is what we commonly known as the Northern Cross. Is this the cross that the Christ teaching brought to us as a cosmic wisdom? If we talk about the 'Creator' and 'His knowledge' then the scientific understanding must measure up to the imparted wisdom.

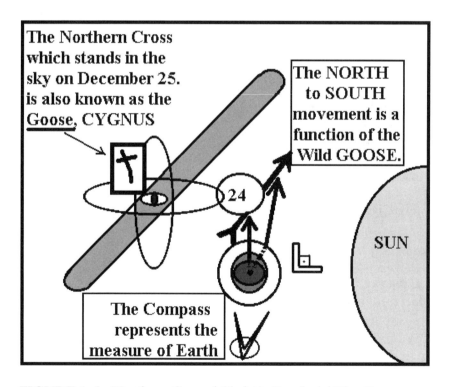

FIGURE 1-4. Northern Cross / Christ's Symbol / The Goose

I am claiming that the Ancients devised a scientific knowledge base, which permeates the Egyptian Hieroglyphics and even Judeo-Christian mythology. The famous Ra Priests were most likely largely Semitic in origin, it would not be surprising to find the Egyptian Mystery School Teachings embedded in Hebrew Wisdom and the well known but largely misunderstood and mis-explained Judeo-Christian teachings of the Holy Bible.

On Figure 1-5 A. one can observe the Goose with the Sun. It means 'Sah-Rah' or 'Shah-Ra', the Son of the Sun. His parents are standing next to him, the 'Delta' is his father and the 'Ankh' is his mother.

FIGURE 1-5A. The Goose is the Son, with Father & Mother
(Egyptian Hieroglyphic Depiction)

The Prince Son is from the Sun, but He is tied to the **Goose** as the marker of the air-born movement creating **Galactic Center's electromagnetic Force,** which shifts the Earths Magnetic North toward the South. The **King** Father is shown as the **Delta Pyramid** shaped 'tipi' or the Sheepherders' Tent to identify him with **the Sunspot Eruption as a male function.** The **Mother** is depicted as an **Ankh,** which in itself is a 'goddess-female' representation.

But I am not sure that the 'sex-minded' ancient scientists were not thinking of dual gender meaning in that symbol by separating the 'oval' shape from the 'T' shape. May be that is why the Coptics picked the 'T' as a male marker in place of the more obvious 'D' of the Hebrews and Greeks.

The Son of the Sun is the Sunspot eruption that tilts the Earth's axis and prepares the globe for the magnetic shift to charge up the fading protective magnetic field. Without that 'evil' force the Earth could not be functioning for too long to keep the harmful cosmic radiation away from us. Life on Earth can only be going on if this periodic destructive force prevails. It is not an angry God, but a scientific one who knows that this has to be done.

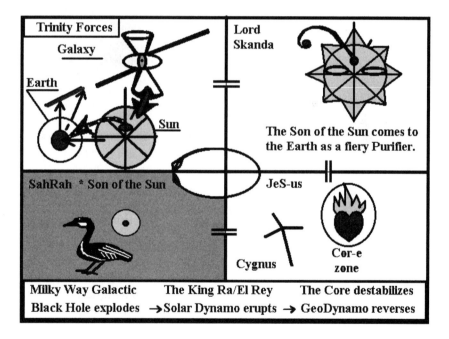

FIGURE 1-5B. The Sun is the Old King of Mythology.

The left lower quadrant of Figure 1-3 of the above diagram demonstrates the Goose with the Sun. It reads Sah-Rah, or Shah-

Ra. Shah stands for the Son or the Prince of the Sun King. Ra is the King, naturally denotes the Sun itself. For now it is enough to know that the Galactic Center controls the Sun eruptions and the Line Between THE MAGNETIC NORTH AND THE POLAR NORTH is exactly lined up NORTH TO SOUTH parallel along the Milky Way GALACTIC PLANE and by action certainly involved in the ending and beginning of any New Ages. Therefore, if a Wild Goose flies above head going from NORTH to SOUTH utilizing the ancient avian PGS system of the ELECTRO-MAGNETISM of the Earth, would that not be the best concept for an animal character to represent the electromagnetic force from the Galactic Center.

Because every 12,000years the Galactic Center destabilizes the Sun and causes it to erupt, the Sun with the circle in the middle on the picture represents the Venus transiting in front of the Sun and also refers to the Sunspot, which calendarically followed the Venus Transit by a year or two. This event is what burnt the earth to ashes. The erupting Sunspot is the Child from the barren old lady in ancient mythology and religious lore, or more clearly the Sunspot is the Son of the Sun. In Hindu mythology the sunspot is placed on the face of Shiva, the Sun as his famous third eye.

In Egyptian hieroglyphic picture the uraeus, the serpent wrapped around the Sun is the resonation, which will strike as a standing up cobra. This explains why the goddess, such as Isis or Cleopatra would wear the uraeus serpent as a headdress. The story of the Serpent and Eve, who is tempted by him, contains the same wisdom. In the Hindu Myths by Penguin Classics a tale about Lord Skanda (he did cause some 'scandals' apparently), the Savior and Purifier, the Son of the Sun came to earth in the following manner:

Lord Skanda the *son of fire* was born in a *forest of reeds beside the river.* (Right next to the star Rigel, which is the <u>foot of Orion</u>, is where the longest constellation of the sky, the celestial 'river' begins.) At the same time the main Hindu god, Indra happened to be looking for a husband for a goddess. Kama, the Harlot was the goddess who passed by. She is Venus, who just passed in front of Shiva, the Old King / Sun. At the sight of so much beauty the Sun then 'raptured' (prematurely!) and out of his body, the arc of the Sun, was born a Child Lord Skanda. And I continue the story with some actual quotes:

> "Then **he who shone like the sun** … saw the battle between gods and demons raging on the Hill of Sunrise. **The God of Hundred Sacrifices** saw the dawn full of blood-red clouds, … A dreadful halo has appeared around the sun and the moon … The **ocean** is carrying great quantities of **blood** against her current, and the **fire-faced jackals** are howling at the sun."(Author's heavyset) (Hindu Myths. Penguin.)

So, from this above quote from the Hindu Myths we can deduce that the Sun bore a Son. The Sun is the Old King and therefore, <u>**Lord Skanda, who is the Son of the Sun, the Savior and the Purifier, is the Sun Spot eruption.**</u> Not only the 'scandalous' name for **Skanda** (Scandal) but also the Sun's easterly direction is pointing to the Seven Stars of the Pleiades, who are called **Krittika** (Critical) in Hindu Myths. These are enigmatically revealing names for the participating celestial gods. The name **Madana** (Madonna) means the '**maddener**' in Hindu Myths. She is properly named as she turns the old Sun King, Shiva sexually 'mad' to rapture and to release the first-born seed. There goes the exalted and faulty believe in the saving grace of a holy 'rapture'. Now we are either dead meat or simply everybody is left behind. I hope that I don't have to feed anybody's horse who, has 'raptured'.

'The God of Hundred Sacrifices' is the secret meaning for the 'hundred' pairs of Venus Transit and the 'Hundred League' between the two north poles whose action marks the End Ages.

The words 'critical', 'scandalous', 'maddener' and others can take on a new cosmic meaning as we learn about the major stars and astronomical players of the cosmic tragedy of Hindu Myths. Certainly this version of our cosmic and cyclically scientific understanding of the Old King, the Savior Prince and the Harlot and the Virgin ('the two Mary') who gives birth to a world-savior puts an uneasy twist on our Dark Age derived literal religious understanding of ancient wisdom.

Let us examine what Professor Barbara S. Lesko; a research assistant in the Department of Egyptology at Brown University writes about the goddesses of Egypt in her book, titled 'The Great Goddesses of Egypt':

> "Isis, giver of life, residing in the Sacred Mound, Satis, Lady of Biggeh, She is the one who pours out the inundation
> That makes all people live and green plants grow,
> Who provides divine offerings for the gods,
> And invocation-offerings for the Transfigured Ones (the dead) ...
> She is the Lady of Heaven, Earth, and the Netherworld
> Having brought them into existence through what
> Her heart conceived and her hands created
> She is the Ba that is in every city,
> Watching over her son Horus and her brother Osiris."

> Prof. Lesko's comment:
> 'Here Isis is credited with being the Creator of All – heaven, earth, and the hereafter. Again, as we saw with the goddess Neith, the Egyptian priests of a goddess had no hesitation in claiming preeminence for her and saw no difficulty in having a female take on the role of Creator. '
> (Barbara S. Lesko, The Great Goddesses of Egypt)

Then two paragraphs later in the same book in Hymn 5 even more exotic powers are given to Isis (Venus), the all-powerful goddess who was the main subject of the praying masses for thousands of years and today may be symbolized by the Sacred Mother, Guadalupe or Virgin Mary. Isis reign ended with the emergence of Christianity, but she cleverly got incorporated into the new religion with almost as much power as she had before.

> "Mighty one, foremost of the goddesses
> Ruler in Heaven, Queen on Earth
> **Sun-Goddess in the circuit of the sun-disc**; …
> All the gods are under her command;
> Great of Magic when she is in the palace,
> Great one upon whose command the King
> gloriously appears on the throne."
> (Author's heavy set and underlining)
> (From Barbara S. Lesko, The Great Goddesses of Egypt.)

In the above hymn, this revered Egyptian goddess is named a 'Sun-Goddess' and is placed in the 'circuit of the sun-disc', the same place from where Lord Skanda of the Hindu Myths originated after his father, the Sun-King sexually 'raptured'. Not only we have a Savior born, but also he accomplishes that sacred event just straight coming from the body of his Father, the Sun. All this is without the physical involvement of a Mother. It sheds some light on a form of 'virgin birth' and explains why the Trinity contains the Father, Son, and Holy Spirit, but no traces of an earthly and sexually active birthing mother.

With this in mind, the Egyptian, Babylonian, Hindu and biblical Judeo-Christian tales will come to light. For some of the skeptics the 'illumination' has to wait until the next Sunspot eruption that can burn everything to ashes to understand the cosmic and human significance of these ancient tales. This cosmic soap opera played out on such a wide podium and with such an awesome celestial power of destruction that it made the successive generations of storytellers repeating it so the next time it comes around we will be collectively ready for it.

Well, the time is here, the stories are widely available, but I do not sense any urgency on the part of our spiritual teachers and I do not see much actual physical preparations. The open-minded minority who actually grasps some of these truths seems to only believe the possibility of the coming Earth changes with their intellect, but apparently not with their Spirit.

In the coming chapter's next few figures I will demonstrate a goddess, the planet Venus passing in front of the Sun. Egyptian mythology and Hebrew Wisdom from the biblical Old and New Testament ties this event to the one hundredth occurrence of the Venus Transit pairs. It is the Judeo-Christian Mary Magdalene and Virgin Mary and the Egyptian harlot Nephthys along with her sister Isis. In the rounded 12,000year cycle the pairs come about every 120years. Thus, they have to come about a hundred times. Not only it is matching the 'hundred leagues', and the Hindu 'God of the Hundred Sacrifice, but also was not even Jesus Christ killed by a 'centurion', which in Latin 'century' refers to one hundred? The letter 'C' also resembled a 'half-cycle' and a celestial 'bow'. One thing is certain from Christian prophesies - that when Christ returns for His Second Coming it will be at the turbulent End Times. His title as Prince or King and the fact that He is tied to a Strong Illumination or Being the Light of the World to me signifies that this specific time will be the or will be coinciding with the Sunspot eruption and the subsequent period of Tribulation. Thus, in this first chapter we realized a number of cosmic secrets that the Ancients hid in their fables. Will we find more secrets and will they fit our expanding puzzle?

Chapter Two
Measuring and The Venus Calendar

One might not assume that the Bible would contain something as important as the Venus Calendar in it, as it would be too much of a New Age concept for traditional believers, but it does. Just like the Egyptians, Babylonians, Hindus and Aboriginal Native cultures, the Bible brought us the Mystery School Teachings of the Ancients. Except it is packaged in historical sounding human stories, which were only meant to hide the real cosmic meaning for the end days of an age. Well, before Noah's famous biblical Flood, the Sun erupted in between the two Venus Transit pairs. These 'two wives' of the main God, the Ram-headed Amun are spaced SEVEN years apart. It is commemorated in the Bible as the 'two wives of Jacob' who were seven years apart. Can you see the sacred Venus Calendar in the ancient biblical stories?

Seven years of famine followed and then the Flood of Noah happened. Those years would fall on the current calendar as the Sun Spot eruption occurring at Harvest of 2006/2007 and the Flood in around 2013 if we extricated the information for our own Mayan Calendar age ending. My earlier work 'The Celestial Clock' expands on the Mayan Calendar ending of 2012. One of the best works on the subject is from John Major Jenkins' book titled the 'Maya Cosmogenesis 2012.' It is a must read!

Later on in this chapter in Figure 2-3 we can observe the astronomical significance of the Two Goddesses, which are the two Venus Transits in front of the Sun and in between the Horns of the Taurian Bull in the sky. The last time it happened was in 1880's and for our age the pair comes again in 2004 and in 2012. Therefore, these are the two goddesses, who have creative and destructive powers in our universe. The first Venus Transit of the pair is termed the Harlot, because supposedly the first one of the Venus pairs in the time of Noah made the Sun erupt and two or three year later Mother Earth would shake and tremble as a loose woman who enjoyed this cosmic sex. One might think that this is not recorded down in the Bible, but it was. I shall swiftly quote a few sentences from the Scripture to show the related story. Not to over complicate the issue, I will go to the Book of the Kings in the Bible, since we already suggested that the Old King stands for the Sun.   "34 Now a certain man drew a bow at random, and struck the king of Israel between the joints of his armor. …
35 The battle increased that day; and **the king** was propped up **in his chariot**, facing the Syrians, and died at evening.
36 Then, **as the sun was going down**, …
37 So **the king died**,-(because the king is the sun!-author)
38 Then someone washed the chariot at a pool in Samaria, and **the dogs licked up his blood** while **the harlots bathed**, according to the **word of the Lord** which He had spoken.   (The author's heavyset and underlining)
(Bible, Kings I, Chapter 22, Verses 34-38.)

Have you noticed above that when the 'word of mouth' of our Lord opens loud, we can always expect some major tragedies? Let me progress on to the Old Testament's celestial revelation from the Book of Kings II:

> "8 So they answered him, "A hairy **man wearing** a leather **belt** around his waist." (Would it be <u>Orion</u>, the Hunter, whose belt with the three stars are world famous?-Author)
> "9 Then the **king** sent to him a **captain of fifty** with his fifty men.
> "10 So Elijah answered and said to the captain of fifty, "If If I am a man of God, then **let fire come down from Heaven** and consume you and your fifty men." And fire came down from heaven and consumed him and his fifty men. " (Bible, Kings II, Chapter I, Verses 8-10.)

Then now that we see from the Bible that God sent us fire from heaven in a particular calendar ending then we should see if in the coming verses would let us recognize the Venus Transit in front of the Sun. So, we are going back to the Bible for more:

> "21 And when all the Moabites heard that the **kings** had come up to **fight** against them, …
> 22 Then they rose up early in the morning, and the **sun** was shining **on the water**, and the Moabites saw the water on the other side as **red as blood**. (The red blood-colored water is from the under water volcanism, which was caused by the sunspot eruption.-Author)
>
> 27 Then **he took his eldest son** who would have reigned in his place, **and offered him as a burnt offering upon the wall**; (Bible, Kings II, Chapter 3, Verses 21-27.)
> ('Burnt offering' a synonym for Sunspot eruption.-Author)

Then enters Venus, the goddess coming in front of the King, the Sun and full fills the sacred birth. Just as other old ladies in the Bible she conceives at an matriarchal age. 'Ven' in Hungarian means 'very old' and it may be derived from 'Ven-us'. These old ladies bare a magic child. See Kings II in the Bible.

> "1 A certain woman of the wives of the sons of the prophets cried out to Elisha, saying, "Your servant my husband is dead . ...
(* As a personal note, here we find another of many of the biblical widows - just as Isis - who are old and barren and relying on the will of God or miracle to have a Child, who will in turn die and needs to be revived! - Author)

> 16 Then he said, "About this time next year you shall embrace a son."
> 17 But the **woman** conceived, and **bore a son when the appointed time had come**. (Appointed time ... as in a calendar? – Author)
> 20 When he had taken him and brought him to his mother, he sat on her knees till **noon**, and **then died**. ...
> 23 So he said, "Why are you going to him today? It is neither the **New Moon** nor the Sabbath."
> 24 Then she saddled a **donkey,** " (Bible, Kings II, Ch.4)
(* What is it with the stubborn donkey and holy people? May be when the Earth's core stopped rotating - it was thought to be a stubborn donkey who would not move! - Author)

Now we only have left the reviving to be performed on the Holy Child and we mainly examined the Old Testament.

> "34 And he went up and lay on the child, and put his mouth on his mouth, his eyes on his eyes, and his hands on his hands; and he stretched himself out on the child, and the flesh of the child became warm."
> (Bible, Kings II, Chapter 4, Verses 1-34.)

This story makes more sense when one reads the corresponding Hindu Myths along with it. Not only the shaking, but also the fact that her underwater volcanism erupted and caused the ocean water to turn blood red make sense. This earned Mother Earth the dubious distinction of the harlot who is having sex with the sun or father sky while she is menstruating. This was the original sin!

The Egyptian Fertility Goddess would be Hathor for that role. 'Hat-hor' means 'the house of Hor or Heru' (Horus) the hero. Having sex, even if it is only between the Sun and Mother Earth, is forbidden when the female partner is menstruating.

As matter of fact, that is how the Hindu Myths interpreted the water turning to blood. The Egyptians or the ancient Jews smearing blood red paint outside the door on their buildings probably referred to the memory of the menstruating Mother Earth in that ancient catastrophe. Professor Lesko writes about the role of Hathor in the next quote:

> "By the Nineteenth Dynasty **Hathor** was described more frequently as the Eye of Re or his **fiery uraeus**. The flying **sun disks** above each temple doorway, to give one example, are accompanied by raised cobra heads. This **uraeus is** then the **god's protection** and is **equated,** not only **with the Two Ladies** but **also with Hathor**. ...
>
> "**Hathor had started** her career **as wife of the sun god Re**. ... Osiris's wife, Isis, also moved into increased prominence in the funerary context by the Nineteenth Dynasty , so **Hathor** may have become much more often **associated with sexuality and fertility** ... ."
>
> (Author's underlining and heavyset)

So why would the planet Venus (goddess) be thought of as the wife of the Sun or even his eye? Just as the 'third eye' of Shiva the Sun in Hindu mythology came to the Earth to burn it up.

The famous Egyptian scholar E.A. Wallis Budge writes about 'The legend of Horus of Behutet and the Winged Disk' in his 1912 classic titled the 'Legends of the Gods: The Egyptian Texts' republished by Dover in 1994:

> "XII. 2. In the three hundred and sixty-third year of Ra-(Heru-Khuti), who liveth for ever and for ever, His Majesty was in TA-KENS, and his soldiers were with him; ... 3. And **Ra set out on an expedition in his boat,** and his followers were with him, and he arrived at UTHES-HERU, (which lay to) the west of this nome, and to the east of the canal PAKHENSU, ... And Heru-Behutet was 4 in the boat of Ra, and he said unto his father Ra-Heru-Khuti (i.e., Ra-Harmachis) "I see that the enemies are conspiring against their lord; let thy **fiery serpent gain the mastery** ... over them." ... XIII. 1. ... And Heru-Behutet flew up into the horizon In the form of the **great Winged Disk,** ... and he **attacked with such terrific force** those who opposed him,
> 2 **that they could neither see with their eyes nor hear with their ears, and each of them slew his fellow.** In a moment of time there was **not a single creature left alive.** And Ra embraced the ... of Ra , and said unto Heru-Behutet,
> **"Thou didst put grapes into the water** which cometh forth from it, and thy heart rejoiced thereat;" and for this reason the water (or canal) of Heru-Behutet is called "(Grape-Water)" unto this day, ...4 And Heru-Behutet said, "Advance, O Ra, and look thou upon thine enemies who are lying under thee on this land; thereupon the **Majesty of Ra set out on the way, and the goddess Asthertet ('Ashtoreth?) was with him, ...**"
> *** (the above female name is close to the biblical Esther, but more importantly it is representing Astoria / Ishtar, who is the planet Venus! -Author)

Therefore, the above Egyptian tale tells about Ra the Sun King who is destructive through a 'fiery serpent'. Then the water turns 'grape' colored. Venus is with him when this happens. This is another proof that our cosmic earth change theory is on the right track.

In another tale from the same book of Wallis Budge a story is told about 'The Legend of the Destruction of Mankind:

> "(Here is the story of Ra,) the god who was self-begotten
> and self-created, after he had assumed the sovereignty
> over men and women, and gods, and things, the ONE god.
> … His Majesty heard the words of complaint, saying: -
> "Behold, his Majesty (Life, Strength, and Health to him!)
> hath grown old, and his bones have become like silver,
> and his members have turned into gold and his hair is
> like unto real lapis-lazuli." His Majesty heard the words
> of complaint which men and women were uttering, and
> his Majesty (Life, Strength, and Health to him!) said unto
> those who were in his train: - "Cry out, and bring to me
> my Eye, and Shu, and Tefnut, and Seb, and Nut, and the
> father-gods, and the mother-gods who were with me, even
> when I was in Nu …
> … Then Ra spake unto Nu, saying: - O thou first-born
> god from whom I came into being … those who were
> created by my Eye are uttering words of complaint
> against me. … Then the gods spake …: "Let thine Eye
> go forth and let it destroy for thee those who revile thee
> with words of evil, for there is no eye whatsoever that
> can go before it and resist thee and it when it journeyeth
> in the form of Hathor." …"

In this above example, Ra again is tied to the destruction of mankind. The goddess Hathor is the Harlot that is the secret representation of the first Venus in the Venus Transit pair.

Let us now switch subjects to see how the 'compass' is tied to the astronomical mysteries. In Figure 2-1 we will talk about the 'Compass' as a measuring device, which the traditional Egyptologist labeled a 'wooden plough'. It could be one of the intended meanings. Although, as one examines the semantic relations of the word 'mer', it will be rather clear that the scribes mainly meant a cosmic 'compass', not a wooden plough!.

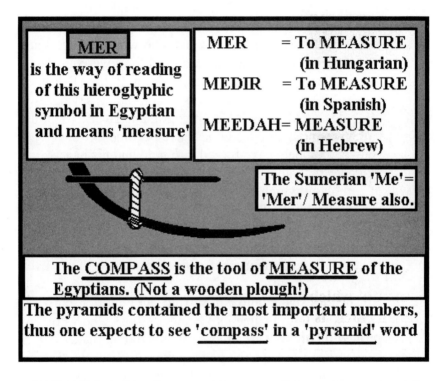

MER	MER	= To MEASURE (in Hungarian)
is the way of reading of this hieroglyphic symbol in Egyptian and means 'measure'	MEDIR	= To MEASURE (in Spanish)
	MEEDAH	= MEASURE (in Hebrew)

The Sumerian 'Me'= 'Mer'/ Measure also.

The **COMPASS** is the tool of **MEASURE** of the Egyptians. (Not a wooden plough!)

The pyramids contained the most important numbers, thus one expects to see 'compass' in a 'pyramid' word

FIGURE 2-1. The Compass Measures. (It's not just a plough!)

The best measure of the ancient Egyptians seems to have been the Pyramids in the old times. Therefore, it would behoove us to investigate the possibility that the written word of PYRAMID in Egyptian will contain the LETTER of the compass – 'MER'. The Hungarian 'Mer' word for 'measure' is identical to the Egyptian.

It is not at all surprising, because the most important word in a language meaning 'God' is said to be 'Isten' in the Hungarian language and almost identical to that of the ancient Egyptian and Hindu god, called the 'pillar' and is spelled 'Istan' or 'Istanu' Tying to this the word for the Goddess Venus in Babylonian is 'Ishtara/Istar'. The Sanskrit word for 'god' is 'Ish'/'Is' and it is found in biblical names such as of Is-mael, Is-rael.

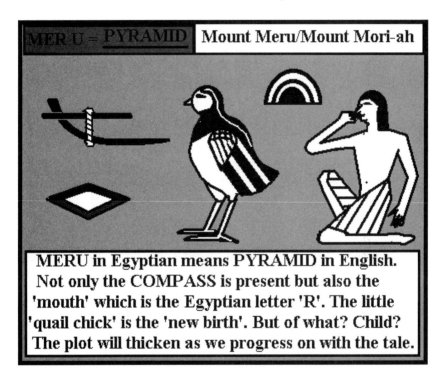

FIGURE 2-2A. Mount Meru is a Pyramid.
(Modified from IHH by Schumann-Antelme & Rossini)

The sacred mountain 'Meru' is also found in the Hindu Myths:
" … and the **king of the gods**, … determined to think of a way to bring about the **birth of a son** of Hara. Then the gods went …**to a peak on the tip of Meru** …"

FIGURE 2-2B. The Compass Measures the Pyramids
(Slightly modified from Wilkinson's Reading Egyptian Art,
'Hoe and obelisks', Tomb of Rekhmire, Thebes, 18th Dynasty)

As one can clearly observe on Figure 2-2B that to measure a
couple of obelisks, one would not need a 'hoe', but might require
a compass. The two obelisks here may represent the two pillars of
the earth, which are the Magnetic and Polar Norths. This is the
same type of obelisk that stands in our nation's capital.

One of the Hindu sacred mountains is called Mount Meru. In
the Bible we find the name Mount Mori-ah. Certainly, both could
be secret references to the man made mountain of measure,
which is the pyramid.

Even when the earth was 'flat' at the beginning of the Dark
Ages in the 13th century, the all-knowing Great Architect of the
Universe was still measuring a round globe with his compass.

The Grand Architect of the Universe.
French manuscript of the 13th Century CE.

FIGURE 2-2C. The Grand Architect of the Universe is using
The Compass to Measure the Earth.
('The Greatest Story Ever Sold' by Acharya S.
Used with permission and consent of the
Adventure Unlimited Publishing, Kempton,IL)

It should not be a great surprise to observe the Creator using the
compass to measure the radius of the Earth on Figure 2-2C, a
rather revealing picture found on a French Manuscript from the
13th. Century. This was just prior to Pope Clement V. single
handedly blowing out the torch of Illumination and allowed the
destructive beginning of the Dark Ages. With the execution of
DeMolay, the leader of the Knight Templars, light, science and
progress almost died out also. It was obviously a sad period in the
time of human kind. It was followed by a destructive witch-hunt
that the corrupt Dark Age church allowed to take place.

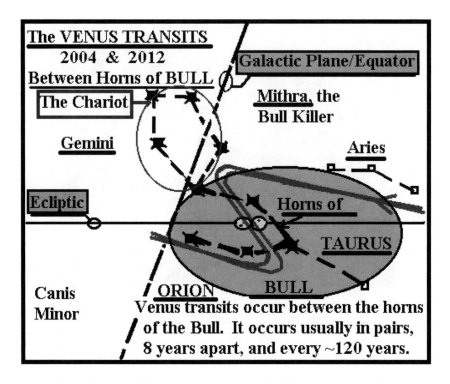

FIGURE 2-3. The Venus Transit Of The Calendar.
(Modified from the article 'The Venus Transit' by
Nick Anthony Fiorenza as posted on his web site)

The reversed 'S' over the horns of the Taurian Bull is the path
of Venus in 2004 and then again in 2012. The two wives of the
old King-Sun, just like in the Bible Jacob has two wives seven
years apart. Makes one ask the question to see if the Scripture is
historical or astronomical. Well, in the above picture this is an
astronomical event, possibly the most important long time
calendar measure. The goddess with the horns on her head and
the sun in between the horns is a well-known Egyptian depiction.
In another article written by Nick Anthony Fiorenza, the sinus
wave pattern of the eight years of the Venus Transit orbit is
shown at the beginning of the path as a phonetic capital 'I' or 'J'.

The last year's sinus wave resembles a 'S', just as we can see in the above Figure 2-3. This suggests to me that the Venus Transit Calendar was a major importance to the Ancients and possibly even the core of the enigmas in the secret societies hierarchy.

As I mentioned earlier the '**IS**' was the Sans-Črit base **word for God**. The **similarly written 'JS' version we could detect in** the names of such important biblical figures as '**JeS**'-us, **JoS**-eph, **JeS**se, **JoS**hua, and a number of others. For example, in the case of Jes-us, we know that the '-us' ending is a Latin addition. Just as Marc becomes Marc-us and Paul becomes Paul-us in Rome. So dropping the '-us' ending from Jes-us - leaves us with 'Jes'. Knowing that neither the ancient Jews nor the Egyptians used soft vowels in their alphabet, thus **the name is reduced to 'J-S'.** And that is exactly what defines the sinus waves of the beginning and the end **of the eight-year cycle between the Venus Transit** years. Is it only a coincidence that the Bible ties Jesus to the Morning Star (Venus) on several occasions, knowing full well that Venus is always associated with feminine qualities? But if the emergence of the main God or the purifying Prince happens in between the two Venus Transits, then the spelling of those biblical names would make perfect sense.

The **bullhorn** in the sky, which angled similar to a **compass**, became the first letter of the Hebrew ABC. This first letter was named '**Aleph**' and it means the '**Ox**' in Hebrew to maintain the relation to the bullhorn. The ancient Greeks turned Aleph 90degrees counterclockwise, thereby making the letter Alpha into the current form of the capital letter 'A'. May be the 90degree square motion performed on the compass shaped 'A' made the 'square and compass' minded ancient Freemasons happy about these secrets. The same thing happened to the half circle shaped letter 'D', which was the Coptic Egyptian letter 'T' (Tau) symbolizing the Spiral Force and the Pillars of the Earth holding up our world.

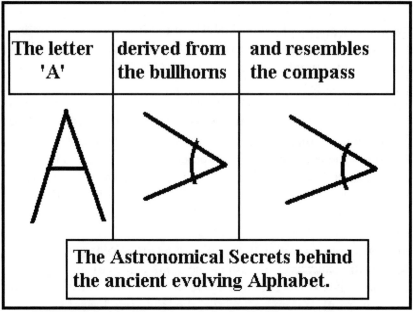

FIGURE 2-4A. The letter A is the Bullhorn or Compass

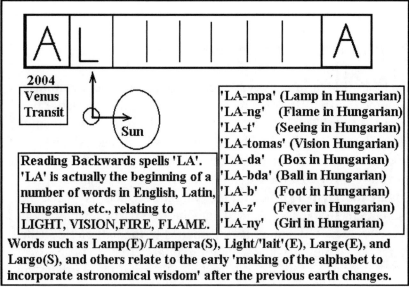

FIGURE 2-4B. Making up the Original Words

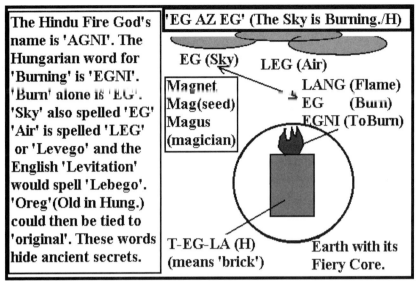

The Hindu Fire God's name is 'AGNI'. The Hungarian word for 'Burning' is 'EGNI'. 'Burn' alone is 'EG'. 'Sky' also spelled 'EG' 'Air' is spelled 'LEG' or 'Levego' and the English 'Levitation' would spell 'Lebego'. 'Oreg'(Old in Hung.) could then be tied to 'original'. These words hide ancient secrets.

'EG AZ EG' (The Sky is Burning./H)

EG (Sky)   LEG (Air)

Magnet
Mag(seed)
Magus
(magician)

LANG (Flame)
EG   (Burn)
EGNI (To Burn)

T-EG-LA (H)
(means 'brick')

Earth with its
Fiery Core.

FIGURE 2-4C. The Sky is Burning in Hungarian

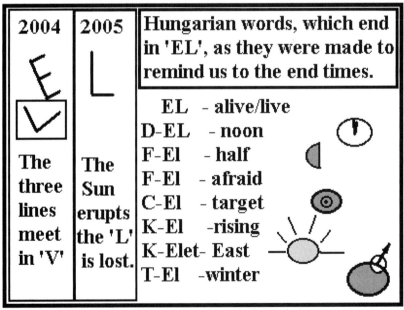

2004   2005

The three lines meet in 'V'

The Sun erupts the 'L' is lost.

Hungarian words, which end in 'EL', as they were made to remind us to the end times.

EL - alive/live
D-EL - noon
F-El - half
F-El - afraid
C-El - target
K-El   -rising
K-Elet- East
T-El   -winter

FIGURE 2-4D. Words are Cosmic in Origin

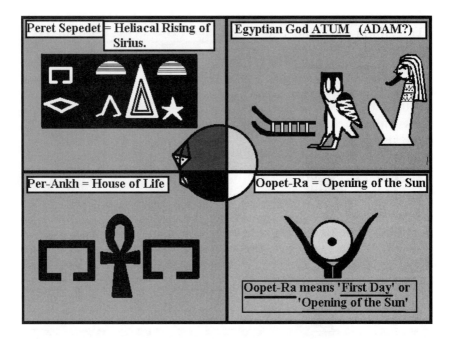

FIGURE 2-4. Opening is Between the Horns of the Bull.
(Modified from IHH by Schumann-Antelme & Rossini)

On Figure 2-4, we are now only interested in the right lower quadrant, which depicts the Sun with a Dot in the middle that likely means the Venus Transit and the Sunspot and may be also the Core. Now this Sun with those three meanings is placed between the Horns of the Bull to signify 'opening'. This Sun 'dot' may also mean the 'Son of the Sun' and it definitely binds the Venus Transit to the sunspot eruption, because that is the only time this whole opening of a 'New Age' matters. This emergence of the 'Young Prince, as the Sunspot eruption' in between the two Venus Transits will be further explored as the examples of the Two Goddesses of the Egyptians and the Two Wives of our founding Biblical Fathers. The word 'Oopet' is even very similar to its English meaning of 'Open'. The Sun opens a new day or a New Age.

FIGURE 2-5. The Two Wives of Amun.
(Modified from Hornung's 'The Ancient Egyptian
Books of the Afterlife)

Returning to the concept of the ram-headed God with two wives we find King Tut, Tut-Ankh-Amun, or simply Amun. As we mentioned earlier the ram-headed God stands for the cosmic scientific concept of spiral galactic forces and the two wives are the Venus Transit pair of the so important Venus Calendar. The two wives in Figure 2-5 also represent the two moving parts of the Earth's geo-dynamo. It will explain the reasoning of why the Lower Egyptian Kingdom was to the North and the Upper Kingdom to the South. The important color designations of Red and White will be revealed. Not only Santa Claus wears red and white, but it will be also tied to the 'Wars of the Roses'. But for now, let us return to the Figure of 2-5 and the meaning of the letters 'T' in the name of King Tut-Ankh-Amun. Thus, the two 'T' letters signifying the Two Pillars of the Earth, the 'W' is the birth of the New Chick. Since for our Milky Way Galaxy the Spiral Forces are the most powerful unseen entities governing our Universe, the Spiral Ram Horns naturally became endowed with mythical powers.

Even in the Bible one can find these two names, King David (DaWooD / TWT) and Ammon (Amun) connected in a battle:
> "1 It happened after this that the king of the people of Ammon died, and Hanun his son reigned in his place.
> 2 ... And David's servants came into the land of the people of Ammon." (Bible, II Samuel, Chapter 10, 1-2)

Historically, it does make the Jewish people the neighbors of the Egyptians and also show that some of them lived in Egypt.

Returning back to analyzing forms and concepts, the letter 'Y' in the name of Y-ah-(weh) meant the male god and it also covered the upside 'delta' shape and combined the two pillars into one. A more amazing assumption is that the ancient Semitic teachers were left with the knowledge of the shape of the male DNA, which is the 'Y'. It is certainly difficult to prove now, but surely the 'Y' or upside down delta shape in several different forms remained the designation for the male gender and mythical kings who never existed. People, who claim descendants from kings such as King Arthur, may not know that he never existed in flesh, but was an astronomical story explaining periodic earth changes. Disappointing? May be.

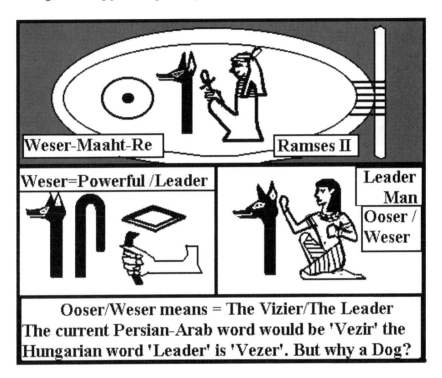

FIGURE 2-6. Osiris the Vizier is the Leader.
(Modified from IHH by Schumann-Antelme & Rossini)

The word 'vizi-er' hides the Hungarian word 'viz' meaning 'water' and 'vizi' is 'from the water', thus the 'vizier' was the 'wise-man' who understood the secrets of Noah's Flood! This word is also detected in the Spanish and English as 'vis-cous'. Furthermore, 'vista' and 'vision' ties this previous concept of 'leader' / 'water' / 'wisdom' to the 'vision' from the Galactic Center's Eye of God to reveal the cosmic connections to these strangely interrelated words. The Hungarian words 'vezer' (leader), 'vezet' (lead / drive), 'vezetek' (electrical wire), 'vezekel' (religious penitence), 'veszely' (danger), 'veszteget' (losing) 'Ar-viz' (Flood) and a number of others relate to this ancient Egyptian Pharaoh who is blamed for this cosmic tragedy.

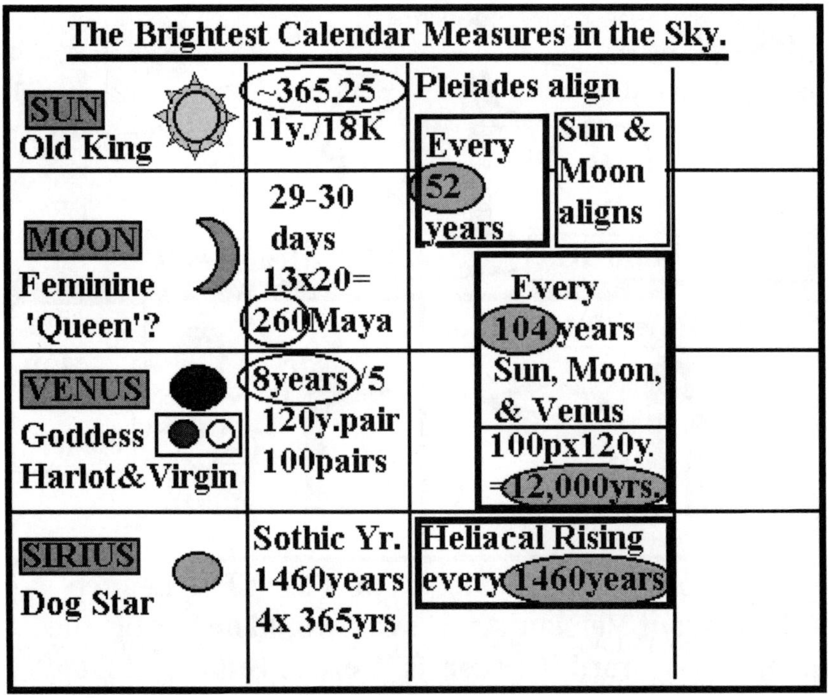

The Brightest Calendar Measures in the Sky.				
SUN Old King	~365.25 11y./18K	Pleiades align		
MOON Feminine 'Queen'?	29-30 days 13x20= 260 Maya	Every 52 years	Sun & Moon aligns	
			Every 104 years	
VENUS Goddess Harlot&Virgin	8years/5 120y.pair 100pairs	Sun, Moon, & Venus 100px120y. =12,000yrs.		
SIRIUS Dog Star	Sothic Yr. 1460years 4x 365yrs	Heliacal Rising every 1460years		

FIGURE 2-7: The Four Brightest Objects In The Sky

Examining the cosmic calendar, the Ancient astronomy priests used the four brightest objects in the sky to measure long times. The Dog Star Sirius is highest in the sky around the last week of July, which is the hottest part of the summer. It is also the beginning of the wheat harvest. How bad can it be during the 'dogs days of summer'? Is it the same dog, which likes to lick up the blood of the King and the Bull in the Book of the Kings I?

The Egyptian Sothic Calendar, based on the rising of the Dog Star, is 1,460year long. 'Eight dogs' would extend to an amazing 8 x 1,460 = 11,680years, very close to the 11,600years end. Even the number '8' resembles two interconnected cycles! Thus, the Dog Star, Sirius - the fourth brightest objects of the ancient Egyptian sky - also became integral parts of the Sacred Universal Calendar. Similar attempts for timekeeping can be seen in other parts of the world. The Mayan Calendar matched the Sun Cycle to the Moon Cycle, which consisted of the gestational length of a human birth, that is 9 months or 260days. The month lasted 20days and there were 13 of them. Therefore, the Sun and the Moon cycle interfaced every 52 years. The 13 & 20 division is displayed in the Hindu Zodiac astronomy where the arc distance between the constellations is broken up by 13'20'' measures. That is like the Mayan Calendar's 13/20 month/days division!

The fifty soldiers usually lead by two brothers are common mythological themes. As matter of fact, Hunor and Magor, the two founding brothers of the Hungarian creation legends of their nation has fifty soldiers who go with them to chase the Golden Elk. In their adventure they stumble on two beautiful princesses who are bathing in a pond with their fifty servant girls. Thus, there are 104 of them. The two brothers take the two princesses and the soldiers take the fifty servant girls and the great nation of the Hungarians are off to a good start. Both the **52 and the 104** are utmostly important cosmic calendar cycles. They are not made up randomly, but provided by the fine-tuning of the Sun, Moon, and the Venus calendar cycles. Therefore, **every about 52 years the 'two most bright objects', the Sun and the Moon would harmonize their calendar cycles,** and every **104 years the 'three brightest objects' in the sky would meet** in a happy calendar reunion. **These are the Sun, Moon, and the Venus Calendar.**

There is a statue of the Bull killing Hero in the basement of St. Clements church in the Vatican. Not only Mithra shares Christ

Birthday on December 25th, but he is also **'sol invictus'** the **'invincible sun'**. In my book titled 'The Celestial Clock' I explained and explored the Bull Killing of Mithra. It represented the 'Chamber of the South Celestial Equator'. The bull-killing scene contains all the constellations that line up on the South Celestial Equator. The sword kills the Bull at the shoulder blade, which are the stars of the astronomical Pleiades. The stars that make up the 'South Celestial Equator' of the earth create the smallest 'third line' in the Cosmic Trinity Powers. Now it makes sense to see the three connecting lines tied to Orion and the divine cosmic birth of a sunspot that rings in the new age.

FIGURE 2-8. Mithra, killing the Bull and the Dog is licking up the Blood. (From 'The Celestial Clock' by Dr. William A. Gaspar)

Always just festivities, partying, marrying, having kids, occasionally sinning, and ritually killing poor innocent creatures in one short cosmic tragedy. Us mere humans are so predictable.

Chapter Three
Family of Gods

If there was a time in the past when gods or aliens intermarried with humans, it would be a difficult endeavor to decipher and verify from the strange mythological tales. When the ancient Greeks talk about 'giants', such as Hercules, the Titans, Hyperion (high heat) and others, it seems to be relating to scorching heat and giant hurricanes rather than the size of humans or aliens.

Let me first mention some of the Greek gods, which are clearly originated from the Egyptian deities. One example would be the Greek Hera-cles, the 'son of Hera' (the Roman Hercules) whom is someway derived from Heru. Another example would be Adonis, whose origin is from Adon/Aton/Aten. The following quote from H.A. Guerber's 'The Myths of Greece and Rome' demonstrates that the mythological 'giants' of the Greco-Romans seem to be the hurricane, volcanism and other gigantic disasters. Then on the next page I will show that Hercules and Adonis are simply derivations of Heru and Aton:

> "There the magic effect of the lotus food soon wore away, and the men rowed steadily westward until they came to the Island of Sicily, then inhabited by the **Cyclopes**, a rude race of **one-eyed giants**. ... but Ulysses and twelve companions landed in Sicily in search of food. The prospect was promising, for on the plains and hillsides great flocks of **sheep** cropped the tender grass; and Ulysses and his followers soon came to a great **cave** filled with rich stores of **milk** and cheese. This was the abode of **Polyphemus, son of Neptune, the largest** and fiercest **among the gigantic Cyclopean race**."

The largest one-eyed giant is the son of Neptune, the god of the sea. Obviously, they are talking about huge hurricanes from the heated oceans. This is how Guerber writes about the Sun myths:

> "Apollo, whose name of **Helios** is pure Greek for "the sun," had therefore not lost all physical significance for the **Hellenic race**, … **Apollo** is beautiful and **golden-haired**, … **Orpheus** is also sometimes considered as the **sun**, … In the story of Phaeton, whose name means "the bright and shining one," a description of the golden palace and car of the sun is given us. … spoke of drought as caused by the **chariot of Helios**, … In the story of Adonis some mythologists find another sun myth, in which **Adonis, the short-lived sun, is slain by the boar,** … One of the **greatest of all the solar heroes** is doubtless the demi-god **Hercules,** born at Argos …"

Now, Adonis above is the short-lived sun, just as Akhen-Aton was a short lived Pharaoh who prayed to Aton, the deity who is always shown as the sun with outstretched arms and a serpent in the middle. 'He' is Aton the Lord of 'Sun eruption'. The idea of the 'golden-hair' is tied to the first pharaohs and obviously stood for the concept of the golden rays of the 'Son of the Sun'.

In the above quote Orpheus is considered the Sun. As we recall, the 'Lyre of Orpheus' is the marker for the Magnetic North. That axis is connected - in a 90degree angle - to the plane of the Sun. The above 'boar' is a common villain in the Hindu Myths. This is how Wendy Doniger O'Flaherty explains the boar mythology:

> "Even in the Vaisnava story of the **boar avatar** there are hints of incidental **destruction** caused by the boar; which exaggerates the **erotic** element … and explains the boar's fatal flaw …**makes love to a polluted woman (as Agni makes love to the Krttikas when they are menstruous)** and is **unable to control his destructive fire …**"

(Author's heavyset) (Hindu Myths, Penguin, pg. 187-188)

"The earth, in the water, is full of desire and behaving like a woman; she has been violated and has conceived a cruel embryo from your fiery seed; she is menstruating, however, and therefore unfit for the embryo with which you impregnated her, O lord of the universe. ... Thus the lord of the world spoke to Visnu, who had a shameful look, about the vicious son begotten by sexual pleasure with a menstruating woman, a son who would do unpleasant things: Abandon this lustful boar-body, lord of the world; you alone are the cause of creation, preservation, and destruction; you are the cause of the world. ... But the boar went to his own mountain, ... and he made love with the earth," (Hindu Myths, pg.188-189)

The above quote will verify our previous statements about the nature of the boar, the lord of the universe and cosmic sex.

Now, as we already covered the Sun myths before, it is time to look at the thoughts of Mr. Guerber on the Fire myths: "The fire myths also form quite a large class, and comprise the **Cyclopes ... The Titans** are emblems of the **subterranean fires and the volcanic forces** of nature, which, hidden deep underground, occasionally emerge, ... In this group we also find **Prometheus**, whose name has been traced to the Sanskrit *pramantha* (or **"fire drill"**). ... **Vulcan (or Hephaestus)**, strictly **"the brightness of the flame,"** another fire hero, is represented as very puny at birth, because **the flame comes from a tiny spark.** The Greek Hestia (or Latin **Vesta**) was also a personification of fire; ... Her office was not limited merely to the hearths of households and cities, for it was supposed **" that in the** center of the earth there was a hearth which answered to the hearth placed in the center of the universe." ..."

The Ancients above clearly state that the Center of the Galaxy is connected to the heat-producing hearth of the Earth.

85

E.A. Wallis Budge also writes about the Greek gods being originated from the Egyptian deities in his 'Legends of the Egyptian Gods: "To this purpose, likewise, is that inscription which they have engraved upon the base of the statue of **Athene** at Sais, whom they **identify with Isis**: "I am everything that has been, that is, and that shall be: and my veil no man 'hath raised'." In like manner the word **"Amoun,"** or as it is expressed in the Greek language, **"Ammon"** which is generally looked upon as the proper **name of the Egyptian Zeus**, is interpreted by Manetho the Sebennite to **signify "concealment" or "something** which is **hidden."**

The word 'Amen' after a Christian prayer may also mean hidden. The next biblical quote also contains the word 'hidden' in relation to the rays flashing from the Lord's hand:
> "4 His brightness was like the **light**; He had **rays flashing from His hand**, and there **His power** was **hidden.**
> 5 Before Him went **pestilence**, and **fever** followed at His feet. 6 **He** stood and **measured the earth**;
> (Bible, Book of Habakkuk, Chapter 3, Vs.4-6)

In an 'Aton' like depiction the bright 'rays flashing' from 'His hand'. Since that represents the Sunspot eruption in the Egyptian hieroglyphs, thus the claim that 'His power was hidden' there is a correct one. These are subtle references that may pass unnoticed.

Probably, this is the time to analyze the ancient biblical name 'Solomon'. The word 'Sol' in the Greco-Roman world means the 'Sun' such as in 'SOL-ar' power. The above quote spells the Greek name 'Ammon' for the Egyptian Amun. Since we know that Amun was put together with the Sun as **Amun-Ra**, therefore placing Sol together with Ammon should not be unusual. This **gives us the name 'Sol-Ammon'** that is the origin of the famous and rich **biblical king 'Solomon'**.

According to the work by Moustafa Gadalla, an Egyptian author who resides in North America, the tales of the biblical King David closely resembles the stories of the Egyptian pharaoh Tut-moses III. There is a king in the Bible named Amon who is tied to a 'Fish Gate', which is the Star Gate of Orion in my theory: "The **word of the LORD** which came to Zephaniah ...

in the days of **Josiah** the son of **Amon, king of Judah.**
2 "I will utterly consume everything from the face of the land," says the LORD; ...
10 " And there shall be **on that day**," says the LORD,
"**The sound of a mournful cry from the Fish Gate**, a wailing from the **Second Quarter**," (Bible, Zephaniah)

In The Epic of Gilgamesh in Tablet V the 'fish' is mentioned along side Enkidu who is the Babylonian Orion:

"Give advice, **Enkidu**, you '**son of a fish**,' who does not even know his own father, "

In 'The First Book of The Kings' (remember KING=SUN) we can find names such as Rei (Ra/Re), Adonijah (Adon/Aton), David (Dwd /Tut) and Solomon (Sol-Amon or Amun-Ra) and Bath-Sheba ('Sheba' is tied to 'star' in Egyptian) all within a few verses or even in the same sentence:

"5 Then **Adonijah** ...exalted himself, saying, "**I will be king**"; and he prepared for himself **chariots** and horsemen, and **fifty men** to run before him. ...
8 ... Nathan the prophet, Shimei, **Rei**, and the mighty men who belonged to **David** were not with **Adonijah**. ...
11 So Nathan spoke to **Bathsheba** the mother of **Solomon**, saying, "Have you not heard that Adonijah the son of Haggith has become king, and David our lord does not know it? " (Author's heavyset) (Bible, Kings I)

In this quote Adonijah is Aton, the young king or pharaoh who is short lived and not ready to rule the kingdom. He is short lived because He is the Sunspot eruption, the Son of the Sun.

In one story, the Egyptians went as far as making the Son of the Sun the product of a Virgin Goddess who was not touched by a male God. This is in the next quote from E.A. Wallis Budge:

> "The Egyptian goddess **Net**, …**the great goddess of Sais**, in the Western Delta. She was self-existent, and **produced her son, the Sun-god, without union with a god**. In an address to her, quoted by Mallet (Culte de Neit, p.140), are found the words, **"thy garment hath not been unloosed**,"

Well, it is time to look at the Egyptian Gods. The Nine Main Gods, better known as The Great Egyptian Ennead of Heliopolis, who are mainly related to the solar myth and mentioned in connection with Ra, are the following:
Ra, Geb, Nut, Shu, Tefnut, Osiris, Isis, Set, & Nephthys.

In a reversed manner to the universally accepted gender designation **Geb** was the male principle for 'earth' and goddess **Nut** represented the 'sky', as in Father Earth and Mother Sky. They had two daughters who were **Isis** and **Nephthys.** The sisters represented the Virgin and the Harlot, the Venus Transit pair. Their two sons were named **Osiris** and **Set.** These two sons are the precursors of the biblical Cain and Abel, astronomically these two characters are the constellation Perseus/Mithra and Orion standing by either side of Taurus, the Bull.

Atum, who is the precursor of the biblical **Adam**, in one story was the originator of Geb and Nut. This is the Earth and the Sky being born from the initial action of the first year of Atum. Thus, as in the biblical claim Adam / Atum becomes the originator of the will of the Creator, but it is not the original Creation, only the Creation of a New Age, New Sun every 12,000years. But why did the Ancients wrapped these stories around the 'original' Creation of the World? Why tackle core emotional issues, such as punishing gods, cosmic sex and marriage, birth of a destructive and purifying son, death, and resurrection? The answer is very simple. There are at least three questions that constantly being asked – and naturally cannot be answered - by any person who is contemplating higher spiritual or religious enlightenment.

   1., **How this all started (Creation)?** We are asking because, although we vaguely understand the concept of 'forever' we still cannot imagine 'eternity' with no end and no beginning.
   2., **Why are we here on Earth, what are the 'right things' to do and if we conduct life well - how goodness is rewarded?** Why bad things can happen to good people if god is love and rewards goodness? Do we know what is the 'right morality'?
   3., **What will happen to us after we die?** Does the body belong to its Spirit? Will the Soul travel separate and the Body perishes? Will we go to Heaven? Is there Hell or Purgatory? Can our body be resurrected, can we live several different lives as reincarnations, or is it only our spirit that lives on forever? Are there more than one existences for humans with simultaneous realities functioning in multiple Universes folded on each other?

Some of these questions in simpler or more complex forms are on everybody's mind at one point or another in their lives. Thus, the secret stories on one hand were manufactured by the wise men to provide answers to the basic spiritual inquiries of humans, but on the other hand they were configured to carry the easily decipherable universal cosmic tales. That is the reason why some of those mythological events sound weird and unbelievable for the educated minds of today. Sure, the stories are not about how our Creator started forming the Earth billions of years ago when there were no humans to witness it. That utterly simplistic literal understanding is for the uneducated and uninitiated. Let their childish mind be satisfied with countless magical tales. For the intelligent readers the stories should signify a Creative Force that 'recreates' the surface of the Earth every 12,000years.

Where we came from before birth and where we shall go after death – I do not know. I doubt that anybody does. People who possess strong faith in an intelligent God understand that if the Creator was smart enough to conjure up several huge galaxies with intricate regenerating capacities and natural laws to govern from the smallest microcosm to the largest one then we should not be worried about what is next. 'He/She' must have designed a recycling system where our indestructible spirits can go and again become useful. Therefore, the stories we grew up with are not feeble attempts of the Ancients to explain poorly understood natural forces, such as the thundering sky and rare eclipses. The tales contain very complex universal scientific ideas and methods to transmit advanced knowledge from a previous era when science may have been more developed then the one today. With this advanced science in mind let us return to the Egyptian gods.

Not your average conservatively dressed guy, **Geb** the male primeval earth divinity was frequently depicted in the ancient Egyptian art as a man **wearing a goose on top of his head.** His athletic wife **Nut**, goddess of the heavens was arching over earth greeting the rising and setting of the sun. She would be openly welcoming the departing souls into her sky body. **Osiris**, their son was the supreme god of the Underworld, and closely tied to the deceased old king who would be replaced by his son **Horus.**

Osiris is often depicted as a deity who died - then afterwards was resurrected to life and was also often associated with the 'pillar' (earth axis). Mainly he is shown in Egyptian art as a mummified king holding the flail and the crook of a ruler. In the Pyramid Texts, Set kills his brother Osiris. He is also depicted as the enemy of Horus. Set is mostly painted in a negative light. He represents the dry desert land. In a biblical fashion of Cain and Abel, the Egyptian Set slays his brother Osiris, who was associated with the green fertile land around the river Nile. This is probably another clue to the earth changes. In another papyrus, the Egyptian god Amun creates Shu and his sister Tefnut by what sounds like expectoration, as in coughing up. It again yields off springs without a sexually active female involvement.

From the union of Osiris and Nephthys (who is very possibly another version of the Harlot, Hathor) comes the heir Anubis. The figure of Anubis the Dog is often depicted resting with a scepter and a flail symbolizing leadership. The *sekhem* scepter was used in funerary rituals held by the leader of the mortuary proceedings. Anubis was considered one of the chief gods of the Necropolis and was associated with haunting in the cemeteries of the desert's edge, another reference to high heat and the dead. Anubis is actually very similar to the god Set who originally was considered a 'desert god' and was mentioned at times when the negative forces stirred up the gods. Some of the tales may even been a restating of the ancient mono-myth with similar characters, animals and pharaohs who appear under varying names in different eras.

FIGURE 3-1: The Canine God Set
(Modified from IHH by Schumann-Antelme & Rossini)

The sign on the left is a **leafless plant** that refers to **drought** in Figure 3-1. The second sign is the letter 'T' or the 'half-cycle' shape of the rising sun above a black sun of darkness.

Interestingly, the core inner circle this time is not a solid color rather it is similar to sand dunes. It may fit with the intended message of 'desert' or drought. Another possibility is a tsunami related mound building from **sand dunes**. It could also relate to the 'building of the high wall' concept in the biblical stories.

Spiritual people imagine God as a Spirit and do not assign a gender to Him / Her /It. From the depictions it seems likely that the ancient Egyptians thought of the Creative Principle as a Male and a Female in a Sacred Union. Definitely, during the earth changes the erupting sun became the male king and the eruption was the prince without a mother. The increased resonation was the evil Serpent and the trembling Mother Earth/Pleiades Sisters was the receptive female harlot. After listening to so many tales about the Queen, the mistress of the King or the bashful Virgin, it is difficult to substitute a suffering Mother Earth for that role.

FIGURE 3-2: Egyptian Family of Gods

Even our Bible will show basic elements of these myths. Also the Scripture will reveal the fact that the early Semitic Biblical Fathers may also imagined a 'divine couple' that was both a male and a female deity. By linguistic analysis even Yah-weh or Jehovah would meet the criteria for a Male-Female God. Let me bring a Bible quote about a male God from Isaiah:

> "2 Behold, God is my salvation, I will trust and not be afraid;
> 'For YAH, the Lord, is my strength and song; He also has
> become my salvation.' " (Isaiah, Chapter 12, Vs.2)

The capitalization of the name of the Lord, **YAH** (Y-AH) in the previous quote is not my doing, but that is how it appears in the Bible. The 'AH/HA' ending/beginning in Hebrew means 'THE'. Since Hebrew reads right to the left, thus it is supposedly reads **'The-Y'** (upside down Delta) the male God. If we think of the letter 'V' as the female designation then it is not hard to see the 'male' in the 'Y' given the extra 'appendage' hanging down from the bikini line. These ancient scribes did posses a bit of pervert humor in those sexual symbols.

Ok, Y-AH is the male part, but who is the W-AH or V-AH. Well, the letter 'V' or the 'W' is the symbol for the female pubic and breasts areas. Even the Roman numeral five = V (5) relates to Venus as the planet takes five 'stations' in her 8year long orbit. Not coincidentally, both the number 5 and the 8 are members in the Spiral based Fibonacci's Sequence (0,1,1,2,3,5,8...). The name 'eVe' or the goddess Venus contains the 'V', just like the words Virgin, Vanity, 'oVum' and 'Venereal'. The 'W' is reminiscent of female breasts and as a letter it is the beginning of Woman, Witches, and Womb, the center of 'eWe' and the shape of the throne of the celestial Queen Cassiopeia. After Noah's Flood the first language had to develop from the accumulated secrets of the cosmic calendar tales.

In Figure 3-3 I will show the Sacred Pair, the Serpent of eruption, the worm, the grail of offering and the bullhorns of opening. This very important group of hieroglyphs represents a tragic sequence of events in our 12,000year old earth change scenario of the Egyptians, but let us see if we can find a Bible quote mentioning the 'worm' along with the sun in reference to the whale of the Flood (Jonah):

> "7 But as the **morning dawned** the next day **God prepared a worm** , and it is so **damaged the plant that it withered.**
> 8 And **it happened, when the sun arose**, that God prepared a vehement **east wind; and the sun beat on Jonah's head,** " (Bible, Jonah, Ch.4, Vs.7-8)

FIGURE 3-3: Sacred Pair and Erupting Serpent
(Picture by Szekely)

In Figure 3-3 under the sacred pair is a **worm or a naked snail,** also called the horned viper. For me it is the worm that represents water from the soil. The explanation for the scientific meaning is the following: - When the Sunspot erupted and the Core shifted, it generated the increased pressure from inside the Earth and caused the **opening of the under water fountains.**

The nakedness of the snail implies a loss of 'house'. Think of that in terms of the 'house of god' or the dissolution of the city palace, which is the Earth. In the same picture, underneath the worm is the **Djed pillar** with four levels. **It is the symbol for four winds** that uphold the Earth. During the upheaval it is both a destructive and recreative power. To the right of the Djed Pillar is the **'was' scepter** symbol. It **represents the 'iron rod'**, the kind that would come out of the Core of the earth, thus it is the symbol of the Magnetic North. Careful visual examination shows that there is a beak on top of the rod, which is tilted in an angle close to the degree that the Polar North would be. The bottom of the iron rod is forked ending in a 'horse shoe' shape. This gives me a feeling that this rod can easily roll over in an earth axis shift.

A Nineteenth Dynasty wall painting in Abydos shows Osiris sitting on the throne holding an ankh in his right hand and the **was scepter** in his left. Seti I is bringing offerings to him. The Eighteenth Dynasty is when Aton the 'Sunspot' ruled, so this Seti I would presumably represent the next year. Seti I's name sound uncomfortably similar to the evil brother 'Set' and I am assuredly convinced that it is for a very good identity reason. Naturally, we look for a quote in the Bible that brings us the iron rod and the ruler ship. If we can find that concept tied to the Father and the Son and on top of it have Venus, the Morning Star involved in this - it would make us really happy. Well, I am glad to say that such a quote exist:

> "26 "And he who overcomes, and keeps My works until **the end**, to him I will give power over the nations –
> 27 'He shall **rule them with a rod of iron**; they shall be dashed to pieces like the potter's vessels' – as I also have received from **My Father**;
> 28 "And I will give him the **morning star**.
> 29 "He who **has an ear**, let him hear what the Spirit says to the churches." '(Bible, Revelation, Chap.2, Vs. 26-29)

The above outlines are self-explanatory with our current knowledge of cosmic science introduced earlier. Father, Son, Venus, ear, end times incorporated in a few sentences. Why would someone give someone else the 'morning star'? A star or planet is not a gift that can be given away. The morning star is the planet Venus. The secret knowledge of the Venus Calendar may be something that can be 'given'. That is a much better explanation for the mentioning of the 'morning star' giveaway.

Let me bring a few examples from the Bible where the Galactic Center's (Sagittarius/Horseman) spiral electro-magnetic force, rattling of the resonation (of the evil serpent), the wind, fire, drought, captivity of the axis are all tied to the opening of the underwater fountains along with the sin of a seductive harlot.

> "3 The LORD is slow to anger and great in power, and will not at all acquit the wicked. The Lord has His way in the **whirlwind** and in the storm, and the clouds are the dust of His feet.
> 4 He rebukes the sea and makes it dry, and **dries up all the rivers.** ...
> 5 The **mountains quake** before Him, the **hills melt**, and the earth heaves at His presence, yes, the world and all who dwell in it.
> 6 ... **His fury is poured out like fire**, and the rocks are thrown down by Him. ...
> 3 The shields of his mighty men are made **red,** the valiant men are in scarlet. **The chariots come with flaming torches** in the **day** of his preparation, and the **spears** are brandished.
> 6 **The gates of the rivers are opened**, and the **palace is dissolved.**
> 7 It is decreed: **she shall be led away captive**,
> 2 The **noise of a whip** and **the noise of rattling wheels**, of galloping horses, of clattering chariots!

3 **Horseman charge** with bright **sword** and glittering **spear.** There is a multitude of slain, a great number of bodies, countless corpses – they stumble over the corpses –
4 **Because of the multitude of harlotries of the seductive harlot,** the mistress of sorceries, who sells nations through her harlotries, and families through her sorceries." (Bible, The Book of Nahum, Chapters 1-3.)
(The author's underlining and heavyset.)

In Tablet II of Maureen Gallery Kovacs' 'The Epic of Gilgamesh the Harlot is mentioned along side of Enkidu (Orion):

"**She** (the Harlot –author) **took hold of him** as the gods do and brought him to the **hut of the shepherds**, …
Enkidu scattered the **wolves**, he chased away the **lions**, …
… for Gilgamesh (Mithra/Perseus - author) as for a god a counterpart is set up.
Enkidu (Orion –author) blocked the entry to the **marital chamber**, and would not allow Gilgamesh to be brought in. They grappled with each other at the entry to the marital chamber, in the street they attacked each other, the public square of the land, The **doorposts trembled** and the wall shook, … "**Your mother… the Wild Cow** of the Enclosure," (That is the commonly mentioned 'Sheep-Fold Enclosure, which seems to refer to the sacred path of the East through Pleiades - Author)

The 'two brothers' fighting is what Christ said would start the end days. There are a lot of speculations about those two brothers. Some might think they are the Germans against the English, or the Arabs against the Jews, but these are neither. The two cosmic brothers are 1., Mithra/Perseus and 2.,Orion, who are placed North to South on either side of the Bull, Taurus.

When the sunspot erupts from the East (Bull) and the Earth's inner Core loses its stabilization, then the Galactic Center (West) allowed to take over control and this causes the Magnetic North (North) to shift toward the South (Polar North). This North to South shift (3 to 4 times) made the **Earth stagger as a 'drunken' body**. This same **North to South** movement allows the **'two brothers'** to engage in a fight and also hides the concept 'of travel to a foreign land'. Following the travel to a 'foreign country' the earth's 'iron rod' (sword) remains stuck as a 'captive' for forty years. This was an ingenious way of the Ra Priests to preserve cosmology.

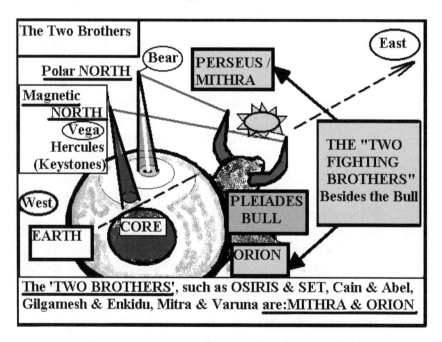

FIGURE 3-4: The Two Fighting Celestial Brothers

The two brothers are Mithra/Perseus with the two edged sword standing above the Bull in the sky **and Orion, the wild hunter** who is positioned below the Bull.

Thus jumping over the bull, running from the bull, rodeo riding the bull, matador fighting the bull, are all sacred ritual to commemorate this astronomical secret. When the North to South axis shift happened - the two brothers were jumping up and down and slapping each other in the sky. This cosmic secret is more befitting of our biblical prophets then the historical minded sacrilegious scholars, who are trying to find ethnic designations to the two brothers. The 'hut of the shepherds' or the 'tent of meeting' as in the Torah is mentioned along with the harlot and a marital chamber in the sky in the previous quote. The wolf, lion, cow are weaved into the story line along with the 'doorposts' (the two pillars) trembling. This is a cosmic marital chamber.

Professor Lesko writes about Hathor, the Goddess of Love in her book titled 'The Great Goddesses of Egypt' in the following manner: "…the first day of the fourth month of Inundation Season celebrated Hathor with drunken revelry (Hathor was also known as Mistress of Drunkenness, and vessels containing wine and beer were often decorated with her image). The ruins of the rambling palaces built by the pharaohs of the late Eighteenth Dynasty have yielded many broken beer jars decorated with three-dimensional blue-haired heads of Hathor (perhaps a reference to turquoise). At Hathoric festivals sexual dalliance was probably the order of the day. New Kingdom Egypt was a permissive society, …"

Now, all of this 'permissive' sexual dalliance was happening during the Eighteenth Dynasty of Akhenaten and the worship of Aton. Obviously, the drunken orgies were caused by the Sun eruption and the free sex was cosmic in origin. This upheaval was needed to reformulate the weakening magnetic field. Without the protective effect of this shield the Earth would be a hot pressure cooker and life would not be possible.

99

So, yes the Creator sacrifices one generation of humans and animals with few survivals every 12,000years, but this killing field will allow countless of future generations to exist in an earthly paradise. In the previous quote the broken beer jars may have been placed into the ruins of the palaces to indicate that the 'broken party' originated with the 'orgies of the gods'. In a lot of other instances at archeological sites the tombs of the dead pharaohs were found in an arranged disarray making the scholars think that there were tomb robbers. Except, as in the tomb of King Tut, there was no evidence of robbery and very expensive gold pieces were left behind. Thus, there is a good possibility that the 'tomb raiders' were the actual 'priest planners' of the disorganized tomb. It was all a prearranged disaster warning.

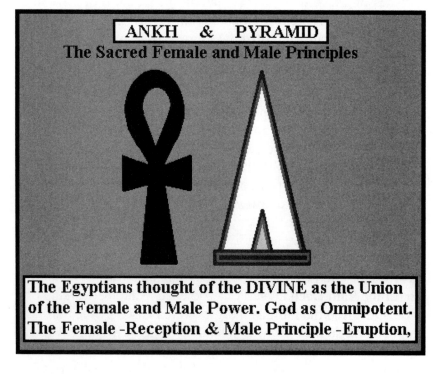

FIGURE 3-5: The Egyptian Sacred Pair.

The Native American 'Tipi', the 'sheepherder's tent' in the Bible and the 'tent of meeting' of the Torah all immortalize this 'Delta / Male' concept. The small pyramid shaped opening in the above Figure 3-5 visually presents a small replica of the large one, thereby stands for the Son of the Big Tent. Again, we can observe the 'large male' to 'small male' depictions. Thus, we are back to the 'Big Sun gave birth to a Little Sun in an eruption'.

Here the Big Tent symbolizing the Sun, and the small pyramid is the Son of the Sun. When the Sun erupts and produces a Child, it does not require a Mother. The cause is identified in the Galactic Center where the Golden Goose lays the Egg of a New Age. We do not need a mother. Therefore, the Feminine comes into the picture with the first member of the Venus pair who is the Harlot. Then she reappears as a Virgin for the second member of the Venus Transit. She has little to do with the birth of this 'fiery embryo' as the Harlot, she is only responsible for teasing the Sun into an eruption. Eight years later the 'virgin birth' of the 'sol invictus' sun is also not a normal human marital behavior.

Now, this 'virgin' designation may hide another clue. That is, if this ancient disaster continued to happen around the third week of August, at the cusp of the months of Leo and Virgo, then the frequent depiction of the Lion and the mentioning of the Virgin would give a double significance to these religious symbolisms. This lack of a sexually active Mother is a divisive absence of the feminine in the biblical concept of Father, Son, and Holy Spirit. A straight quote from God provides us with an exact date for this fiery Day of the Lord (**Aton!**), on the **Day of Atonement. Thus, counting from December 25, it will take us to early August**:
> "26 And the Lord spoke to Moses, saying:
> 27 "Also the **tenth day of this seventh month shall be the Day of Atonement**. It shall be a holy convocation for you; you shall afflict your souls, and offer **an offering made by fire to the Lord**." (Leviticus, Ch.23. Vs.26-27)

FIGURE 3-6A: Sacred Family: Son of the Sun, Delta and Ankh.
(Egyptian Hieroglyphic depiction)

Looking at Figure 3-6A, we have terrific good news; the Sacred
Family delivered a Child. His not walking straight yet, there is a
little bit of waddling in his stride, but regardless the parents
seemed to be proudly standing by his side. In appearance He does
not closely resemble either of his parents, but what do you expect
if one mates a 'key hole' to a 'tent'? As far as the proud parents
are concerned if the Sun shines on the little rascal it cannot be a
bad day. His name is 'Sha-Ra' / 'Sa-Rah'. It is **worth comparing
Figure 3-6A with the Figure 3-17 for contents**. Naturally, the
Father by being the 'Shepherd', is represented by the 'shepherd's
tent'. The Mother has an interesting 'Key Hole / Ankh' shaped
'Oval Opening' whose sides are pulled together to represent
virginity. It is a 'Key Hole' that has not seen a Key yet, but is
bursting full of cosmic enigmas. Unfortunately, opening up a
Pandora's box of cosmic secrets can bring instant destruction and
at the very end may be only a few surviving witnesses remain to
sing the songs of the bards. The King, Queen and the Goose are
showing up in the sky in mid-September during the Virgo sign in
Figure 3-17. We understand that the 'Son of the Sun' is tied to
the birth of the young Prince there shown as the Northern Cross,
that is Cygnus the Goose positioned in the Galactic Center.

It is the astronomical Cross of Christ. Furthermore, this ties the last twelve hours of Christ on the Cross - as the last twelve years of the Earth changes - to that tragic period 12,000years ago.

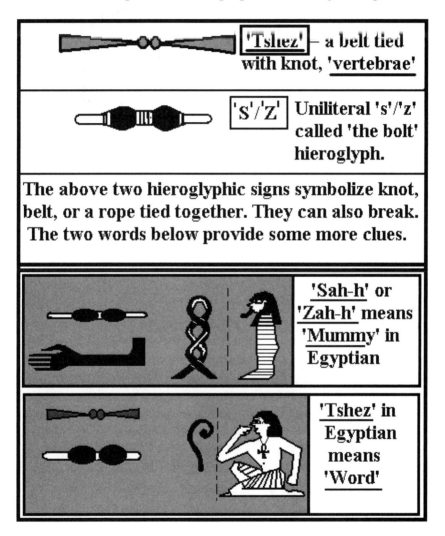

FIGURE 3-6B: The Knot Breaks and the Word Sounds
(Adopted and modified from Illustrated Hieroglyphic
Handbook by Schumann-Antelme & Rossini)

Analyzing the pictures in Figure 3-6B provides us with more clues about the simple scientific concepts emanating from the Egyptian Hieroglyphic depictions. The triliteral expression **'tshez'** is shown as a **'belt'** (Orion!), which is **fastened with a knot** that we assume can be 'untied' at the end of an age. Using this symbol in the bottom section of Figure 3-6B, along with the **'tied rope'** that **can also break** when there is an **'eruption' (spiral sign)** gives us the whole meaning that is **'WORD'**! Thus, again when the divine 'words' resonate or erupt from the mouth of God then the 'rope' can break at the timing of the unbuckling of the 'belt' of Orion. Another noteworthy rope amongst the constellations would be the one that ties the two fish together in Pisces. I am wondering how all this collections of hieroglyphic symbols made sense to the scholars until we just realized that the depictions were carefully chosen by the Ra Priests to represent astronomical knowledge of cosmic breaking points.

The depiction above this bottom one in Figure 3-6B reads the **'MUMMY'**. Examining the hieroglyphic signs we first encounter the **'rope' that is ready to break**. Below it, is the **'arm'** placed in the 90degree angle representing 'Hercules' /'Sun' / 'King' and naturally the 'Square' as we learned by the spelling of the Sun King Ra in earlier chapters. These two signs followed by the **'DNA helix'** sign that looks like **'braided rope'** and it stands for the Egyptian unilateral letter **'H'**. The ancient message to me reads like this: *"When the 'rope breaks' by the 'strong arm' of the 'Giant King' of the Sun then the 'Two Kingdoms' will unite and become ONE "*. This concept is cleverly represented by the 'braided rope', because not only we will see that braiding two ends of the rope will create one unified entity, but because it resembles a DNA helix we should also understand that a 'New Creation' or birthing process is taking place. In this act of uniting the 'two poles', the old Sun King dies and the Earth stops moving. These two things are hidden in the concept of the 'mummy'.

Returning to the concept of the 'ankh' there are legends about a 'knot' of Isis that may be untied at a certain time.

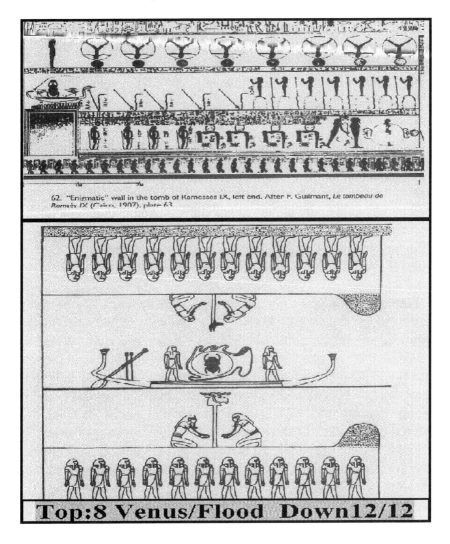

FIGURE 3-7: Venus Calendar on Top, 12K on Bottom
(Adopted and modified from Erik Hornung 'The
Ancient Egyptian Books of the Afterlife')

The top part of Figure 3-7 is the 'Enigmatic' wall painting from the tomb of the pharaoh Ramesses IX. It is mysterious because the depictions are not the traditional hieroglyphic signs. Then what are they? From left to right the top row shows a standing god whom in today's time would be representing 2003. That is because the next symbol stands for the first Venus Transit of a time 11,600years ago. Today it would parallel the year 2004.

There are EIGHT Venus symbols in that row representing the parallel years prior to Noah's Flood to the current Venus Transit pairs between 2004 and 2012. The two Venus Transits in front of the Sun is hidden in the biblical wisdom of the 'two wives' of Jacob, David, and Samuel. Furthermore, Jacob in the Bible married Leah who he did not love (Harlot). Then He had to labor 'seven' years for Rachel (Virgin) who he admired. The name 'Rakhel' in Hebrew means 'EWE' and if Jacob was not a 'Ram', such as the Egyptian god 'Amun', he would not marry an 'ewe'.

Figure 3-8 shows a close up of two Venus symbols that are the third and the fourth from the left. Above them are hieroglyphs that are not clearly seen in the previous figure and are modified for clarity in this one. Above the third Venus symbol from the left is the 'Son of the Son – Shah-Ra' symbol is displayed. Today it would be 2006. Was the second or the third year after the first Venus Transit of the pair is the one when the Day of the Lord played out nearly 11,600years ago? It is difficult to establish. If the first year of the last 12 in our calendar would be 2003 then the third year would fall on 2006 and the fourth is on 2007 and the fifth is on 2008 and so forth and so on. Therefore, reading the 'fourth' and the 'fifth' hour of the last twelve hours of the Amduat in 'The Ancient' Egyptian Books of the Afterlife' will make us recalculate the exact year of that ancient tragedy.

The upside down woman in Figure 3-8 surrounded by the circle resembles Leonardo Da Vinci's 'vitreous man' drawing.

Did he know about the Venus Calendar in the Dark Ages? Drawing not one, but two figures in the circle Da Vinci must have known about these secrets, although it is difficult to be certain how much he knew. For us it does represent the Venus Calendar and the upside down legs resemble the famous 'V',

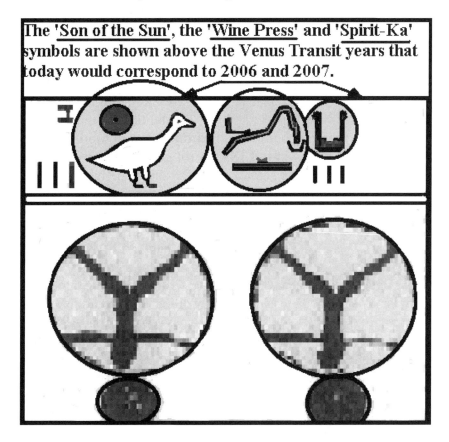

FIGURE 3-8: The Son of the Sun is above 2006

An Old Testament quote from Isaiah and another one from the New Testament's **Revelation mention the 'winepress'** along with the 'garment', the colors 'red' or 'white' and the 'blood' **along with the coming of the 'fury' of the Lord**:

"2 Why is Your apparel **red**, and Your garments
like one who treads in the **winepress**?
3 **'I have trodden the winepress** alone, and from
the peoples no one was with Me. For I have
trodden them in My anger, and trampled them in
My fury; their blood is sprinkled upon My
Garments, and I have stained all My robes."
(Bible, Book of Isaiah, Chapter 63, Vs. 2-3)

"12 **His eyes were like a flame of fire**; and on His
head were many crowns. **He had a name** ...
13 He was clothed with a **robe dipped in blood**
and **His name is called the Word of God**. ...
15 Now **out of His mouth goes sharp sword**, that
with it He should strike the nations. And He
Himself will **rule them with a rod of iron**. He
Himself treads the winepress of the fierceness
and wrath of Almighty God."
(Bible, Revelation, Chapter 19, Vs. 12-15)

I will demonstrate again with an Old Testament Bible quote
from Isaiah that the 'West' is the 'Powerhouse of Grandfather'
and the 'East' is where 'Kings and Princes' come from. Also, the
'sacred tree' is connected to kings and the milk of the breast that
sits in the sky:
"19 So shall they **fear the name of the Lord from the
west**, and **His glory from the rising of the sun**; when
the enemy comes in like a **flood**, the **Spirit of the Lord
will lift up a standard against him**. ...
(Bible, Book of Isaiah, Chapter 59, Vs.19)
"3 The **Gentiles shall come to your light**, and
kings to the brightness of your rising. ...
16 You shall drink the milk of the Gentiles, and
milk the breast of kings; ..."
(Bible, Book of Isaiah, Chapter 60, Vs. 3-16)

The 'brightness of the rising of the Sun ('on that special day'– I may add) is tied to the Kings. The 'breasts' of the kings are likely reference to the astronomical picture of Virgo transposed on the Milky Way Galaxy shown later in Figure 3-17. Between two stars named 'breast' sits the astronomical 'king' and 'queen' above the dragon. One of the stars named breast naturally belongs to the Queen Cassiopeia 'W' and the other one is the breast of the constellation Cygnus, the Goose who is an Egyptian Hieroglyphic symbol for the 'Son of the Sun'.

The ancients attempted to wrap all of these royal family relations together into an airtight case, so when we start understanding the science of the sky again we would have ample 'amo' to 'prosecute' the old tales to a universal conclusion. The trial only started recently and at this point I do not feel like we are winning the case. This serial potential mass killer 'Sha-Ra' who masquerades as a 'Goose Prince' might have to be set free soon and if He kills again then we may be able to wrap up the case. His 'rap sheet' is long and the numerous circumstantial evidences are abounding, but we do not have a living eyewitness who could come forward. Therefore, all we can do now is to build a case against Him and see if He does his evil deeds again.

The Ancients used all the tools that were available for their disposal to fine-tune the exact time when this disaster happened and might again occur in the future. Therefore, they monitored the crossings of Jupiter and Saturn. It was Saturn who took rulership over from Jupiter in Classical Greek mythology. It is similar in design to the Old King losing his kingdom to the Young Prince. That is the old Sun giving ways to the New Age by erupting and producing a new heir. This story is displayed in so many different ways in all of the continents where uncles and evil brothers involved in this chilling family feud. In Greek mythology this change of rulership also involves Saturn, Jupiter and Ouranus.

This may be a reference to the ancient disaster happening at one of those Saturn – Jupiter conjunction. How the 'neutering' of his father Ouranus is tied into this mystery is a little more complicated. Figure 3-9 will show the work of the medieval astronomer Kepler researching the Great Conjunctions of Jupiter and Saturn.

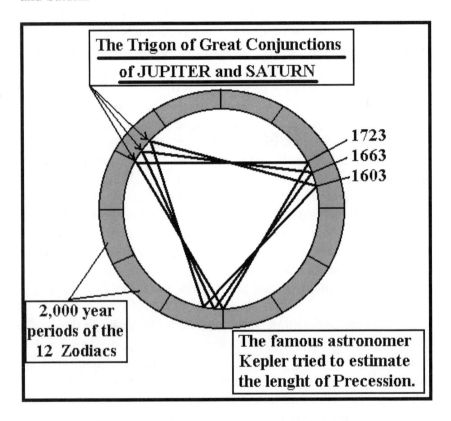

FIGURE 3-9. The Trigon of Great Conjunctions

The Trigon of Great Conjunctions of Jupiter and Saturn were used by Kepler to study the Precession of the Equinoxes. It happens every few decades and deemed important due to the stories of the Greek gods taking ruler ship from one another.

The importance of those planetary conjunctions is still debated in astronomy. The names of the largest planets along with the name of the main gods are still widely open to varying interpretations

Let us examine then the Greek mythologies to see if the same or similar concept about the cosmos is hiding behind the tales.

H.A. Guerber writes about Neptune, Laomedon and Hesione in his collection titled 'The Myths of Greece and Rome':

> "Neptune, the personification as well as the god of the sea, was of an exceedingly encroaching disposition. Dissatisfied with the portion allotted him, he once conspired to dethrone Jupiter; ... and Jupiter, in punishment ...exiled him to earth. There he was condemned to build the walls of Troy ...
> **Apollo**, also banished from heaven at that time, volunteered to aid Neptune by **playing on his lyre,** and **moving the stones** by the power of sweet sounds. ...
> ...**Neptune created a terrible monster,** ...
> To save themselves from the awful death which threatened them all, the Trojans consulted an **oracle,** who advised the **sacrifice of a beautiful virgin,** ...
> **Hercules,** ... came to Troy to punish him for his perfidy. The city was stormed and taken, **the king slain,** and his wife and children carried to Greece as **captives**."

Apollo is the Sun and He is able to move stones just by playing on his lyre. Again, here we find the Sun controlling the stone, that is the Foundation Stone, which is the Core of the Earth. How we know that? By the simple reference to the lyre and Hercules. Vega/Lyre/Harp and the giant Hercules stand for the Magnetic North - the Core of the earth, which is controlled by the Sun. When the Core shifts is when Neptune, the sea god can create the terrible monsters, earthquakes, hurricanes and huge tsunamis.

The sea came to the land as a giant tsunami and it built huge sand dunes, 'city walls', or the above called 'walls of Troy'.

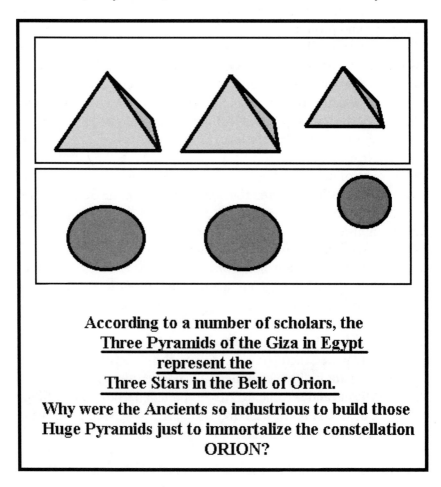

According to a number of scholars, the
Three Pyramids of the Giza in Egypt
represent the
Three Stars in the Belt of Orion.

Why were the Ancients so industrious to build those Huge Pyramids just to immortalize the constellation ORION?

FIGURE 3-10. The Orion Belt

A common Egyptian word is 'papyrus' that is found in all major languages. Taking off the Latin '-us' ending we are only left with the Egyptian 'PAPYR'. It corresponds to the Hungarian 'PAPIR, the English 'PAPER' and the Spanish 'PAPEL'.

Another mythologically important word is 'child' pronounced 'KheredJ' in Egyptian. Reading that backwards, as it should be, it yields 'Djerekh'. The Hungarian word for 'child' is 'Gyerek', but it sounds and pronounced as 'Djerekh', as written in Egyptian. Furthermore the Hungarian dictionary provides other clues, such as the word 'mag' meaning 'seed', 'magus' as 'magician', the word 'magas' meaning 'high/tall' and 'Maga' meaning 'Sir'. Thus, this 'MAG' root word obviously relates to the cosmic electro 'MAG'-netic force, which governs our Universe. The Latin 'Magna' and the word 'Magnifico/Magnificent' are also derived from that most important basic cosmic root word for 'MAG'-netism. "Maga' in Hebrew means 'touch' or contact and 'maga meenee' would mean 'sexual intercourse'. 'Magal' stands for the 'sickle' in Hebrew and it likely relates to the early harvest and the 'winepress'. It will make perfect sense why the sickle was such an important concept in astronomy when we arrive to our last chapter. The communist Soviets placed the sickle on their national flag less likely to impress us with their work ethic, rather to preserve the ancient symbolic knowledge of what it stood for in the earth change scenario. How cleverly the ancient root race arranged cosmic concepts around important and related items.

This is how Knight & Lomas write about the connection between Jesus and the planet Venus and also talk about the Magi:

"Jesus was born in a cave to the light of a bright star that shines brighter than any other from the east. And that means Venus! ...

Magi distinguished themselves with high hats, they also professed knowledge of astronomy, astrology, and medicine, of how to control the winds and the weather by potent magic and how to contact the spirit world. ...

The 'magi' were originally a class of priests among the Medes, but in Hellenistic time the word stands for men from the East (or Egypt) who possess astrologic / astronomic wisdom."

Returning back to linguistics on another continent, the Hindu word 'kuta' or 'kuti' means 'dog' and it is written as 'kutya' in the Hungarian language. Going to Mexico to visit the ancient Mayans, their word for 'father' is 'Aphu', which practically equals the Magyar word 'Apu' and 'Apa' for Father. The Mayan 'First Father' is called 'Hun-Aphu'. The 'Hun' part of the Hungarians' called themselves the 'first people of the Earth'. The Spanish word for 'One' is also '(H)un'. The obvious similarities between the names 'Maya' and 'Magyar' are worth mentioning. Interestingly, both the Hindu and the Egyptian mythology mention a Prince named 'Maya' that may gave the 'Mayans' their name. In Egypt Maya was the treasurer of the pharaoh Tut-Ankh-Amun in the famous XVIII. Dynasty when the rule of 'Aton', the Sun King established 'monotheism'! Design or co-incidence?

These are not historical or linguistic coincidences, but emerging truth that at one point the world population may have spoken a common root language as it is claimed in the Old Testament. The language similarities are well researched and documented by Joseph Greenberg, Ruhlen and their students about this supposed proto-language. Jumping to another continent, the Lakota Sioux Indian word for '**blood**' is '**we**'. The Hungarian word for 'blood' is '**ver**', and the related artery is '**er**'. Is it only coincidence that the letter 'V' from 'Venus' is the first letter of these important words symbolizing the lifeline of human existence?

On Figure 3-11, **Vesica Piscis** covers more secrets than Sacred Geometry can conjure up. The meaning of 'Vesica Piscis' is '**the urinary bladder of the fish**'. It hides the enigma of the star gate of **Orion where the three cosmic lines meet and perform the cosmic birth.** Through this connection to Orion, the long sought secret of Sacred Geometry has been solved. The interconnected two circles create the obvious vertical geometric shape that is universally recognized as a 'vagina'. When turned horizontally it resembles the divine 'mouth'. It is a very complex simplicity!

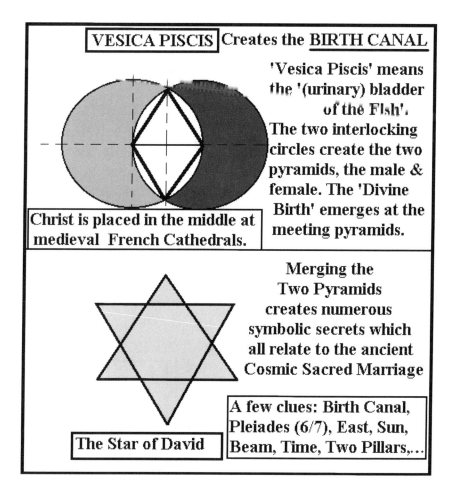

VESICA PISCIS Creates the BIRTH CANAL

'Vesica Piscis' means the '(urinary) bladder of the Fish'. The two interlocking circles create the two pyramids, the male & female. The 'Divine Birth' emerges at the meeting pyramids.

Christ is placed in the middle at medieval French Cathedrals.

Merging the Two Pyramids creates numerous symbolic secrets which all relate to the ancient Cosmic Sacred Marriage

The Star of David

A few clues: Birth Canal, Pleiades (6/7), East, Sun, Beam, Time, Two Pillars,...

FIGURE 3-11: Vesica Piscis and the Star of David

When viewed from the top to the bottom along the vertical center 'the Star of David' also displays the same 'birth canal'. It is the 'bee hive' extended by the upper little male pyramid and the bottom female pyramid that is upside down. After one would extract this 'birth canal' out of the Star of David, we would be left with the two 'sand timepieces' on the sides. Thus, cosmic union happens in between the two halves of time. Marvelous!

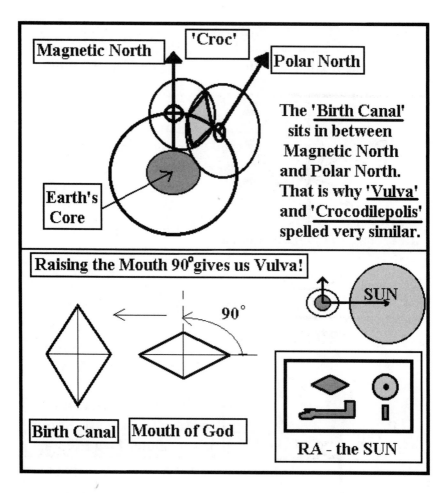

FIGURE 3-12: The Mouth and the Vulva

In Figure 3-12, in the lower right hand corner we can observe the hieroglyphic spelling of Ra, the Sun. Each symbol is carefully chosen by the ancient Priesthood to demonstrate their knowledge of the Earth, Solar and Galactic mechanics. The 'mouth' symbol represents the 'word of god' from the Galaxy. The extended arm in a 90degree angle is a reference to the Sun's stabilizing effect on the core and the strong arm of Hercules and the King.

The Old Testament has a quote about the strong arm of God:
"8 The Lord has sworn by **His right hand** and by **the arm of His strength,**" (Bible, Isaiah, Chap.62, Vs.8)

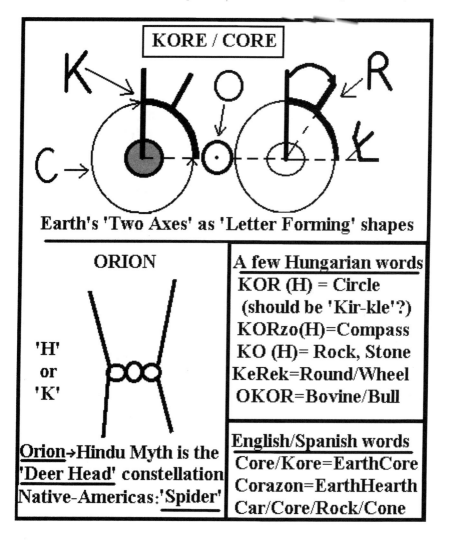

FIGURE 3-13: The Letter Origin of Earth Mechanics?

In astronomy there are two main characters that commonly shown with the arm in a 90degree angle. The most obvious is the

Babylonian portrayal of the King. He is depicted with the right arm in a 90degree angle while he is giving an offering. The other strong-armed astronomical hero is Hercules in the Magnetic North position. Their significance is obvious in our ancient cosmic tragedy.

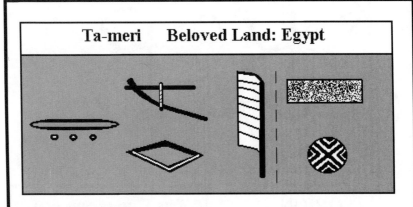

Ta-meri   Beloved Land: Egypt

The Belt of Orion, a Compass, Mouth of God and a Feather ---means Beloved Land : Egypt.
The 'Block of Stone' likely relates to the 'CORE' and the 'Circle' is the 'Four Direction' crossroads.

FIGURE 3-14: Beloved Land: Egypt

A 90degree turn –an important cosmic dependence of the Earth's Core on the stabilizing Sun - would symbolically transform that 'Mouth' into the 'Divine Birth Canal'. Tying all of this to the 'vesica piscis', which is the secret representation of 'Orion' in the 'crossroads' of the celestial spheres truly demonstrates a superb scientific base knowledge of the Egyptian Priesthood of Ra.

One can detect the letter 'A' in most ancient names of gods. The Egyptian 'R-A' (R = Mouth/Resonation, A = Ox/Compass) is the most obvious. If 'A' stands for the Ox horns and the letter 'V' is representative of Venus then the female '**Ava**' would be an appropriate name for the last Venus Transit periods when the purifying god emerges. The male would be '**Ada**'. Both of those names closely resemble the first biblical pair '**Adam & Eve**' A number of the Egyptian, Hindu and Babylonian divinities are also gifted with the letter 'A', such as Ishtar, Ishtanu, Aton /Aten, Atum, Agni and others.

The letter 'A' stands for so many important cosmic concepts in our earth change scenario. The letter 'A' is 'Aleph' meaning 'Ox' in Hebrew. It is the 'Horn of the Bull', the 'Compass', the 'Two Axes' of the earth, the shape of the 'Pyramid' / 'Delta' / 'Tent', and so much more. The ancient Greeks and Hebrews decided to use the basic Phoenician Alphabet that was based on these secret astronomical concepts. The symbol for the celestial 'Bullhorn' or even a 'Compass' was stood up on its side, turning it 90degrees and that became the letter 'A' or 'aleph' (that means 'Ox' in Hebrew). It does also look like a compass, which secretly represents the opening between the 'two norths' where the Dragon lives. It is also very similar and symbolic to the Delta sign or the Pyramid.

Turning a **compass** by a **square** 90degrees up contains the two most important Freemasonic symbols. And this is only the first letter of the Alphabet. How much more secrets the ancient priesthood hid from us in plain view? Now, the same thing happened with the Coptic Egyptian letter 'T' that was written as a half circle or as a letter D lying on its flat side. This letter was stood up also 90degrees and became the letter 'D'. The civilizing function of Thoth, the Scribe had to involve the development of a new language to incorporate the symbols that will remind future generations of the ancient cosmic disaster. Using the Hungarian language that I am familiar with I theorize that some of our early words were assembled from the cosmic astronomical secrets.

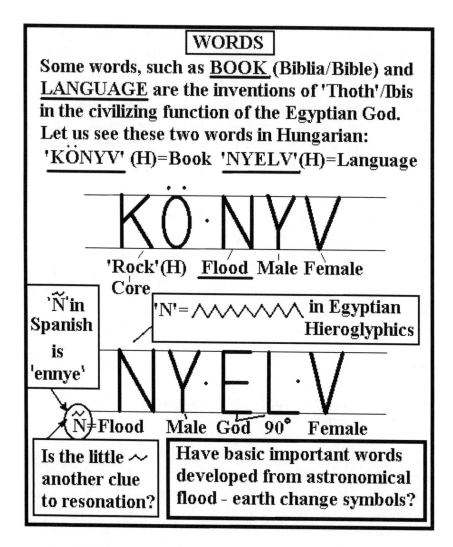

FIGURE 3-15: Some Words May Be Cosmic In Origin.

In Figure 3-15 the Hungarian words 'book' (konyv) and the 'language' (nyelv) may hide important cosmic concepts. The word 'DIVINE' is common in different languages. Figure 3-16 will show that it is a **'divine cosmic sex act - causing flood'**.

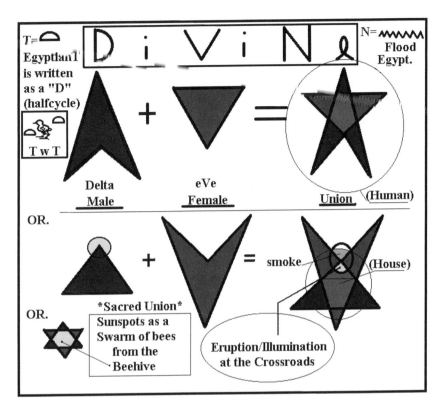

FIGURE 3-16. The Egyptian Sacred Union.

The word 'DiViNe' is spelled out from the above symbols. The 'Delta' sign is the 'D'. The next letter in 'DiViNe' is the obvious 'V' shape or female pubic line. Beginning with the initial bright and enormous solar flare 'illumination' these two cosmic forces 'intermarry' at the end of each 12,000year half-cycle endings. The 'living water' of the Flood pours out of the birth canal. The Egyptian letter 'N' is the symbol of Flood, thus our D+V=N.

Progressing further to Figure 3-17 that shows the astronomy of the sky in mid-September in the Virgo Sun sign. Even in the sky we can see the Sacred Couple, the Queen and the King and Cygnus the Goose. Compare this to Figure 3-6A.

The upside down 'Delta' sign for the male King can be observed besides the Dragon. Next to it is the 'W' shape for the Queen of Cassiopeia. One of the stars in Cassiopeia is called the Breast, and another star in the nearby Goose is named Breast ('Sadr' in Arabic) also. The Goose is the Northern Cross and it is near the Galactic Center. In parallel to the Vega and Polaris, sits the mythical fiery Dragon. The Dragon causes the polar axis shift, but it is the Prince who will come in between the breasts to ignite the fire of the heart (Earth's Core / Corazon) when the Old Kind, the Sun (Re/Ra/Ray/El Rey) erupts. How cosmically beautiful these strange astronomical tales can be.

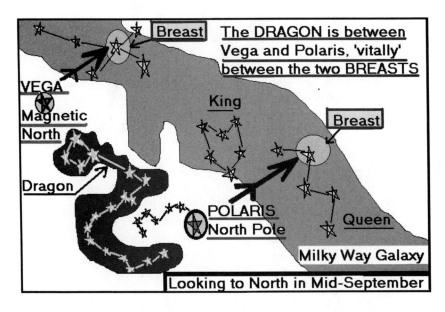

FIGURE 3-17. The Fiery Dragon sits between the Breasts.
(From 'The Celestial Clock' by Wm.Gaspar)

In the picture of Figure 3-17, the King is shown upside down as the Pyramid /Delta / Tent / Tipi shape representing the Male. The female Queen is shown as the 'W' shape of the astronomical constellation of Cassiopeia.

Possibly the W shape represents the breasts of the female, but also it is the shape of the throne the Egyptian Goddess who sits on while she is carefully breastfeeding the *New Child*. Since we are positioned in the Milky Way, the milk producing 'breasts' is even more motherly appropriate and brings to attention the Galactic Center. It is not at all surprising that the letter 'W' is represented in the hieroglyphic alphabet by the New Birth symbol, i.e., the one-day old Quail Chick, which looked like the throne of the Queen. This is how the classic book on mythology titled 'Hamlet's Mill' from Santillana and Dechend ties the goddess to the cosmic mysteries:

> "The constellation …('menat'/**mooring post** - author)
> …- occurs in two categories of astronomical monuments, namely (1) in the **Ramesside Star Clocks**, and (2) in the ceiling pictures of royal tombs, **in the zodiacs of Dendera**, etc. In every case the peg or post rests in the hands of Isis disguised as a hippopotamus; fastened to the mooring-post is a rope or chain, to the other end of which is tied Maskheti, **the bull's thigh**,… and in one of the text it is stated (Brugsch, Thesaurus, p. 122) that "it is the office of Isis-Hippopotamus to guard this chain." …
> …**Isis-Hippopotamus holding the mooring-post, and carrying upon her back a crocodile, with a constellation very near the Pole.** … We do not dare to molest the reader with impenetrable text (Brugsch, Thesaurus, p.122), out of which we quoted only one sentence which states that **Isis-Hippopotamus is guarding the chain;** this much at least is recognizable, that **this text jumps from the Big Dipper- via 'the middle of the sky' to positions 'South of Sah-Orion'** …"

Please, this is very important, there is a **JUMP** from the **NORTH** position toward the **SOUTH** in the **DIRECTION OF THE CONSTELLATION ORION!**

This quote again ties the Goddess to the Polar North, Pleiades (shoulder blade of the bull) and the constellation Orion. The peg is a reference to the fact when the 'millstone' (Precession) is jolted, the 'peg' fell out of the middle of the millstone, thereby allowing the quiet revolving notion to come to a sudden halt. It is not written in an easily understandable manner. I can see why an average person without mythological and astronomical interest or background would have a difficult time trying to make sense out of these stories. But for us it starts making sense.

The constellation Cassiopeia with its 'W' shape does lend itself to a 'throne' shape, and even resemble the 'human breasts'. Furthermore, it is the 'quail chick' or 'golden colored as the Sun Easter chick' letter 'w' of the Egyptian Alphabet. May be by coincidence, it is also resembling the 'zigzag' shaped arrow inside the 'Sacred Bear' of the Pueblo Indians in the Santa Fe area. This in my theory ties the Bear to the concept of the axis shift when the Earth was drunk. It is truly amazing how many religious symbols of different cultures can be tied to this single chain of events that happened 11,600years ago.

On Figure 3-18 Horus (Heru / 'Hero') is being fed by Queen Isis. Actually, there is an old legend contained in the Harris Papyrus kept in the British Museum. W.M. Flinders Petrie popularized it in his 'Egyptian Tales' and Gaston Maspero has it in the 'Popular Stories of Ancient Egypt'.

In the story, there was an old king who never had a child. He prays to have a son and they listen to him and grant him and his old wife a son. The Seven Hathors come by as they have the ability to tell any child's destiny. These seven Hathors prophesize that the 'boy' shall die by either the 'crocodile', 'serpent' or by the 'dog'. The Child grows up to be a Prince and travels to Syria in search of love. There he later dies by the action of his dog, but not before he gains the love and the hand of a Syrian Princess.

He is introduced to the princess and her king father as the 'son of a soldier of chariots' who is a foreigner fugitive from Egypt. After the doomed prophecy is full filled and he dies, the gods, Ra and the Seven Hathors take pity on the lovers and bring them back to life. (The Egyptian name of 'Hathor' is 'Het-Heru' that is currently translated as 'the House of Heru', but 'Het' in Hungarian means the number 'Seven' and I suspect that it is the same meaning in Het-Heru. The 'Het' or the 'Seven' would most likely stand for the Seven Years of Famine that followed the Sunspot eruption. - Author) This short synapse of the Doomed Prince contains the cosmic elements we have been talking about. There is the King/ Sun God Ra, goddesses, even the Seven Hathors representing the seven years in between the two Venus Transits, a Prince whose demise is tied to a Crocodile (Dragon), a Serpent (Resonation / Sun Eruption), or a Dog (Sirius). The Chariot and the Rebirth are also necessary elements of this myth. Is it about the 'Son of the Sun'?

The Divine Birth of the goddess' child was celebrated in the temples associated with Hathor and Isis. Female cult members dressed up as the goddesses to read the proclamation, which announced Horus, the son of Osiris as the supreme ruler of the Earth, thus equated to the Pharaoh. This Divine Birth, the Sunspot eruption happens in ONE DAY. This is what the Book of Revelation predicts about the Babylonian Harlot.

> "7 In the measure that she glorified herself and lived luxuriously, in the same measure give her torment and sorrow; for she says in her heart, 'I sit as **queen**, and am no widow, and I will not see sorrow.'
> 8 "Therefore her plagues will come in **one day – death** and mourning and **famine.** And she will be utterly **burned with fire**, for strong is the Lord God who judges her. " (Author's heavyset)
> (Bible, Revelation, Chapter 18, Verses 7-8.)

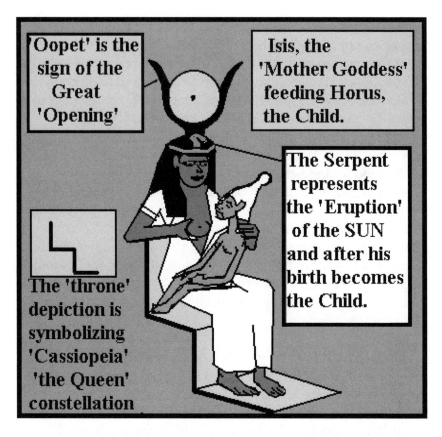

'Oopet' is the sign of the Great 'Opening'

Isis, the 'Mother Goddess' feeding Horus, the Child.

The Serpent represents the 'Eruption' of the SUN and after his birth becomes the Child.

The 'throne' depiction is symbolizing 'Cassiopeia' 'the Queen' constellation

FIGURE 3-18: Isis, the Mother Goddess feeding Horus the Child

The above Figure 3-18 depicts the goddess Isis who is feeding the Child. We just observed earlier that this goddess has a throne that is the letter 'W', which is the golden little 'chick' in the Egyptian Hieroglyphic Alphabet. This 'W' is 'new birth' that takes over the 'throne'. Since the 'W' also appears to resemble the 'breasts' and feeds the future kings of the galactic kingdom it is not a surprise that we see that one of the stars in 'Cassiopeia', the Queen is called the 'Breast'. In Arabic the name for 'Breast' is spelled 'Sadr'. This is well demonstrated in Figure 3-17.

The previous quote from Revelation is quite self-explanatory in
view of our earlier discussions. At this junction I will also
entertain a few quotes from the New Testament to see whether
the teachings of the Prince of Peace falls in line with what we've
discussed so far.

> "31 'Now is **the judgment of this world**; now the
> ruler of this world will be cast out.
> 32 ' And I, if I am **lifted up from the earth**, will
> draw all peoples to Myself.'
> 33 This He said, signifying by what death He
> would die.
> 34 The people answered Him, 'We have heard
> from the law that the Christ remains forever; and
> how can You say, 'The Son of Man must be lifted
> up'? Who is this **Son of Man**?'
> 35 Then Jesus said to them, 'A little while longer
> **the light** is with you. Walk while you have the
> light, lest darkness overtake you; …
> 36 'While you have the light, **believe in the light**,
> **that you may become <u>sons of light</u>**.' These
> things Jesus spoke, and departed, and was **hidden**
> from them' …
> 38 '…**And to whom has the arm of the Lord**
> **been revealed?'**   (Bible, John, Ch.12.)
>   (Author's underlining and heavyset)
> (Please, take a peek at Figure 3-6 to have 'the arm
> of the Lord' in 'light' been revealed to you!)

In this previous quote Christ answers the Disciples in a
somewhat elusive manner. The old teaching, which precedes
Him, is explained. The fact that 'the Son of Man must be lifted
up' is explained with the presence and the disappearance of light,
which can be easily understood as the events following the
sunspot eruption and the Hindu 'boar' tusking up the Earth. The
'light' is 'hidden' (Amen).

The ancient 'law that the Christ remains forever' does not seem to personify the historical Jesus, but it is written in a manner of the Egyptian Sun Child as a Cosmic Force of the Creator. This force includes the creating, and re-creating powers, which is best identified with the Light. In Chapter XVII of The Book of the Dead, Wallis Budge quotes a hymn about the identification of the body of Osiris with the various gods:

"THE CHAPTER OF DRIVING BACK SLAUGHTER IN SUTEN-HENEN. Said Osiris: " O land of the scepter! O white crown of the divine Form! O holy resting place**!** **I am the Child**. I am the Child. I am the Child. Hail, you the goddess Aburt! You say daily, 'The slaughter block is made ready ...' **I am the holy knot** within **the tamarisk tree'** ... To be said four times. **" I am Ra** who establishes those who praise him, I am the knot within the tamarisk tree, **more beautiful in brightness than the disk** of yesterday ... going forth on this day. My hair is the hair of Nu. My face **is the face of Ra**. My eyes are **the eyes of Hathor.** ... My teeth are the teeth of Khepera. My neck is the neck of Isis, the divine lady. My hands are **the hands of Khnemu,** the lord of Tattu. ... My privy member is the privy **member of Osiris**. ... My breast is the breast of the awful and terrible One. My belly and my backbone are the belly and backbone of Sekhet. My buttocks are the buttocks of the **eye of Horus**. ... I am like Ra every day. None shall seize me by my arms; none shall drag me away by my hand. ... I come forth and advance, and **my name is unknown**. I am yesterday, and my name is 'Seer of millions of years.' I travel, I travel along the path of **Horus the Judge**. I am the lord of eternity; I feel and I have power to perceive. I am the **lord of the red crown. I am the Sun's eye**, my seat is on my throne, and I sit thereon within the eye. I am Horus who pass through millions of years. **... I am the only One born of an only One**, who goes around about in his course; **I am within the eye of the Sun.**

Things are not evil nor hostile unto me, nor are they against me. **I open the door of heaven. ... I shall not die again. ... I am he who is unknown.** ... I am the unveiled one. ... I cannot be held with the hand, but I am he who can hold you in his hand. Hail O Egg! Hail O Egg! I am Horus who live for millions of years, **whose flame lights upon your faces** and **blazes in your hearts. ...**" (Author's heavyset)

I would like you to look back to the previous page where we have the quote from the Book of John from the Bible. It ends with the question; '...And to whom has the arm of the Lord been revealed?' Well, after reading the above Egyptian quote about Horus and Osiris and their arms and hands and the rest of their divine body parts, I feel like the arm of the Lord has been revealed to me. But if you do not believe me - as I don't want to only rely on the ambiguity of the previous two quotes - I would like to present to you in Figure 3-20 the hieroglyphic revelation of the 'arm of the Lord' as a letter in the Egyptian word 'Rah', the Sun.

If one thinks that only Christ can be 'raised' up according to the New Testament then I will provide a quote from the Book of Romans to demonstrate that the early Christians also tied this 'raising up' concept to the Pharaoh:

> "17 For the **Scripture says to the Pharaoh**, 'For this very purpose **I have raised you up**, that I may show My power in you, and that My name may be declared in all the earth' "
>
> (Bible, Romans, Chapter 9, Vs.17)

To understand the mysteries of the Holy Bible one needs to study the Egyptian teachings, because most of our hidden marvelous Judeo-Christian wisdom that are contained in the Scriptures were transmitted to us by the Priests of Ra from Egypt.

For a moment, let us return to the Bible quote from the Book of John a couple of pages ago. Certainly there is a connection in that previous quote from the Book of John between the 'judgment of this world' and 'the light'.

Now, some spiritual leaders would tell me that this is about 'spiritual enlightenment' rather than a very strong light from the Sun. To them, I shall continue quoting from the same chapter.

"40 '**He has blinded their eyes** and hardened their
hearts, …
44 Then **Jesus cried out** and said, 'He who
believes in Me, believes not in Me but in Him
who sent Me.
45 'And he who sees Me sees **Him who sent Me**.
46 '**I have come as a light into the world,** …
47 'And if anyone hears My words and does not
believe, I do not judge him;" (Author's heavyset)
(Bible, John, Ch.12, Vs. 40-46)

Well, I sure don't want to turn this into a one sided Bible study,
but clearly there is a blinding light and He was sent by Him the
Father and He has 'come as a light'. Thus, Jesus came from Him,
the Father, the Old King who is the Sun. Therefore He comes as a
Light. The secrets are not lost, they are actually rediscovered, and
thus it is a powerful metaphysical lesson to the 'Illuminati'.

The story of Moses, Jacob, Joseph, Jesus and so many others in
the Bible is tied to Egypt. We need to return to the original
teachings, which were unalterably carved on the walls of various
tombs and pyramids long before we knew anything about ethnic
divisions of the world. The only way to decipher a true scientific
meaning to the ancient wisdoms is to compare the oldest teaching
of the world, which are the Egyptian and the Hindu myths. One
can compare the animal symbols at the birth of the Hindu gods
and the birth of Christ at the Nativity scene to realize the same
cosmic teaching. Clearly, the word 'mesi' as in Mesi-ah, or
'mose' as in Moses implicates an Egyptian origin for the biblical
names. It would be difficult to deny that these hieroglyphic
pictures meaning 'to give birth to …' hide something more than
just childbirth. It would be easy to just show a baby or a child,
rather than having an abstract seemingly meaningless hieroglyph.
Three lines meeting in one point is not an easily visualized birth,
unless it is about Orion.

The symbol 'mes' according to Wilkinson means the 'Child'. This Child might even stand for two different occasions. The first is at the end of summer when the Sun erupts during early Harvest time and the second is three or seven years later at Christmas when the New Sun is reborn after the 'Three Years of Darkness',

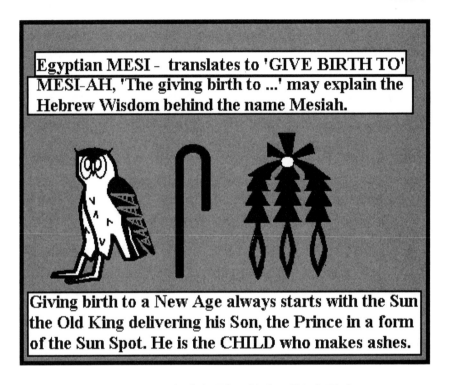

FIGURE 3-19. Mesi-ah is The Giving Birth To?
(Modified from Schumann-Antelme & Rossini's IHH)

The 'owl' or the 'cane' hieroglyphic symbols bring a cosmic 'divine birth' to mind. This happens at the point of Orion when after the Sunspot erupts it will cause the death (owl) of the Old King Sun, which is followed by a three years of darkness (owl) before the birth of the New Sun. This was accomplished by the axis deviation of the Magnetic North (cane). This makes sense.

I know it is difficult to digest these cosmic events on just a few stick and circle shaped hieroglyphs. That is why I am showing so many examples that point to that same cosmic scenario. The spelling of the name for the Sun is another of those examples.

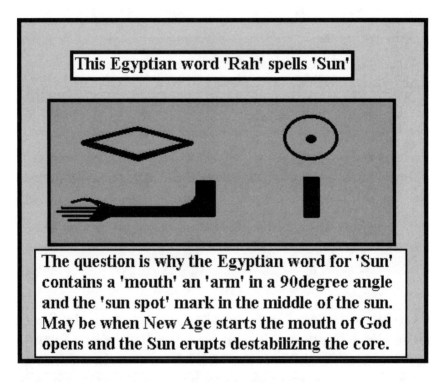

This Egyptian word 'Rah' spells 'Sun'

The question is why the Egyptian word for 'Sun' contains a 'mouth' an 'arm' in a 90degree angle and the 'sun spot' mark in the middle of the sun. May be when New Age starts the mouth of God opens and the Sun erupts destabilizing the core.

FIGURE 3-20. Ra (Rah / Re) is the Sun.

The Opening of the Mouth ceremony involving the Crocodile was one of the most important depictions inside the tombs of the pyramids. It likely involved the Mouth as the opening and closing of space in between Vega and Polaris, which houses our mythical fiery dragon /crocodile. In the Hebrew Wisdom from the Ra Priests this opening of the Mouth became the Mouth of God. The 'Word', which resonated out from the mouth of God was depicted as a Serpent or resonation.

This is how the Hindu Myths tie the mouth of God to the fire:
"Since **creation** has been performed by Brahma, I will therefore **destroy, cutting off my own seed**. When he had said this, **he released from his mouth a flame which burnt everything**." (Author's heavyset)

In the figures of Chapters 3 and 4, the Face of God, the Word from the sacred Mouth is tied to the Serpentine Resonation, the Two Goddesses and the Two Pillars, along with New Birth, Axis Shift, Orion's Leg, Wick of the Oil Lamp, The Stork who brings the New Baby. This stork likes to nest on smoky chimneys not even worrying about improperly blocking Santa Claus' entry through the roof at Christmas.

FIGURE 3-21: The SECRET of the FLOOD - Tied to the Chick, Two Ladies, Sun Rise, Leg, Cane, Fish, Scroll, Arm, Braided Rope, Stork and Pyramid

The Hungarian word for the English 'Leg' is spelled 'Lab'. The capital letter 'L' does resemble a leg. But whose leg is it? Is it the leg of that famous hunter **Orion** and the foot **star called 'Rigel'?** When the astronomical pointer reaches Rigel, the leg of Orion it **starts the** longest constellation Eridanus, the **'River'**. A clue? It is documented in my earlier work titled 'The Celestial Clock'.

Let us see a few quotes from the Bible to demonstrate the references for the 'leg', 'river' or 'riverbank':
> "Then it came to pass, at the end of two full years, that **Pharaoh** had a dream; and behold, he stood by the **river**."
> (Bible, Genesis, Chapter 41, Vs.1)
> "17 Then Pharaoh said to Joseph: "Behold, in my dream I stood on the **bank of the river**.
> 18 "Suddenly **seven cows** came up out of the river, ..."
> (Bible, Genesis, Chapter 41, Vs.17-18)

Let me provide a few more quotes about our stubborn Donkey. The secret of this 'wild ass' will be revealed in our last chapter.

> "24 A **wild donkey** used to the wilderness, that sniffs at the wind in her **desire**; in her time of **mating**, who can **turn** her away?   (Bible, Jeremiah, Chapter 2, Vs. 24)

> "5 Does the **wild donkey** bray when it has grass, or does the **ox** low over its fodder?(Bible, Job, Chapter 6, Vs. 5)

> "12 For an empty-headed man will be wise, when a **wild donkey's colt is born a man**." (Author's heavyset)
> (Job, Chapter 11, Vs. 12)

This 'wild ass' will be a major player in the tragic beginning of an era that brought us a Sunspot eruption followed by an axis shift. The seven years of famine was a natural out growth of the initial disaster and the flood of Noah washed down the rest.

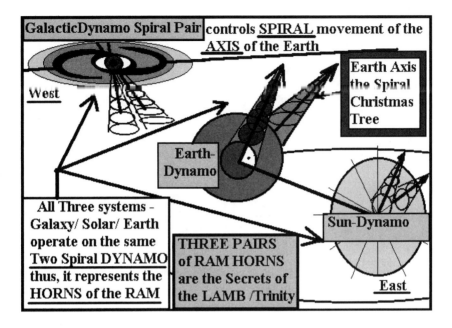

FIGURE 3-22. The Trinity Power Lines and the Lamb /Ram

It is Orion in the tail of the 'Fish' or biblical whale, where the celestial equatorial lines cross. Therefore, it makes perfect sense that the Egyptian word 'Bes' that means 'SECRET' (Fig.3-21) is designated by the 'FISH' and the 'Scroll'. The scroll is a written document that is contained between two 'sticks' that represent the two pillars of the Earth. By rolling open the 'two pillars' one symbolically opens up the 'mouth of god' or opens the compass or even the mouth of the Crocodile deity. A simple 'rabbinic' act can hide so much cosmic knowledge!

Figure 3-22 demonstrates the Three Planes –Galactic, Solar, and Earth – that each function as 'Electro-Magnetic Dynamos'. Since the essence of the 'two axes' of each systems controlled by SPIRAL pairs the concept became represented by the Spiral Horns of the Ram or the Lamb in religious mythologies.

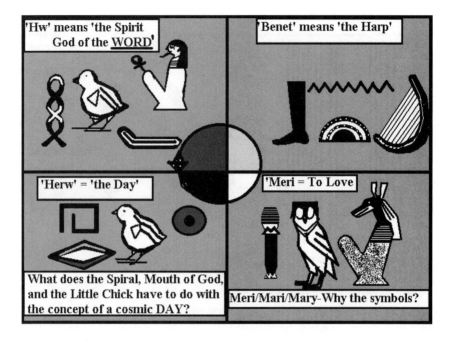

FIGURE 3-23. Meri / Mari / Mary is to Love.
(Modified from IHH by Schumann-Antelme & Rossini)

It is interesting to ponder on the word for 'Heru' (Horus) that is similarly pronounced and means both 'Hero God' and the 'Day'. This 'Cosmic Day' is shown in Fig. 3-23 as a Sun with a 'Spot' in the middle, thus tying the Sunspot to the 'Day' of the Lord. The '**Cosmic Day**' to the '**Earth Day**' is derived from the fact that when Heru fights, it is usually at 12 noon (12,000year end) or at midnight of the 24,000year Cosmic Day. The 24hour Earth Day resembles the 24,000year long Precession. In the same set of hieroglyphic pictures '**Meri / Mari / Mary**' is '**to Love**' makes perfect sense if the lovemaking is about '**cosmic sex & birth**'. A quote from the Bible underlines my claim that the 'Birth' is thought to be from the 'celestial womb'. I will demonstrate - that the noise of a 'word', tied to Venus 'morning star', and to earth's core. **Fire and flood** is the result of this **cosmic birthing** event.

The Lord also encourages knowledge and shuns ignorance. The mentioning of planet Venus as the Morning Star, and later on the Orion and the Pleiades in the Book of Job, has a very important cosmic significance.

> "1 Then **the Lord** answered Job **out of the whirlwind**, and said: 2 Who is this who darkens counsel by words without knowledge? 3 Now prepare yourself like a man; I will question you, and you shall answer Me. 4 "Where were you when I laid the **foundations of the earth**? Tell Me, if you have understanding. (Book of Job. Chapter 38, vs.1-4) (I need to comment here: There were no people present at the creations of the earth foundation, and the Creator knows that! But this is not an 'angry, and jealous God', but a wise One who knows science. The foundation stone of the earth is the 'keystone' body of Hercules, who lies to the Magnetic North direction -the Core of the Earth.- Author)

I will now continue with my quote from the Book of Job:

> "5 Who determined its measurements? Surely you know! Or who stretched the line upon it?
> 6 To what were its foundations fastened? Or who laid its **cornerstone**, (Only one 'stone'- the core, not four! Author)
> 7 When the **morning stars** sang together, and **all the sons of God** shouted for joy? (Author's underlining, heavyset) (A question:- Is there more than one sons of God?- Author)
> 8 "Or who shut in the **sea** with **doors**, when it **bursts forth** and **issued from the womb**; (Job, Chapter 38, Vs. 5-8)

Please, take notice. **1. 'Doors' hold the 'Flood' from the sea. 2. The 'Flood' is ISSUED FROM THE WOMB.** And let me tell you, it's the enigmatic **'Womb of the Milky Way Galaxy'**!

Returning to the Egyptians, in the temple of Ramesses II in the Sanctuary the deified pharaoh Ramesses is positioned next to Amun-Ra, Ra-Horakhty and Ptah. (Ramesses is in the Bible!)

Two times in a year the rising sun shines straight into the Sanctuary illuminating the gods Amun-Ra and Ramesses. The Egyptian Book of the Dead and related papyri sound very similar in context to the Bible. Amen (Amun) or Amen-Ra, is written about as such in the following papyrus quoted in The Egyptian Book of the Dead by the famous E. A. Wallis Budge:

> "The extract from a papyrus written for the princess Nesi-Khonsu, a member of the priesthood of Amen, is an example of the exalted language in which his votaries addressed him.

> "This is the **sacred god, the lord of all the gods, Amen-Ra,** ... the sacred soul who came into being in the beginning, the great god who liveth by right and truth, ...the One of One, the creator of the things which came into being when the earth took form in the beginning, whose births are hidden ... The sacred Form, beloved, terrible **and mighty in his two risings** ... He shone upon the earth from primeval time the Disk, the prince of light and radiance. ...He is the prince of princes, the mightiest, he is greater than the gods, he is the young bull ...He is the firstborn god, ...the terrible one of the two lion-gods, **... the lord who shooteth forth flame ... he is the aged one who reneweth his youth**; ... his rays are the guides of millions of men; ... and they are under the protection of **his face**. ... He is the **young bull that destroyeth the wicked**, ... and he cannot be known. He is the King ... gods and goddesses bow down in adoration before his Soul by reason of **the awful terror which belongeth unto him**. He is the Being who cannot be known, and he is more hidden than all the gods. He maketh **the Disk** to be his vicar, and he himself cannot be known, and **he hideth himself from that which cometh forth from** him. **He is a bright flame of fire** ...He is the king of the North and of the South , Amen-Ra, king of the gods ... "
> (Author's heavy set and underlining.)

Well, let me summarize this a bit:
- So this was about the Creator God, Amen-Ra, who had 'two risings' and he shoots forth flame, he is the old king who can renew himself, thus it is not about the original creation but renewing an already old sun king to his youth.
- He is a young Bull,
- He has a face, but he is hidden and nobody can know him.

- He made the (Sun) Disk and hid himself from what came out of him. He is a 'bright flame of fire' who unites the North and the South. He is a young bull who destroys the wicked.

I think, this is the appropriate time to say: **I rest my case!**

ONLY my cosmic scientific theory can explain this strange concept in its entirety! It is a bloody crying shame that, famous professors who receive doctorate degrees in these disciplines and spend their lifetime studying this ancient culture would leave the correct cosmic interpretation to outsiders such as myself. The quote on the previous page almost sounds biblical, but also it is very revealing as to the equating the unseen force recognized in our Creator to the destructive force arising unexpectedly as a sunspot eruption. The same force can be creative or destructive.

First of all before we say anything else, let me state something very important: - Please, notice that <u>this is not about a historical Pharaoh king</u>, the kind the traditional Egyptologists are talking about. Second, that the Creator God is tied to a peculiar 'two rising' of the Sun in a manner of being 'reborn'. He shines as the Sun, but He is not the Sun, and actually is known to come from the Disk of the Sun and awful terror belongs to him. So, I feel comfortable restating my position, that is:
- That, the Creator God is equated to the unknown and unseen magical electromagnetic Force in the Universe, which in this instance is best represented by the erupting Sun.
- When the Sun erupts, and the Earth's axis tilt, the Sun that day will appear to come up twice within 24hours. If I have to bring up examples from the Bible about the early Dawn and the Noon Sun going dark or reappearing, and the Child who is revived by magic - then I would be wasting my time.
- The uniting of the North and South Kingdom of Egypt is about 'uniting' the Magnetic North (North) and the Polar North (South) during a time of an axis shift.

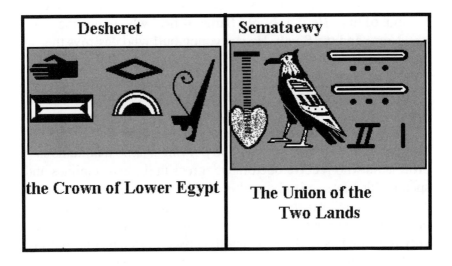

Desheret	Semataewy
the Crown of Lower Egypt	The Union of the Two Lands

FIGURE 3-24. Union of the Two Land.
(Modified from IHH by Schumann-Antelme & Rossini)

In Figure 3-24 the Crown of Lower Egypt is showing a spiral eruption. Since we agreed that the Lower Kingdom of Egypt is a synonym for the Core-Magnetic North of the Earth, the dark or red color would be appropriate for the hat. The hand, pool, the mouth and the half cycle horizon symbols had been discussed in previous pictures and they certainly fit the theory. In the right hand side of the same figure is 'The Union of the Two Lands'.

The traditional interpretation of the first symbol on the right hand side is 'lungs and trachea'. Being myself a practicing Internal Medicine doctor I have a little problem with the anatomical accuracy of how a pair of lungs would be depicted by a society who practiced embalming. To me the symbol appears as if a 'heart' would be pierced by 'resonation' from above. When the Savior is depicted in religious pictures, the heart is either pierced or it has the color of blood and occasionally flames on top.

140

The Egyptians understood resonation and that is what they are
showing here. When the resonation (serpent) erupts from the Sun,
it affects the Core (Cora-zon = Heart in Spanish) of the Earth.
Following that the erupting underwater volcanism releases
sulfuric acid and that is what turning the water to blood color.
Thus, it gives a cosmic meaning and scientific significance to the
religious iconography.

The 'II' and 'I' type of symbols on the bottom portion of the
right hand side of Figure 3-24 is almost identical to the markings
seen on the 'Face of God' in Figure 4-4, marked about eight
waves between his mouth and above his 'serpent beard'. In my
opinion, these two markers are the representations of the two
Venus Transits eight years apart. In between those Two Venus
Transit ladies is when the three power lines meet in Orion and
that is when the 'two kingdoms' unite. Thus in Figure 3-24, the
two elliptical cycles with the three dots are probably representing
the belt of Orion. Still continuing with the interpretation of
Figure 3-24, the second symbol from the left is the hawk or
vulture. The 'hawk' of the Magnetic North is the one that
happens to shift during the 'Orion meeting'. Reading the sentence
analytically, it certainly yields a much better and clearer
understanding to the terms used in the Egyptian expression 'The
Union of the Two Land'. This cosmic interpretation transfers to
the reading of the 'Two Kingdoms' in the Bible. Even the light
and the Lord is connected to 'living waters' and oneness:

> "6 It shall come to pass in that day that there
> will be no light; the **lights will diminish**.
> 7 It shall be **one day**, which is **known to the Lord**.
> 8 And in that day it shall be that **living waters
> shall flow** ...
> 9 And the **Lord shall** be **King** over all the earth.
> **In that day it shall be – "the Lord is one," and
> his name is one**.   (Author's heavyset)
> (Bible, Zechariah, Ch. 14, Vs. 6-9.)

Is the Lord name (Aton/Adon) is 'one' on that day because the 'Two Lands/Earth Axes' of Egypt is unified? The answer is yes. **The monotheist Aton/Aten was** usually not shown as a human pharaoh, but as **the Sun disk with rays of hands** shooting out. This is depicted on Figure 3-25. The **evil serpent** (resonation / sunspot eruption) is also featured **in the middle of the Sun disk**.

I will quotes from the Bible about the **'arm of God' and fire**:
"9 Have you an **arm like God**? Or can you thunder with a **voice like His**?" (Bible, Job, Chapter 40, Vs. 9)

"2 ... "The Lord came from Sinai, and dawned on them from Seir; **He shone** forth from Mount Paran, and He came with ten thousands of saints; **from His right hand came a fiery law** for them" (Deuteronomy, Ch.33, Vs.2)

"And it came to pass in the sixth year, in the sixth month, on the fifth day of the month, as I sat in my house with the elders of Judah sitting before me, that the **hand of the Lord God fell upon me** there.
2 Then I looked, and there was a likeness, **like the appearance of fire** – from the appearance of His waist ..." (Author's heavyset) (Ezekiel, Chapter 8, Vs. 1,2)

The Hindu Myths by Penguin Classics write about a fiery law and also has the Christ-like infant Krisna tied to the fire and the ashes: "The **supreme purification** of the entire universe is to be **accomplished by ashes.** ... By means of ashes, my seed, **one is released from all sins.**"

"The infant-swallower, searching for children, happened to come to the house of Nanda, and she saw there on the bed the **infant Krsna**, whose true **energy** was concealed, like a **fire covered with ashes**." (Author's heavyset)
(Hindu Myths, Penguin Classics, pg. 215)

FIGURE 3-25. The Sun King Aton /Aten (Tomb of Ay, Amarna, modified from Wilkinson's Reading Egyptian Art)

Thus, Aton (the Hebrew Adon/Greek Adonis = biblical Lord) is clearly and picturesquely depicted as the erupting Sun. The artist even gave seventeen rays with hands coming out of the Sun to clue us in on the secret that it happens in between the two pillars where the dragon rules who has exactly seventeen named stars.

The obvious nakedness of the people on the streets may be coincidental, but it almost appears that the 'serpent' of the Sun made them jump out of their shower. This nakedness scene may be the basis for the references in the Bible and in the Egyptian Book of the Death about nakedness of the father, skin boils from the sun eruption and the 'revealing one's nakedness'. The intense heat from the sunspot eruption likely made even the most prudent religious people lose their clothing fast. The biblical 'boil of Egypt' came next. Thus, the 'lepers' needed the healing.

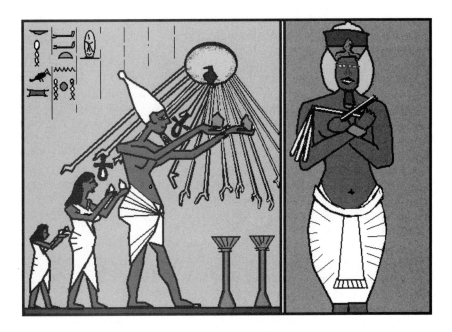

FIGURE 3-26: Aton Adored By Akhenaten

Figure 3-26 provides us with another depiction of Aton from the Great Palace at Tell el-Amarna that is found on a sculpted block where the rays of Aton are 14 in numbers. A small goddess stands to the left then a larger goddess in the middle and the pharaoh Akhenaten is to the right. The arms of rays extend toward the two goddesses. The second arm of ray coming from Aton the erupting Sun and it is over the face of the second goddess. This second hand is holding the 'ankh' toward her face. Then four rays later the 'ankh', is held toward the face of Akhenaten who is a male, but interestingly and obviously depicted with wide feminine childbearing hips. On the right hand side of the picture I show the contours of a colossal sandstone statue of Akhenaten from the Gempaaten temple at Karnak. We see a male god with two female consorts referring to a period of the 'Two Venus Transits' as a marker for the sunspot eruption. Aton does appear as a 'eunuch' on the right hand side picture.

The number fourteen refers to the seven years of bounty and the seven years of famine. The **feminine depiction of the male** Akhenaten is reminiscent of the **biblical 'eunuch'** and likely symbolizing a fact that we have a **'castrated old King'** or even a 'pregnant' male pharaoh at hand who gives birth through the action of the erupting sun. Scientifically it symbolizes the fact that after the Sun eruption the Earth forces stay within a **'neutral state' magnetically** until a new field starts fortifying.

Akhenaten's new religion reveals his emphasis on 'One Lord', the Disc of the Sun itself. According to the hieroglyphic writings on the walls of the tombs of Akhenaten, he sent his soldiers all throughout Egypt with the instruction to destroy the statues and blot out the names of other deities. But we know that this is not a historical story, but a cosmic teaching. If it would be a historical fact, then the excising of the names of other deities would have started in his own town, where next to his stories are carved the tales of other cosmic deities. Apparently the popularity of Aton had been growing since the beginning of the New Kingdom. Even Tuthmoses I had taken on the royal title; "Horus-Ra who comes from the Aton" and also Amenhotep III had named his vessel "Glorious is the Aton" By the time of his reign there was a temple erected to Aton at Karnak. The Sun Disc Aton became the representation of Ra-Horakhty, the solar deity that was a hawk-headed god with the sun disc on his head. A few generations after Akhenaten's death, his name was erased from the lists of the Kings of the New Kingdom. Was it historical fact or was it set up as a plot from the beginning? So Akhenaten attempted to abolish the old polytheistic religion and offer lotus flower only to one deity, one Lord, the Aton/Aten. When his name came up in later Dynasties, he was referred to as 'the heretic pharaoh' or simply 'the rebel'. This, as we know by now, was done because his role as the 'Sunspot' was scandalous and rebellious to so drastically end an old age and to start a new one.

We also understand that it was not about bringing a new religion, but starting a new half cycle. It was a swift entry and a quicker exit, but in that short reign this Prince of the Sun impressed us enough to generate countless 'religious' tales about his short lived Kingdom.

This is how The Egyptian Book of the Dead on Plate XXV writes about the 'making of the transformation'. This sounds as an Egyptian spell to promote 'shape shifting' through flame.

> "Making the **transformation into a swallow**. Ani Osiris, the triumphant said: ' I am a swallow, a swallow that is **a scorpion, the daughter of Ra**. Hail you gods. Sweet is your smell, twice. **Hail flame**, coming forth from the horizon. … O grant me your two hands that I may pass the time in the **Island of Flame**."

Even in the symbols of their tombs or the shrines a connection can be noticed to the intended geological meaning of the two parts of the geo-dynamo. The Upper Egyptian Shrine on Figure 3-27 has a cupola, which is off center as the Polar North axis would be. The Lower Shrine shows an inner pillar or a three layered inside to symbolize the Core of the Earth.

A few quote from the Bible about Temple, fire and light :

> "11 Our holy and beautiful temple, where our fathers praised You, is burned up with fire; and all our pleasant things are laid waste."   (Isaiah, Chapter 64, Vs.11)

> "22 But I saw no temple in it, for the Lord God Almighty and the Lamb are its temple.
> 23 The city had no **need of the sun** or of the moon to shine in it, for the glory of **God illuminated it. The Lamb is its light.** "   (Bible, Revelation, Chapter 22, Vs. 22-23)

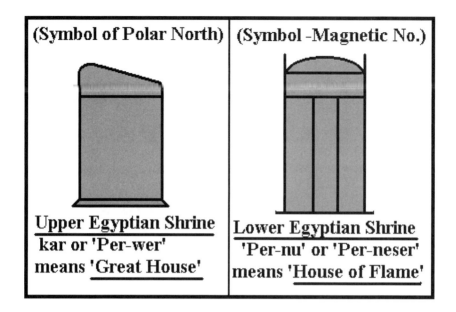

(Symbol of Polar North)	(Symbol –Magnetic No.)
Upper Egyptian Shrine <u>kar or 'Per-wer'</u> **means 'Great House'**	**Lower Egyptian Shrine** <u>'Per-nu' or 'Per-neser'</u> **means 'House of Flame'**

FIGURE 3-27. Upper and Lower Egyptian Shrines
(Modified from Wilkinson's Reading Egyptian Art)

Let us now look at a picture from Lesko's book. Here they unified a male and a female into one figure. They also gave her extra heads of a hawk and a lion. In this one creature they seemingly incorporated the biblical four beasts of the Apocalypse into one big warning.

To me the combining of the 'hawk' head with the head of the 'lion' means that the sunspot eruption (the swooping down of the hawk as the Magnetic North) happened at the Age of Leo and in the Sun sign of Leo, which is the month of August. Why the ancients combined the 'goddess'' and the 'phallic' symbols is not as obvious, but one thing seems clear that they meant these female and male forces as cosmic power references. The phallic symbol alone should symbolize the Sunspot eruption of the male sun king.

FIGURE 3-28. The Three-Headed Goddess Mut
(Modified from Lesko's The Great Goddesses of Egypt)

Professor Barbara S. Lesko depicts in her book the goddess
Mut, apparently from a late Book of the Dead. In figure 3-28, I
show the Three-Headed Goddess of Mut from Lesko's book. She
has three heads, a feline like human skull, along with the separate
lioness head and the hawk head. She also displays wings of a
hawk and a ***phallus, symbolizing the sunspot eruption.***

Lesko also remarks that the goddess Mut was responsible of
burning the enemies of the Pharaoh in a box like furnace.

This opens the door for a detailed discussion on the phallic symbol representing the eruption of the Sun. The hawk symbolizes the sun or simply the Sun's effect on the Magnetic North. The goddess Mut is connected to the North and as a further clue to her relationship to the Core of the Earth is memorialized by the fact that her divine husband was Ptah, considered god of the craftsmen, including workers in the metal smelters. **The mythical blacksmith is a secret representation of the core of the earth** where the molten iron plays a significant part in maintaining or disrupting the power balance of the earth.

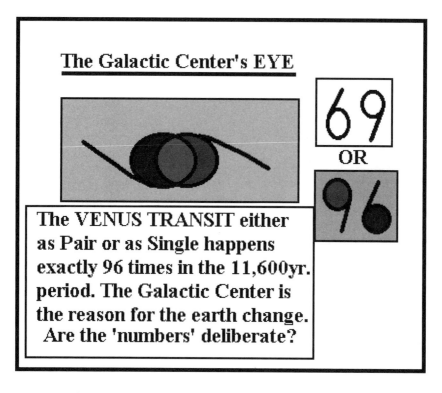

The Galactic Center's EYE

69 OR 96

The VENUS TRANSIT either as Pair or as Single happens exactly 96 times in the 11,600yr. period. The Galactic Center is the reason for the earth change. Are the 'numbers' deliberate?

FIGURE 3-12: Ninety-Six Venus Transit Periods

Was the above concept meant to be 69 or 96?

HATHOR, the Cow-headed Goddess

Why would the Egyptians depict one of their most favorite goddesses as a cow-headed human freak unless there was a superb cosmic scientific meaning hidden behind the picture?

Hathor, the Goddess of the West represents the first of the pair of Venus Transit, which happens between the horns of Bull.

FIGURE 3-13: Hathor, the Cow-headed Goddess

We conclude this chapter with the picture of Hathor, the cow-headed goddess who represented so many things for the early Egyptians. She was the Goddess of Fertility, Songs and Dance, but also she stood for the role of the Goddess of the West who welcomed the departing souls into the Afterlife. Astronomically, for us she is the representation of the first coming of the Venus Transit pair. This first Venus Transit that happened about 11,600years ago, just prior to Noah's Flood, began a tragic period in the lives of the ancient Egyptians. The cosmic resonation that slowly increased following this Venus Transit - and eventually resulted in the Sunspot eruption – earned the 'Harlot' designation for Venus and Mother Earth. In the next chapter we will further explore the roles of the 'two goddesses' in this ancient disaster.

Chapter Four
Two Ladies and a Dung Beetle

The Two Ladies in ancient Egypt represented several different aspects of cosmology and earth mechanics. First and for most, they were the representatives of Upper and Lower Egypt. This is one of the most misunderstood and falsely explained concepts in traditional Egyptology. The Egyptian beauties definitely had strange tastes for headdresses. They were not worn for the shock value, rather these headdresses were meant to convey a specific cosmic scientific message.

For the Egyptologists at the beginning it must had been difficult to make any sense out of these Two Ladies. The early French, Italian, English, German and Hebrew scholars, who started the deciphering in the late 1700's, were still in their initial steps of scientific development. Without advanced science the message cannot be explained correctly. To that effect allow me to quickly manufacture a parable. For example, in those early years if someone from our time would have had the ability to travel back in time and give the main scientists and also the priesthood of that era a 'Holy Handbook' on the mechanics of a Ford Mustang automobile, and tell them:

- *"Listen folks, this writing is a holy book on the concept of fast travel for even the average person. This fast machine will revolutionize travel and free people from bondage. The book contains the blueprint of this awesome vehicle, which will make all your horses and oxen obsolete for travel. Its design comes straight from one of the greatest industrial powers on Earth. Handle this book carefully and when the time comes, a few hundred years from now, you will understand the wisdom contained in this book."*

Now, I have a feeling that a few priests, scientists, Sunday school teachers and even laypersons would take a stab at the meaning of this 'holy machine book'. Most, if not all of them, would get the majority of the writings wrong. But it would not matter, because most of those charismatic preachers would draw on an even less educated and less complex thinking crowd two hundred years ago. The collection bin would still be full and everybody would be happy. I can see them reading the manual and trying to make heads and tails out of the special sections:

"Let me see ... and it says here ... the carburetor mixes the fuel and the air to a special ratio. ... Ok. I think I understand it. The fuel is the liquid of the gods, like manna. Air is also needed, because it is like the Spirit of God.. All right, in my sermon tomorrow I will impart this knowledge to the faithful."

My exact point with this is that a lot of people interpret things that they have not much scientific knowledge about. In any sacred book, the real knowledge can only be understood and deciphered if the reader is up to the scientific complexity of those ancient Ra priests who carefully recorded down the information. Those preachers who do not possess this higher scientific mind should stay with strictly 'moralizing' the stories and not touch the more spiritual or cosmic interpretations of the sacred stories.

In defense of the theologians I must admit that the scientific information, which was needed to crack the main purpose of the Two Ladies and their role of unifying the Two Lands of Egypt was only made public in 1994. Since then the Roberts-Glatzmaier Geo-dynamo is at least known to a few scientists, but really not known in traditional Egyptologist's circles. So, why do we expect them to come up with the right answer? Well, I don't. The training, like still so many other fields of expertise, is based on an old school system. Likely the aging professors - who developed the curriculum for today, that the currently lecturing new professors grew up on - were riding in the saddle of their four-legged mustangs to get to work, rather than driving it.

This is not to say that our knowledge base did not expand by incredible leaps and bounds in the last few decades, but the scientists from Los Alamos National Laboratory, NASA or NOAA are not necessarily invited to the reunions of the mainstream Egyptologists for some scientific refreshments.

I will bring up the Two Ladies in Figure 4-1A one more time again as a reminder. They are the consorts of Amun the Ram-Headed god. In this picture they are wearing the headdresses reminiscent of their role as the goddesses of the Two Lands, the Upper Kingdom and the Lower Kingdom. We are not talking about the possibility of two actual historical kingdoms with two living goddesses. Rather, I would like to discuss the teachings of the Earth's mechanics and the calendarical, astronomic and cosmic importance of these two goddesses. Before we progress to that let me mention the two other significances these ladies carried besides being the goddesses of the two kingdoms. The second aspect was the cow or bullhorns on their heads to identify their relation to the Venus Transit. Thus in general the cow horns with the sun in between referred to the secret Venus Calendar.

**The TWO LADIES
& the Ram-Headed God AMUN**

FIGURE 4-1. The TWO LADIES
(Modified from Erik Hornung's 'TAEBOTA')

The third aspect of the goddesses' symbolism was their animal and flower decorations (Figure 4-2). One of them would be wearing a snake headdress or even depicted as an actual Cobra ready to strike. The other goddess was commonly pictured either as an Egyptian Vulture or most of the time as a goddess wearing a headdress of a vulture. These headdresses never actually caught on in the fashion industry, not like the mascara of Cleopatra, but even she could not market the serpent headdress.

Well, let's think about what cosmic scientific concept these two ladies can teach us. The Cobra is the striking aspect of the wavy resonation coming at us from the center of the galaxy and from the sun. The Vulture - eight years later, after the seven years of Famine - obviously refers to what everybody would be thinking of when seeing **vultures** hovering overhead. It is **the *sign of death***. Not the Pharaoh's death, but the larger population during those earth changes nearly 12,000years ago.

The **flower symbols** for the two goddesses were the **papyrus** and the **reed** / lotus / water lily. We find that clearly mentioned in the Bible in the same paragraph.

> "11 Can the **papyrus** grow up without a marsh?
> Can the **reeds** flourish without water?
> (Bible, Book of Job, Ch.8. Vs.11)

The 'red sea' is a mistranslation of the 'reed sea' or the 'sea of reed' according to a few esoteric sources in research societies. In my opinion, it is both. Besides the symbolic meaning of the reed, commonly mentioned in the Egyptian stories and in biblical tales, the turning of the sea red is also an important concept during the earth changes. All of this is tied to the Venus Transits. Before I get fully emerged in the functions of the two ladies, I have to get a few scientific 'pains' off my chest. One is the current strange solar minimum and the other is the proper length of the Precession of the Equinoxes. They are both ways off!

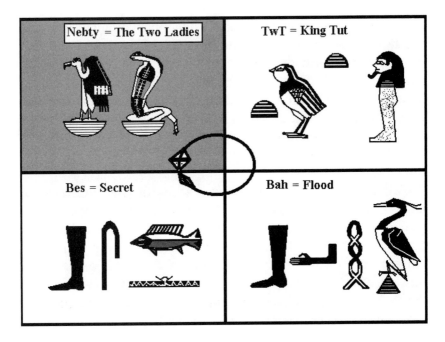

FIGURE 4-2: Vulture & Serpent. Nebty means Two Ladies.
(Modified from IHH by Schumann-Antelme & Rossini)

Before I analyze those pictures in Figure 4-2 above – well, wait a minute, as matter of fact I will let you dissect them on your own. We already know enough to trust that most of you will come up with the proper cosmic scenario. In the meantime, I will respectfully take a short detour into our current world affairs.

Since we talk about Sunspot eruptions, let me first remark on the fact that today we are entering into a dangerous active solar minimum. The year of the solar maximum was around 2000 and will again come in 2011, but the low years in between 2003 – 2008 should resemble lessened solar activity. We know that, but the Sun does not seem to be aware of that! It is still acting up in these years of solar minimum. Strong solar eruptions and galactic flashes are effecting our environment even today.

The popular media does not tie this to the strong hurricane seasons we just had in the summers of 2004 and 2005, although they are very closely and causatively related. The Sun has acted up in October and November of 2003. **The largest ever eruption happened on November 4th, 2003** It was an **X-28 solar flare,** which luckily blew away from the Sun in the opposite direction of Earth. Then in the spring of 2004 about 60% of our ozone has been destroyed over the poles by solar storms. This is truly global warming, except it is regulated by the powerful 2.6 million solar mass Galactic Center Super Sun and following in his footsteps is the overheating Sun of our Solar System. I assure you, that our Almighty God is personally responsible for this global warming. Unless, someone would explain to me how our earthly pollution is heating up the distant gigantic Sun. We seemed to forget the 'pecking order'. It is - first in order of strength and importance - the Galactic Center, second the Solar System's Sun, and then our tiny Earth. Not the other way around! Someone again is deliberately lying to us? Why?

We are sinking deeper into the solar minimum, but the solar flares have not stopped. We have seen ample evidence of that a few months ago on January 20th 2005, when the sun was producing major solar flares scaring the Russian military into deep subterranean mountain hideouts. The latest major eruption – actually, the second largest ever on records, an X-17 solar flare – just happened now on September 7th 2005. As I am finishing up the editing of this book and I am wondering when the next fiery 'Day of the Lord' will come for our age. Will it repeat the events in the same sequence as it happened 11,600years ago? Would it come between the Two Venus Transits of 2004-2012? Or are we safe to go another round before our great-great-grand children have to worry about this same issue? Only the Creator knows and I am afraid to ask, because anytime He opens His mouth serious trouble follows. So, we will just remain humble, hope for the best and quietly try to guess the exact time of the next one.

According to Dr LaViolette, it is a very likely possibility that a Galactic Flash (Magnetar explosion) detected by astronomers on the 27th of December 2004 caused the 'Tsunami' in Asia. The explosion was 40-50,000 light years away. In comparison, the Galactic Center is about 23-24,000 light years away. When I published my first book 'The Celestial Clock', several scientists told me that my theory was wrong because the galactic center is too far from us to cause any damage to Earth. Really?

Since we are on the subject, let me remind you that Dr. Paul LaViolette, an astrophysicist wrote a few excellent books. One is the 'Earth Under Fire' and it promotes the 'Super Galactic Wave' theory. He theorized over 20years ago in a thesis and now seems to be proving it right, that periodic eruptions of the Black Hole in our galactic center are responsible for earth changes.

Very interestingly and certainly not coincidentally, **the distance between the Galactic Center and the Earth is the same** as far as the thousands of **light years and the number of years** of the dominant **ice volume collapse** cycle detected. **The Galactic Center is about 23-24,000light years away from us, and the dominant ice age cycle found in the Milankovitch Ice Age strata is also 23-24,000years. This is also the actual length of the Precession of the Equinoxes according to my theory and clear scientific evidence.**

Sadly, there are several highly intelligent scholars who still prescribe to a 26,000year long Precession. This 26,000year Precession was roughly calculated by the ancient Greeks 2,500years ago probably using sticks and pebbles in the sand! They assumed a perfect circle with 360degree angle for the path of the Earth's orbit. Now we know that it is not true! I cannot believe that anybody would try to fool us over something as important as this. **The Precession of the Equinoxes determines the earth changes.**

The ice age cycles demonstrate a roughly 11,600year half cycle, thus a 23-24,000year long full cycle of Precession or Ice Volume Collapse cycles. The problem with the ancient Greek estimate that even the half cycle is not a perfect half circle; rather it is a half spiral or elliptical shaped orbit of the traveling Earth. Why would Earth trod in a perfect circular motion when any other planets in our solar system display elliptical orbits even on a yearly scale.

Over 100years ago an amateur American scientist, Mr. Chandler correctly hypothesized that the Earth's polar axis is wobbling in a progressively growing spiral fashion. It was measured in the 1960's and 70's by our government scientists and proven correct. Therefore, if it is the accepted theory called the **Chandler Wobble** that is taught at the main universities. I don't understand why we keep insisting on a perfect circular Precession? Whose interest it is to misguide us? May be – if we are lucky - some upper echelon scientists or secret societies know the Truth? I hope so! I pray that when the 'Day of the Lord' will commence on our age - we will have enough smart government scientists around the world who are prepared to disable the large arsenals of atomic weapons.

Otherwise, it would prove to me what I already suspect, that the human species are not ready to take on the title of the 'crowning members of Creation' as far as stewardship for the well being of the Earth is concerned. Guys, please get this right now! We are not populating any distant galaxies! Forget that. First we have to prove it to ourselves that we can take care of this little rock. Let's all of us agree on that for now! Ok? Unfortunately, very few scientists or 'mind' people muster up just enough 'spirituality' to make sound decisions including their hearts and brains. The old adage still stands. Body, mind, spirit! Harmonizing the function of the 'body, mind, and spirit' is still a very important concept when we are playing with weapons of mass destruction!

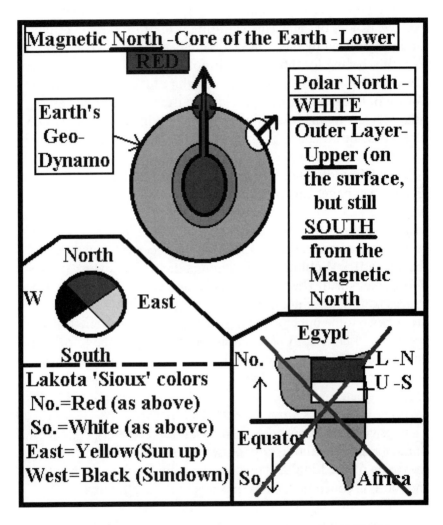

FIGURE 4-3. The NORTH AND SOUTH OF EGYPT.

Let us turn our attention now to another nationally important subject. It is the 'faded glory'. Well, we salute the flag, but are not being told of the symbolic meanings behind the colors we bow to. May be if our leaders would tell us about the deeper cosmic meanings of the colors we would not burn the flag.

On the previous Figure 4-3, one can observe the meanings of the two-colors of the Two Ladies. **Lower Egypt** was to the North and symbolized by the Red, because it represented the **Magnetic North** standing for the **Core of the Earth**, which is surrounded by *red lava*. That is straight up North and is called the Magnetic North. Interestingly what we call North that is the **Polar North** was secretly **designated 'South'**, since it is positioned south of the dominant Magnetic North. Therefore, the Polar North, which fell south of the Magnetic North received the designation for **Upper Kingdom**, since it was above the core at the surface, rather than being Lower in the inside of the Earth. The snow cover gave the Polar North its natural **white color. Even Santa Claus sports red & white in honor of the two norths**. Thus, the Upper Kingdom was the Polar North, designated by white color, but it was the 'Southern Kingdom of Egypt' as it fell south of the Magnetic North. The East and West were already taken up by the Sun's path, thus only the south was open for the polar north. I am hoping that it is not too confusing. Regardless, this is how the Ancients clued us in to the fact that they were aware of the North to South alignment of the two axes lining up parallel with the controlling Galactic Plane. The East direction was obviously painted golden yellow from the color of the Rising Sun, and the West became black from the darkness created by the Setting Sun. This is how the Lakota Sioux Indians depict the four directions. The oral and ritual tradition amazingly lasted for the whole duration of the 12,000years. Likely, as all others, they also forgot the cosmic principle behind the colors.

The secret of the 'bloodline', 'the Sacred Feminine' and the 'Rose Line' of The Da Vince Code is contained in the concept of the Magnetic North (Red Rose) shifting to the Polar North (White Rose) and causing the 'Holy Grail' (astronomical Grail in the middle of the Chamber of the South) to turn the Waters of the Oceans 'BLOOD RED' during the Divine Birth, Death and the Resurrection of the Son of the Sun!

Amazing secrets to hide! How much easier it is to write this down in a paragraph, rather than build hundreds of cathedrals?

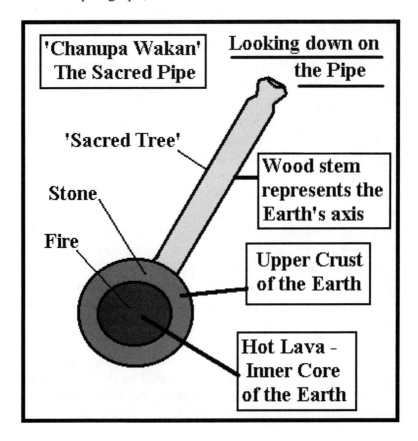

FIGURE 4-4: The Sacred Pipe Represents the Heated Earth

In Figure 4-4 we can observe the 'Chanupa Wakhan' that is the Sacred Peace Pipe of the Lakota Sioux Indians. Looking at It from above when can observe a hidden cosmic meaning. The 'Catlinite' hollow red stone bowl represents the Earth. The hole in the stone, where the fire goes is the core of the Earth. And finally the wood stem represents the axis of the globe.

Commonly, green sage is tied around the stem standing for a good green harvest or remembering that early tragic harvest.

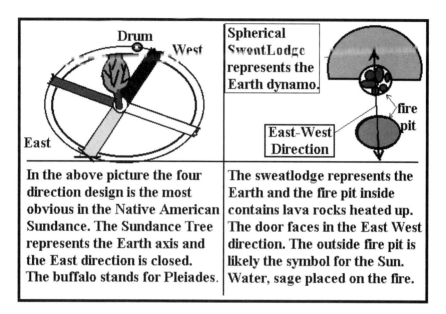

In the above picture the four direction design is the most obvious in the Native American Sundance. The Sundance Tree represents the Earth axis and the East direction is closed. The buffalo stands for Pleiades.	The sweatlodge represents the Earth and the fire pit inside contains lava rocks heated up. The door faces in the East West direction. The outside fire pit is likely the symbol for the Sun. Water, sage placed on the fire.

FIGURE 4-5. Native American Ritual Cosmology

One might ask why are we talking about Native American rituals and biblical concepts when the book should be about the Egyptians. Well, it is. I believe that the Egyptians were in direct communications with the Mayans and others. The presence of cocaine and tobacco residues that only grew in the Americas was actually found in some mummies in Egypt. Therefore, there had to be oceanic travels and intercontinental communications even several thousands of years ago. All the knowledge around the world must have originated from the ill-fated continent of Atlantis and then subsequently came out of Egypt.

Looking at Figure 4-5, on the left side the circular Sundance Ground of the Lakota Sioux Indians display the four directions. Usually, one or two female dancers guard the gates.

A young virgin girl is designated to select the Sundance tree in the nearby forest before the dance is set up and she is the one who swings the ax first at the tree to be cut. These may be long forgotten ritual references to the secret Venus Transit Calendar. When the male dancers 'pierce', the rope attached both to the sacred tree and to their chests. This rope ends in a 'Y' shape at the two ties at the chest of the dancers. The 'Y' shape upside down is almost identical to the 'delta' shape of the male part of the five-pointed star or the Egyptian tipi. So tying them with the 'Y' is likely the male symbol for god. The two ends tied between the two breasts where we can find the heart. Looking at Figure 3-17 can give us some cosmic clues about the meaning of the breast and heart. This closely relates to some Judeo-Christian depictions and even to important secret society rites.

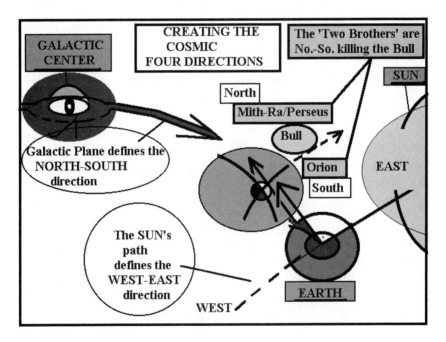

FIGURE 4-6: The Cosmic Four Directions

There is one more ceremony that I would like to briefly write about. It is the 'Heyoka' Dog Ceremony tied to the Cattle Dance. In it a 'white puppy dog' is boiled in a kettle and the initiate has to grab the dog meat out of the boiling water without himself getting burned. This strange medicine man called 'Heyoka' is like a clown, who does things mainly backwards. Interpreting this in a cosmic sense to me means the following: - When the Sunspot erupts shortly after the Dog Star is highest in the sky, the rivers will be boiling and the earth axes will reverse. Sirius Dog Star, intense heat, 'comic/cosmic' axis reversal. Very simple Native Wisdom surviving 12,000years in oral and ritual traditions!

Well, the Dog who licks up the blood of the bull after the Mithraic bull sacrifice and in the Book of the Kings I is hiding the same celestial enigma. From this bloody carnage, let us return to the peaceful plants and the flower symbols of the Egyptians. In Egypt it was the lotus and the papyrus, which stood for the two pillars. Representing Upper Egypt was the 'lotus' or water lily. This is how Richard H. Wilkinson writes about the symbol of the lotus/water lily in his excellent book titled 'Reading Egyptian Art':   "Because the water lily closes at night and sinks underwater – to rise and open again at dawn – it was a natural symbol of the sun and of creation.   …
The concept of **the young sun god appearing as a Child**, a lotus is described in Chapter 15 of the Book of the Dead, …   … the lotus was used representationally as a symbol of Upper Egypt … "

Please, note above 'the young sun god appearing as a Child' seems to be well established in scholarly circles, thus when I call the 'Child' of the Old Testament the 'Son of the Sun' I am not far from the Truth.

On the next page of the same book Wilkinson describes the significance of the 'papyrus':

"**The papyrus** was thus a natural symbol of life itself,
... Because the plant was a symbol of the primeval
marsh from which all life emerged, and **papyrus
"pillars" were also said to hold up the sky**, ...
Hathor, as a **goddess of heaven and the necropolis,**
sometimes appears **as a cow with papyrus umbel
between her horns as a symbol of the sun or** of the
papyrus **marshes of the west**, ... Mehu or Ta-Mehu:
"Land of the Papyrus," which was used to denote
the kingdom of Lower Egypt.

Those science priests of old were not confused about their
North and South. They used the word 'Egypt' to designate the
powers and the Kingdoms of the spherical Earth. Thus, the two
warring Kingdoms were about the fight between the Magnetic
North and the Polar North. If someone searches geographically
for the exact locations of the places in Egypt, such as the Lake of
the Jackal, the Lake of Fire, the Field of Reeds and the Field of
Offerings, would actually have a hard time pointing to the
specific location. The reason for that is because these names are
not about geography, but cosmology. Just as with the Egyptian
gods, we don't expect to believe the Greco-Roman tales that Zeus
and Poseidon were sky gods falling in love with earthly humans.

With the strange young Egyptian 'pharaoh' Aton, who was a
'monotheist' One-God believer, his rule was symbolically short
lived as a large sunspot would be. Since the sunspot eruption
destabilized the core of the Earth, it allowed the Magnetic North
to be pulled to where the Polar North was located and thereby
'unified the two kingdom'. After the sunspot eruption, one of
the two 'ethnic enclaves' or kingdoms **traveled to a 'foreign
land'**, just as if an exodus would have happened. **The magnetic
North became the 'captive'** of the Polar North. That is why in
the Old Testament of the Bible we find of one kingdom enslaving
another and later allowed to return to its own land.

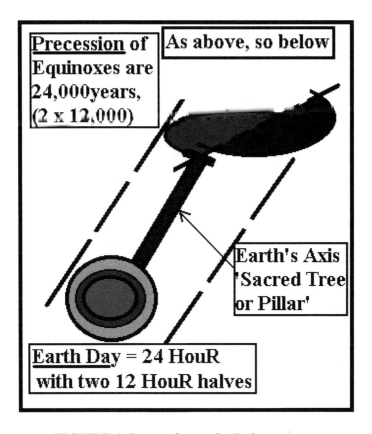

FIGURE 4-7. As Above, So Below

The twelve Labors of Hercules did not much differ from the struggles of the Twelve Knights of the Round Table, or the twelve trials of Gilgamesh in the Babylonian Epic. Jesus Christ similarly trained twelve apostles and spent twelve hours on the cross, after he went through the stations. The tribes of Israel were twelve and they consisted each of twelve thousand members. The number 12 and 12,000 was another clever cosmic reminder of the last 12years of a period and its year-to-year progression along with the concept of the 12,000year half cycle. The Egyptians also showed twelve gods on each side of the solar bark, which had at each end a watery disaster. See Figure 4-8.

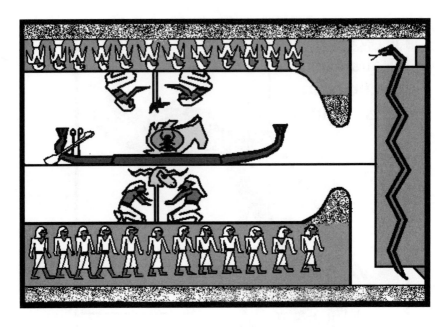

FIGURE 4-8. The 12 and 12 is 24.
(Modified from Hornung's The Egyptian Book of The Afterlife)

In Figure 4-8 we can observe the 12 gods above and below. This represents the 12,000year catastrophic half cycles. The 'solar bark' in the middle is also a boat. The Scarab Beetle (Kheper or Khepri) was already discussed as the depiction of a male son having a male offspring without female involvement. Another way to say it, that it represents the major earth shaking Sun spot eruption. The Lamb or Ram being adored on the boat by two persons is the representative of the 'Spiral' force of the Sun and the Galaxy. It is also the 'hidden' representation of the East direction, from where the Sun erupts. And because the Sun erupts at the end of the 12,000years in a particular year during late summer when the Dog Star, Sirius is highest in the sky, it explains why the Dog is also being adored. The Serpent guards the Gate on the right side of the picture standing in front of the 'door', which is mentioned in religious writings so many times.

Interestingly, the hinges of the door represent a 90degree angle and a tilted, 1/3degree angle to clue us in on the 'two norths'. In the next graph Figure 4-9 I will introduce a new concept.

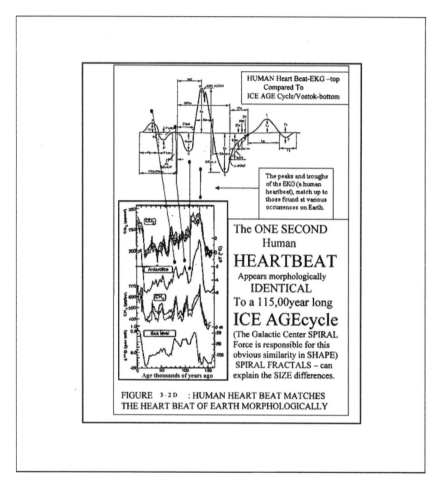

FIGURE 4-9. Human Heartbeat matches Earth's Heartbeat.
(From 'The Celestial Clock' by Wm. Gaspar)

It is so amazing to me to see that a Human Heartbeat matches the Heartbeat of the Earth morphologically.

There are 4 'fingers' on the graph of the Ice Age rhythm, which stand for the 4 cold periods and the actual 5th and larger wave is the warm period. That represents the 'heartbeat' in the EKG. It is like the fingers on the hand. It is no surprise as Creation works in the fashion of 4+1=5. That is the breakdown of the Spiral. It is in my earlier book titled 'The Celestial Clock'. See Figure 4-10.

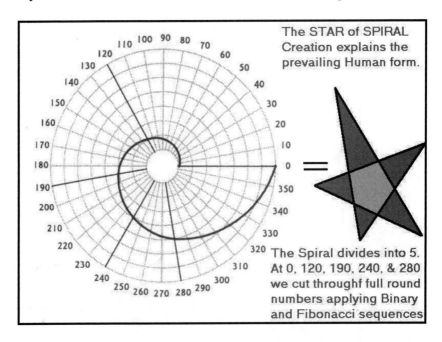

FIGURE 4-10. God Creates in a Spiral, Which Divides to 5
(From 'The Celestial Clock by Wm.Gaspar,
slightly modified from Drunvalo Melchizedek)

For our purposes now we need to know that each of those waves, which the researchers found in the ice, were between 23-24,000years long, and since those waves are bifid –meaning have two halves- the half cycle periods are about 11,500–12,000years long. That is where the about 11,600year half-cycle originates from in our cosmic calendar. It is a SCIENTIFIC FACT!

That is why the biblical teaching emphasizes 12,000 members of the Tribe of Israel and 12 gods that are shown on each side of the boat in Figure 4-8. Thus, every 12,000 years there is a major Flood. One cannot have just an immense fire from the sun, huge earthquakes, heated oceans and not expect the melting of the few miles thick polar ice caps. I don't care who promised us 'no more flood' that is not feasible scientifically. And since our Creator is the only true scientist - and 'He / She' knows better – thus He would have not promised us something so unscientific. The 'no more flood' may have been promised to the scared members who survived Noah's Flood. The promise came from Noah, but I honestly don't think that our Almighty God was involved in something so unscientific as that old claim.

Another historical sounding 'human' example of the Egyptians was the different ' human ethnic' types on those wall paintings. They depict Nordic or Southern phenotypes along with Eastern and Western people. The Ra Priest did not mean to show specific ethnicity, but only one of the four directions assigned to them in the Egyptian hieroglyphics. Cosmology, not ethnic strife! This was a display of superb and altruistic scientific thinking from these science priests who were not interested in local warfare and ethnic hatred. That would have been 'pity' human soap opera for them. They were only concerned with saving the accumulated advanced scientific knowledge of the Atlanteans for the future generations. They knew that after the world-destroying Deluge, it would take several thousands of years for humans to start accumulating real scientific knowledge. They understood that from the protective comfort of the cave we would not be shooting for the Moon right away. They hoped that our scientific understanding would reach a level equal of theirs for us to be able to decipher the intended meanings. They also were aware of the facts that before that time happens a lot of generations of simple cultures will be looking at those hieroglyphic pictures. Thus, they needed to depict the people in a comparably simple way.

Helicopters and airplanes, space suits and automobiles would not have been appropriate depictions. Even in today's modern world we have religious fanatics blowing up ancient Buddha statues in Afghanistan, just because Buddha did not look exactly the right ethnic make up or did not have beard. So, let's not be fooled by the simplicity of the country side of ancient Egypt, the Ra Priest were extremely intelligent scientists with the understanding of the limitations of the coming generations.

Very little, if any history made it to the stories as we are learning now. That is why the 'history' based understanding of any sacred writings will not have the required depth to the complex science needed to decipher the intended messages.

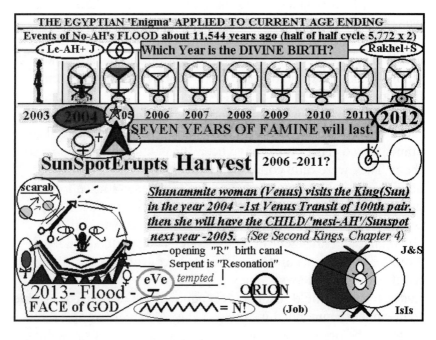

FIGURE 4-11: The Seven Years of Famine between Venuses

In the Tomb of Ramsses IX there was a painting on the wall, which the scholars called 'enigmatic', since it contained none of the known hieroglyphs, rather it had eight pentagrams with an upside down female figure and the sun on her head, supposedly representing the seven years in between the two Venus Transito. Figuro 1 11 is by no means the original wall painting, but it is my brainstorming about the possibilities that it is related to our own Mayan Calendar ending of the year 2012. If we use that logic, then the 'Face of God' would represent 'Noah's Flood', which in my calculations happened about 11,500-11,650years ago. That is a rounded number of 100pairs (96 in actuality) of Venus Transits. They are occurring 121.5 then 105.5, or on average 131.5 years apart.

In Figure 4-12A the 'mouth' in 'The Face of God' represents another form of the 'chalice', a type of the Holy Grail. This mouth-grail is the 'birth canal' of the New Age. It is the 'womb' of the Milky Way Galaxy. Very cleverly it is made into a 'boat', because every 12,000years when god opens His 'mouth', the Earth cleansing Flood pours out of this galactic womb. Even more revealing the shape of the boat is fashioned into a snake. The fourth wave of the 'serpent beard' is all of sudden noticeably larger than the first three. So what does that represent for us now, if we consider a parallel occurrence to the Mayan Calendar ending of 2012? Is it the huge X-28 Flare Sunspot eruption of November 4, 2003? Or is it the intense solar storms of the spring of 2004? Or may be it is the representative of the December 25th, 2004 Asian 'Tsunami', which was caused by the 'magnetar' galactic blast 50,000 light years away?

Most importantly, the **right temple** on the face is an arrow like **penis** that is **erupting.** This exploding 'male instrument' was the best way of the Egyptians to record down pictorially the eruption of the 'Old King Sun'. The dung beetle is holding the Sun or may be his own male larva at the 'third eye' position of 'Shiva / Sun'.

FIGURE 4-12A: The Face of God may be Noah's Flood.
(Modified from Hornung's The Egyptian Book of the Afterlife)

The picture in Figure 4-12 is from the enigmatic wall painting from the Tomb of Ramsses IX. It seems obvious that the beard of the 'Face of God' represents at least two other significant scientific concepts. The one clearly shown is the **beard**, which stands for the **'water'** under the boat, the vessel the Egyptologists keep calling the 'solar bark'. They make us think that it is a solar bark, as the 'Sun floating through the sky' and it would have no connection to a flood. Then why is the beard shown as water? Is someone trying to mislead us about a 'solar bark' explanation?

'Heru'/ 'Her' /' Hr' means 'Face'

'Herru -renpet' means 'the 5 epagomenal days'

FIGURE 4-12B: The Face and 5 Unlucky Days
(Modified from IHH by Schumann-Antelme & Rossini)

It is not a mystery why the 'face' and 'mouth' hieroglyphs are tied to the 'five unlucky epagomenal days'. These are the days in early August when the five main Egyptian gods were born and the time when the Sacred Cosmic Marriage was performed.

The Mayans also celebrated these five unlucky days in August. As we will learn in the last chapter, the hot summer period is the most likely time of the year when this ancient tragedy happened. It fits the early Harvest designation, the astronomical markers and it is also the time when the hurricane season is in its full force.

The significant scientific meaning, - that I explored earlier - but really deciphered from this strange 'Face of God' picture, is the fact, that the 'beard/water' is also a 'Serpent', which is increasing in height! It caused a 'Eureka' shout from my beardless mouth. I have seen this strange 'Face of God' and it made me realize that the **'Serpent'='Resonation'** in ancient mythology and religious tales. How obvious after the fact. So, if Noah's Flood was tied to the coming of the Venus Transit pair, the first of which was 'Eve', then the connection of the 'evil serpent' to the catastrophe would make perfect sense. Adam was 'Eight' generations away from Noah. These eight biblical generations must have meant the 'EIGHT' years between the Venus Transits. This 'serpentine' resonation must have come shortly after the first Venus Transit.

I already knew that the **'sin'** was not the female's fault as we learned about *Mother **Earth's menstruation** is what **was the original sin in the Hindu Myths**.*

Tying a Native American culture to the scientific concept of 'snake = resonation, which is coming from the mouth of God', one needs to look at the Hopi Indians in Arizona, who display the Snake Dance and the Antelope Dance at their major religious festival. Figure 4-13 depicts an imaginary Hopi dancer who dances with a snake in his mouth. During the ritual the spiritual dancer holds the live snake in his mouth by biting gently behind its head and holding up the rest of the snake's body with his left hand. This is the same scientific concept as in Figure 4-12A.

FIGURE 4-13. Hopi Snake Dancer

Even in the Bible we have passages, which promote dancing with the snake. Some 'offshoot southern fundamentalists' even took those verses verbatim and perform the psychedelic dance with the venomous snakes in their hands. Several times the Bible states that God is Spirit, eternal, and unseen and we will never see the 'Face of God'. I believe that. But a few other places say that 'when we will see the face of god' we will also see some trouble. Now I understand why that is so. In reality we know God is an Omnipotent Almighty Spirit, which we will never see in His physical manifestation or if we do then we would recognize Him in everything around us in all 'His' divine forms. I completely understand that. Well, in Figure 4-12A we see His face. I hoped that 'He' had more hair, but totally understanding that 'He' has been around for several billions of years 'He' is still strangely handsome for an old bald man.

In this Egyptian face of god, the 'mouth' obviously represented the 'chalice' or the 'cosmic womb' and explained to me the uselessness of the search for the 'holy grail'. A little more disturbing was, what I found at the right temporal region of the 'Face of God' on Figure 4-12. If I did not know what it stood for I would have been a little upset, but then I remembered the 'phallic' symbols of ancient primitive cultures and it made me smile. *So, those aboriginal guys were scientists, not perverts!*

A male eruption can only represent the 'rapture of the Old King, the Sun'. The Old King 'raptured' and released his 'Son'. No need for a wife, a cute harlot passing by in a safe distance can facilitate things, especially if it is that round planet Venus.

So now I fully comprehend; the Father, the Word (resonation from his 'mouth'), and the Holy Spirit. Or even better yet; the Father, the Son, and the Holy Spirit. A truly marvelous trio!

I would be a pinch more excited if this Holy Trinity was not about the 'holy burning' of the whole Earth. Hmm, now I really feel bad knowing that a number of people let the priests smear 'ash' on their foreheads on Ash Wednesday. And the priest does not even hide the truth. He is smearing it right where the 'third eye' of Shiva would be, the one that erupted and burnt most everything to ashes. It makes me think twice before I do another 'burnt offering', smear ash on my face or even think about accepting Lord Skanda, the fiery Purifier to be my personal Savior.

With names as 'Skanda-L' (The Purifying Lord), 'Krittika-L' (Pleiades) and 'Madana, the harlot Maddener' (Venus) it is an amazing wonder that the Hindu religion survived as long as it did. As matter of fact, I am glad it did otherwise we would be lost with a lot of our cosmic stories that sound historical.

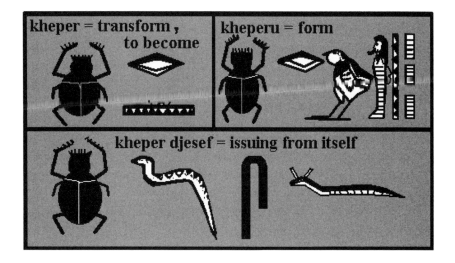

FIGURE 4-14. Kheper, Issuing From Itself
(Modified from IHH by Schumann-Antelme & Rossini)

Studying the concept, 'issuing from itself' in Figure 4-14 in this hieroglyphic writing there is an interesting picture design. The word definitely starts with the 'dung beetle', implying a 'male issues from itself another male'. Probably, insignificant details, but even the 'seven' projections on the front of the scarab's head reminds me of the Pleiades and the five hair-like projections on the front legs might represent the five stations of the Venus cycle in eight years. Further discussing Figure 4-14, the 'transform' word above also contains this same concept. Besides depicting 'Kheper' the scarab beetle, there is also a divine 'mouth', and a sacred 'scroll', the type the Hebrew Rabbis still use in the synagogues.

Thus, for earth 'transformation' to take place one needs a 'male to male' birth, also the mouth of God to speak His secret 'Word' and if one wants to know more, then one needs to read the sacred scroll! Simple enough.

FIGURE 4-15. Kheper, The Dung Beetle God
(Modified from Wilkinson's Reading Egyptian Art)

In Figure 4-15, Kheper sits on a throne, which has a red brick in the right lower hand corner. That is symbolic of the earth's core. In the ancient Babylonian Epic of Gilgamesh, it is referred to as a foundation stone, fired to a red brick in a kiln. This concept even brings the core together with the lava-like high heat.

When the Sun erupts, the core will over heat from the friction of the geo-dynamo. This is how the idea is presented in Maureen Gallery Kovacs' book in the Tablet I of 'The Epic of Gilgamesh':

"Anu granted him the totality of knowledge of all, He saw
the **Secret,** discovered the **Hidden,** he brought
information of (the time) **before the Flood.** ...
Take hold of the **threshold stone – it dates from ancient
times!** Go close to the Eanna Temple, the residence of
Ishtar, such as no later king or man ever equaled! Go up
on the wall of Uruk and walk around, examine its
foundation, inspect its brickwork thoroughly. Is not
**(even the core of) the brick structure made of kiln-
fired brick,** and did not the **Seven Sages** themselves **lay
out its plans?"** (Author's heavyset)

Clearly the 'secret' information is about discovering the
'Hidden' that originated even before the 'Flood' tied to the
foundation 'stone' that sounds like the 'Core' of the Earth.
All of this is weaved in with 'Ishtar' (Venus) and the Seven
Sages who are the seven stars of Ursa Minor, the Bear that stands
for the North Polar Axis. The throne is bringing the Queen
Cassiopeia and the scarab beetle together.

On the following picture in Figure 4-16 the Sun is actually
shown as hitting the 'throne' by six rays. The brick shape inside
represents the core of the Earth. The earth mounds carry they
own secret meaning. A strong wave of tsunami would build those
impressive sand dunes. On the other hand, the fast flying
swallows represent 'fast' solar wind coming from the sky. In one
of the funniest comedies of all time, the hilarious performers of
the Monty Python crew in the movie 'The Holy Grail', the fast
flying swallow is comically immortalized. It makes more sense
when a cosmic meaning can be tied to a mythological animal.

"2 Praise the **Lord** with the **harp;** ...
7 He **gathers the waters** of the sea together **as a heap;**
He lays up the deep in storehouses."
(Bible, Psalms, Chapter 33, Vs. 2,7)

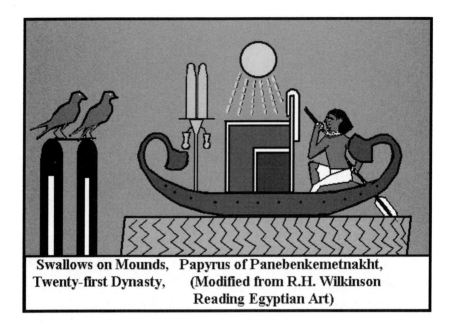

Swallows on Mounds, Papyrus of Panebenkemetnakht,
Twenty-first Dynasty, (Modified from R.H. Wilkinson
Reading Egyptian Art)

FIGURE 4-16. The Sun Hits the Core of the Throne
(Modified from Wilkinson's Reading Egyptian Art)

I would love to listen to the explanations of the traditional
Egyptologist concerning these 'strange habits of ancient pharaoh
kings exchanging their heads or noses for the manure smelling
dung beetle to attract their sister to marry them', as let's say part
of a 'valley folks fertility ritual'. Returning back to the 'Two
Venuses' who are so crucial in the ancient calendar time keeping.
In a museum piece, which was unearthed by an American
archeologist in the 1800's, while searching for the Temple of
King Solomon in Babylonia, we can readily see that the Ram-
Headed Babylonian God embraces two bulls. (Figure 4-17) The
Dog carries the 'time piece' defined by two pillars and on top of
it are animal heads and the infamous 'shoulder blade of a bull'.
The Lion offers the 'oblation' and he carries the 'Aquarian Vase'
defining the **12,000year cycle endings** with the **'Age of Leo'** and
the **'Age of Aquarius'**.

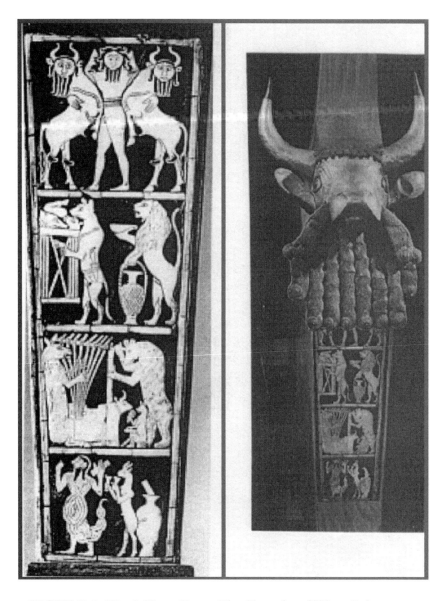

FIGURE 4-17. A Harp From The Temple of King Solomon
(From Wm. Gaspar 'The Celestial Clock')

This 4,600year old 'Harp' with the picture carvings, displayed in the University Museum of Pennsylvania, alone can tell so much to the seekers of astronomical mysteries. **The 'Donkey'**, who is commonly tied to the holy people, **plays the 'Harp'**. I can hardly wait to get to chapter eight where I can reveal to you the secret astronomical meaning of the donkey. **The 'Bear'** (Polaris) pushes **a staff** through **'the shoulder blade of the Bull'** (Pleiades) while an **'Eastern Bunny'** creature is looking on. The bottom picture of Figure 4-17 depicts a **'Goat'** with a vase behind him offering to what looks like a **'Scorpion King'**.

I can hardly hide my excitement at the multiple connotations this one enigmatic museum piece offers to us in our search for the cosmic-astronomical mysteries of the end age 11,600years ago. The 'Donkeys' are contained within the Cancer constellation and the 'Goat Star' with his 'kids' is part of the constellation of the 'Charioteer', as in the 'Chariot of Fire'. A 3-D view toward the East and also monitoring the movement of the stars through out the year would tell us why the constellation of Cancer along with the Northern Donkey and the Southern Donkey was the time of this ancient Magnetic Polar axis shift. Certainly, the goat can also signify the time around Christmas, thus it could relate to the Capricorn sign of the December divine birth of 'Sol Invictus'.

In one of his labors, Hercules steps on the Crab who bites him. The gods in turn transform the Crab into the constellation Cancer. That is how the Greco-Roman tales maintained the knowledge that these legends were about celestial events. How the Cancer constellation and the two upper stars, the Northern Donkey and the Southern Donkey lines up in the sky when the cosmic tragedy happened? We will see it in the conclusion of Chapter 8. The designation of Northern and Southern Donkeys make me suspect that if we were lining up with the Cancer constellation that the North to South shift happened from the upper donkey to the lower donkey. Chapter 8 will give us the answer on that one.

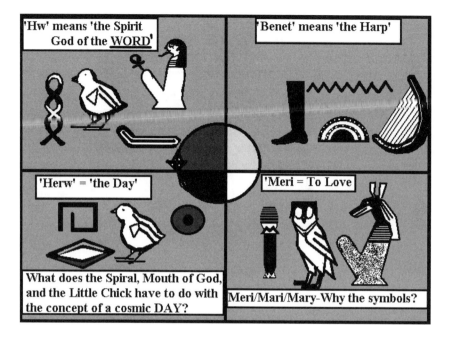

FIGURE 4-18. The Egyptian Dog And The Harp.
(Modified from IHH by Schumann-Antelme & Rossini)

The 'Goddess – Angel' depiction on the next Figure 4-19 is shown holding 'two ankhs/cartouches' in her out stretched hands. The ankh relates to Venus, the female goddess thus reconfirming that the most important cosmic event, the birth of the 'main Lamb or Ram Headed God', 'Son of the Sun', 'young Prince of the old King' happened in between the coming of the rare events of the Venus Transit Pairs. This was counted out to be about a 'Hundred Pairs' in the rounded 12,000year cosmic cycle. The real actual number is likely between 96 and 100pairs.

Religious preachers are usually concerned with finding human moral explanations in the sacred stories, as that is what sells the message to the 'sinners'. Unfortunately, focusing on our own small or large - but in a cosmic sense definitely pathetically insignificant private parts - will make us forget, that these tales are about cosmic sex followed by incredible earth changes!

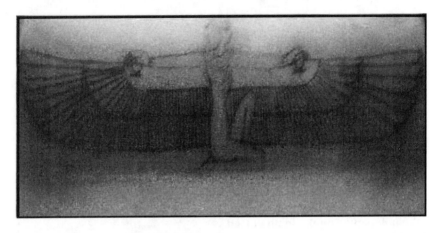

FIGURE 4-19. The Goddess-Angel With Two Ankhs/Cartouches
(Picture taken by Szekely)

Even the New Testament emphasizes that the legend of the 'two wives' are symbolic tales:

> "23 But **he who was of the bondwoman was born** according to the **flesh, and he of the freewoman thorough promise,**
> 24 **Which things are symbolic**. "
> (Bible, Galatians, Chapter 4, Vs. 23-24)

Another animal that transcends from nomadic tribes to civilized cultures is the 'deer' or the elk. In a sense the closely linguistic connotations even tie the deer, antelope or the elk to the 'ewe'. A rarely mentioned constellation around the North Pole is the 'three skip of the antelope', which likely refers to the movement of the Earth during the 'drunken' phase of the globe.

A comparison of the Egyptian, English, Hungarian and Finnish languages about the 'ewe' and the 'fish' is an interesting study.

Figure 4-20 will show us interconnectedness through the analyzing of the pronunciation.

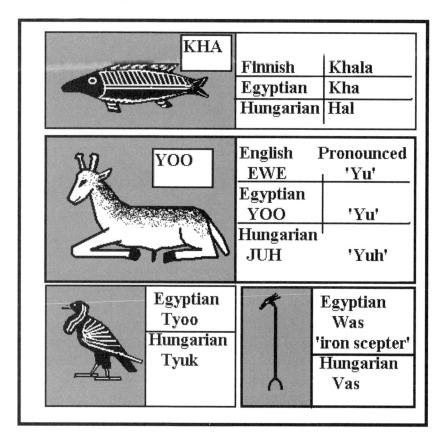

	KHA
Finnish	Khala
Egyptian	Kha
Hungarian	Hal

	YOO	Pronounced
English EWE		'Yu'
Egyptian YOO		'Yu'
Hungarian JUH		'Yuh'

| Egyptian Tyoo | | Egyptian Was | 'iron scepter' |
| Hungarian Tyuk | | Hungarian Vas | |

FIGURE 4-20: The Unexpected Linguistic Connections

These above linguistic similarities strengthen my argument that at one point most cultures spoke the same languages.

The last diagram in Figure 4-21 will demonstrate the rounded approximate time periods that were noted by the Venus Transits. The seven years between the 'two wives' of Jacob were secretly about the 'seven years' between the 'two Venus Transits'.

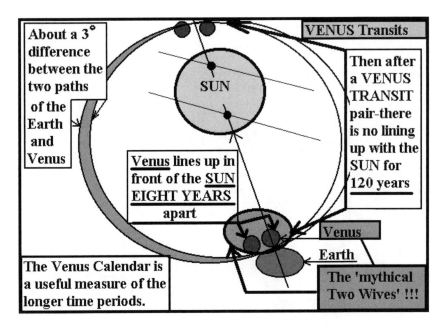

FIGURE 4-21: The Two Wives and the Two Venus Transits

The greatest secrets of ancient mythology were the 'Two Wives' and the 'Son of the Sun'. The countless moral stories we were brought up with all attempted to incorporate some aspects of the Venus Transit Calendar that marked the Sunspot eruption when the Earth got drunk and the Two Brothers began the fight against each other. For thousands of years, we did learn a tremendous amount of twisted wisdom about angry gods and strangely constructed moral tales, but the cosmic lessons remained elusive until now. How many innocent scientists and spiritual reformers had to be burnt at the stake or hung from the tree by the religious majority to arrive to this point in time when we can finally understand the enigmas?

Chapter Five
Festivities, Legends, Spells and Judgment

Similar to other cultures, the Egyptians did not lack in festivities. There were occasions to celebrate the Harvest, the Union of the Two Lands, the Union with the Sun's Disc, and the Divine Birth of the Goddess's Child, the New Year and others.

The celebration of the "Sacred Cosmic Marriage' was held at Edfu and it lasted fifteen days. Two weeks before the New Moon, the celebrations began in the town of Dendera, the headquarters of goddess Hathor. The third month of summer at New Moon the festivities began to shift to the Nile and the Goddess was placed into a boat to be transported upstream toward the south. The lovemaking and drunken singing and music lasted from New Moon until the Full Moon of that same month. In a fashion probably not dissimilar to a Brazilian fiesta, the Greek Bacchus, god of wine celebrations, or the Mardi Gras of New Orleans - Hathor, the beautiful goddess of fertility and sexuality was shipped to Edfu, to the hometown of Horus, where his temple was located. There, the two, a god and a goddess spent two weeks together in 'meri'-making. This Egyptian and Babylonian 'meri/mari' word means 'love or making love', i.e. cosmic sex, thus the name Mari-A(H) is likely derived from cosmic sex act.

The Male God was clearly represented on the walls of the Pyramids with nakedness and an obvious phallic symbol. It was not done for the pornographic 'shock value' or to represent the 'fertility' of a coming harvest. It was representative of that single day event, which changed the lives of billions of people almost

189

12,000years ago. That one gigantic 'male eruption' destroyed civilizations in a blink of an eye, and probably earned a 'male' designation to the genderless Creator Spirit.

FIGURE 5-1. Isis Stands Behind A Male God.
(Picture taken by Szekely)

Another related festival was held at the Temple of Luxor or at Medinet Habu. It was designated the Feast of Opet. Possibly, the 'feast of opening' was related to the opening of the mouth of the Crocodile (Dragon), but by inference also the opening up the New Age. According to Lesko, there were food offerings of 11,341 loaves of bread and 385 jugs of beer. Together it amounted to 11,726 pieces of food offerings. These odd numbers may represent the 11,500 – 12,000years between the time periods of major disasters.

The temple calendar of Medinet Habu listed a few other feasts, which were held there locally. These were the Feast of the Valley, the Feast of Amun, and the Feast of Lifting Up the Sky. This last feast reminds me either the 'cosmic boar' or a return of the sky to its previous position after the initial displacement

Another major celebration, which lasted twenty days, was the Feast of Coronation. This was marked in the twenty-second year of the reign of the king. May be relating to this was a celebration of the thirtieth year of the reign of the pharaoh Amun-hotep. This gave an opportunity to the ruler to officially declare himself transformed into a cosmic deity, the sun disk itself. Interestingly, in the last eight years of his reign – from 22 to 30 - he is depicted much younger, as if he was reborn. By today's calendar supposedly the 30 would fall on 2013 and thus, the 22 would be 2006. The reason why I am assuming that is because the Egyptian showed eight gods leading up to the Judgment Hall of Osiris. Those eight gods seem to line up with the two Venus Transits of 12,000years ago, but by today's counting it would be 2006-2013. Although, it is difficult to determine with any amount of accuracy what different cultures understood as the first year of those turbulent changing times.

The Sunspot eruption seemed to be a few years after the first Venus Transit. This was eight years prior to Noah's Flood and the Flood itself happened a year or two after the second Venus Transit. Although, nobody seems to be worried about those events repeating themselves today, interestingly the Sun is acting up in the last 2years. November 4th 2003 brought us an X-28 solar flare, which if it would have been Earth directed could have been a devastating event to our current civilization. But fortunately it blew 180degrees away from the globe. The second largest sunspot eruption happened days before that in the last week of October 2003. This initial eruption was an X-17. This was matched again just recently on the 7th of September 2005.

Are we getting ready for the 'Big One' in the coming few months or years?

Should we trust the ancient Egyptian pictures along with a Mayan Calendar to estimate when the next one will hit or should we simply trust our scientists? Unfortunately, I feel that the calendar is more accurate. The scientists who I contacted kept arguing with me that 2003-2008 is not a solar maximum, thus we don't have to worry about a sunspot eruption. Then November 2003 the NASA scientists were on the edge of their seats, because they did not understand how a large eruption could have happened. The solar wind speed increased from an average about 250mile/sec to over a 1,000mile/sec. The instruments were only calibrated to a maximum of 1,000. Thus, it has actually even passed that 1,000 mark. And that was from an eruption of the overheating Sun, which shot to the opposite direction of the Earth. What if one of these days it will hit the Earth as it had done it before. Will the eight-minute warning be enough?

Increasingly more scientists jump on the bandwagon of stating that our air pollution is responsible for the observed global warming. They are wrong! The Sun would not overheat from the pollution we put into our atmosphere. The Sun is too huge and too far from us to expect it to overheat from our tiny earth's atmospheric pollution. If there were no human activity on Earth, if there were no industry what so ever, the cosmic Mayan Calendar would still be accurate and it would foretell when the Earth's axis marches in front of the Galactic Center. Polluting our air is wrong for several different reasons. We do pump a lot of CO_2 into our atmosphere. So much, that we have passed the upper limits by 40%, but strangely the earth's axes have not shifted, because it does the shifting on a very punctual cosmic calendar. According to John Major Jenkins, the alignment with the Galactic Center happens between 2006-2014. Those years would befit the time frame of the Tribulation.

Since I am using biblical terms here, might as well let me say this also. The prophetic Book of Revelation in the Bible does not say the End Days will come when industry pollutes too much, rather it is using warnings about the 'two olive trees, which have power over heaven to shut down when the fiery dragon comes'. Those words hide an astronomical and calendar event and no feeble human activity will alter the cosmic events.

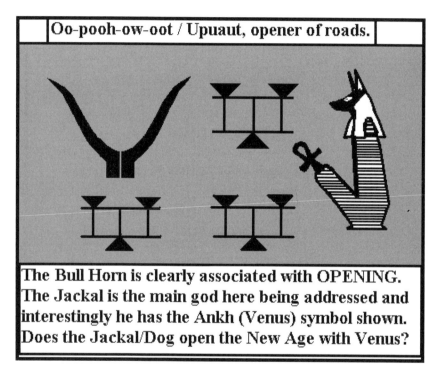

Oo-pooh-ow-oot / Upuaut, opener of roads.

The Bull Horn is clearly associated with OPENING. The Jackal is the main god here being addressed and interestingly he has the Ankh (Venus) symbol shown. Does the Jackal/Dog open the New Age with Venus?

FIGURE 5-2A. Opener Of Roads
(Modified from IHH by Schumann-Antelme & Rossini)

The opening of the road to the 'End Days' began with the first Venus Transit, thus the Bull Horns are shown. The fiery Sunspot eruption happened in the third month of the Egyptian summer at early harvest, when Sirius the Dog Star was highest in the sky.

The Canine God became associated with that particular 'dog heat of the summer'. The 'three scales' are the three back and forth movements of the 'drunk earth' between the two fighting brothers Mithra and Orion. But one can think of it as the mythological 'three skips of the antelope' or one can even picture the Pueblo Indians' 'Sacred Bear' with the three waves of the arrow running through the inside of its body. The scale itself is carefully designed to show the 'male' pyramid in the middle of the two upside down pyramids representing the 'two females' of the Venus Transit pair. Two blocks or 'two half cycles' are enclosed in this same drawing. The design of a simple genius if one understands the intended cosmic astronomical message.

Giorgio De Santillana and Hertha Von Dechend in their classic on Comparative Mythology from 1969 titled "Hamlet's Mill' tie Horus to the Opener of the Way:
> " … when Geb / Kronos declared Horus the eldest, cutting out Seth / Typhon completely, as reported in the Shabaka Inscription. **Actually Geb claims Horus to be Upuaut, the Opener of the Way** – Upuaut being the Upper Egyptian Jackal or Wolf."   (Author's heavyset)

Therefore, the birth of the divine Child is tied to the opening of the gates of heaven and the calendar of the Dog Star, Sirius. It makes me smile whenever I hear the theory of a meteor impact as the culprit for the end days. Childish misinterpretation. Sure, I understand that it is easier to publicize a 'big rock hitting earth' as it is brutally more visual. It is also more physical, thus even a simple mind can imagine that. The false belief is that 'God only throws a stone'. In actuality, the force that arrives from the Black Hole to the Sun and subsequently to Earth is an unseen electro-magnetic super-wave. It will cause a great 'illumination' from the Sun when his 'son' is born. That ancient depiction of a fiery star-like phenomenon with a smoky tail approaching Earth was about an enormous solar flare rather than a random meteor.

The meteor idea is so innocently 'Hollywood'. If you noticed even in the wildest sci-fi movies, the last battle that decides between good and evil - the last fight of the main characters - always have to rely on something as rudimentary and barbaric as their fists. Or who can run faster. Technology rarely enters the scene in those crucial last moments when the story decides between the winners. Well, that is how most of our scientists publicize the earth change scenarios. Not much finesse, rather a lot of caveman age 'stone throwing and meteor flinging'. Basic, brutal, but it is visually much more rewarding. The unseen electromagnetic forces radiating or erupting from the Galactic Center and all of a sudden causing the Sun to rapture out of nowhere is a technically much more difficult concept to sell to the public. The rigidly meticulous science is much less equipped than mythology to foretell an event, which tends to happen out of its season and disruptive to the idyllic harmony of cyclically predictable Nature.

Returning back to Egyptian festivities, a figure of Hathor was ceremonially carried to the roof of the Temple of the Goddess in Dendera at the change of seasons. The priests piously walked to the top of the temple with the sacred bust of the goddess to expose her to the rays of the sun. This they did to mimic the unification of the goddess to the Sun disc. An engagement ceremony before the true sacred cosmic marriage would take place between the Sun and the Goddess. Isis role as the married goddess was tied to the Sun and cosmic laws. According to Professor Lesko, charms were made to honor Isis, which promised that it would help make a woman love a man as much as Isis loved Osiris. Well, who ever made the charm must had not been aware of the burning cosmic fire and destruction, which accompanied that kind of celestial love. It was certainly a sizzling cosmic romance that most of us would love to live without.

The same kind of charm was employed if the man was after a married woman. If she would be already married then she would hate her husband as much as Isis hated Seth. The knot of Isis was usually made out of red jasper, which would symbolize the blood of Isis. The amulet was sent with the mummies to the afterlife to gain protection from evil harm.

'Tiet'
Isis Knot

The 'Knot of Isis' is similar to the 'Ankh' sign, and is often translated as 'Life'.

To the left is a personified 'tiet' / 'Isis Knot' from the coffin of Ankhefenkhonsu, the Twenty-Fifth Dynasty.

FIGURE 5-2B: The Isis Knot can mean Life or Cosmic Sex

Then according to The Egyptian Book of the Dead by E.A,
Wallis Budge recorded down in the Paris Papyrus - Osiris is
glorified in the following manner.

> "(Osiris) …you are established as the Bull of the West,
> your son Horus is crowned on your throne, all life is
> with him. Your son, to him are given millions of years,
> the fear of him is for millions of years; fear him as the
> cycle of the gods."

Another spell in The Papyrus of Ani is instructing the reader
through the transformation into a divine hawk.

> "Chapter of making the transformation into a divine
> hawk. Osiris Ani said; 'Hail mighty one, come then to
> Tattu (the two pillars). Arrange for me the ways, make
> me go around my thrones. May I renew myself, may I
> become strong. O grant me your fearfulness, create for
> me your terror. May the gods of the underworld fear me
> in their habitation they are for me. Let not the One come
> near me that would do harm to me, may I walk through
> the house of darkness' ."

**An interesting function of the goddess Isis was her search to
reveal the divine name of her father, the sun king Ra.**
According to legend, the old king Ra was having a walk one
night and because he was so aged and senile he was drooling bad
from his mouth. The saliva from this drooling fell on the earth.
Isis went and scooped it up and mixed it with earth and fashioned
a snake out of the resulting mud. The snake then bit the old king
Ra – I should add at this point that it was very similar to the way
the Greek hero Hercules got bit by the astronomical 'Cancer'.
Ra, the old sun king begged his daughter to use her magic to get
relief from the misery of the snakebite, but Isis remained stern.
She would only attempt to use her magic for his benefit if Ra
would reveal his secret name to her.

Finally, Ra could not stand the agony of pain and revealed his secret name to her. From that moment on Isis obtained enormous powers from knowing the name of the sun king Ra. This 'name' is unknown because it is the 'resonation', which comes out of the mouth of god and causes some major earth changes. That is why 'knowing the secret name of god' or knowing 'the lost word' gives extraordinary power to the sages. <u>Listen, I will tell you the two main secrets: - 1. Unimaginable destructive Earth changes come regularly every 12,000years, regardless whether we are good or bad. 2.The well-awaited Purifier Savior Prince is the Fire and the Destroyer! (No sinners left after He cleans house!)</u>

> " ... lord Bhava ... replied with a sorrowful heart, ...
> **What will be comes to be, and no one can prevent it;**
> what has been, has been. Now, immortals, listen to the
> matter at hand: who will now take my seed, the semen
> of Siva, that has been shed?...Then having cursed Visnu
> and all the gods, **the empress of everything spoke in
> fury to the Purifier, who had eaten the seed of Siva:
> Fire,** you will be omnivorous, constantly tortured in your
> soul." (Author's heavyset) (Hindu Myths, pg. 164)

On Figure 5-3 the Judgment Hall shows the main god seated on the right side. The Dog/Jackal is at the Scale. The head of the goddess Ma'at, who stands for 'Truth', is at the center of the Scale. There are seven seated gods on top above the scale bearing ankhs on their knees, likely standing for the seven years of famine, which happened in between the Two Venus Transits. The next seven gods are the seven years of bounty leading up to the seven years of famine. Thus, the story of the Pharaoh's dream with the seven fat cows and the seven skinny cows in the Genesis of the Bible must have originated from this and similar Egyptian hieroglyphic pictures. The two goddesses behind the Pharaoh are the two Venuses and also stand for the concept of the 'two kingdoms' of the Core/Magnetic North and Polar North.

FIGURE 5-3. The Judgment Hall of the Dead
(Modified from Erik Hornung's The Ancient
Egyptian Book of the Afterlife)

The 'throne' contains within it **the square foundation stone**, which stands for the core of the Earth. The 'Hawk King' represents 'Vega' the 'Swooping Hawk/Swooping Eagle' The 'Ibis/Stork' Thoth is the Scribe who also delivers the Child. In a style of Chucky, a Hollywood horror story, the birth of the Child causes the death of most everybody else. This whole morally interpreted and insane appearing Judgment scene can make perfect sense if the cosmology is known. No, the Egyptians originally were not animal worshippers as we wrongly assumed, but rather they established a cosmic science using animal symbols, which only had meaning to the initiates of the sacred Ra Priesthood. This knowledge reached us in a less decipherable way in the form of the written words of the Holy Bible.

The falcon or hawk-headed god, the king or the prince who will rule the Earth with the sword or a rod of iron, the wolf or dog, the two brothers commonly appear in the mythologies of different nations and on the pages of most sacred books. Since we discussed the Latino and the Hungarian cultures along side the biblical stories let us see what is stated in their Creation legends. It was Romulus and Remus, the two Latino brothers who founded Rome and by that established the Great Roman Empire that was so instrumental in the formation of civilized European laws and nations. As babies, Romulus and Remus were saved from starvation and lovingly fed by a Mother Wolf. Is this a reference to Sirius and the two brothers as Mithra and Orion?

In Hindu mythology we find Mitra and Varuna (Orion) as the two brothers. Besides the Babylonian Epic of Gilgamesh, it is the Hindu tale that preserves the obviously cosmic origin of their battle.

In Egypt there is also a tale of the two brothers. Their names are Anpu and Bata. In the book titled 'Egyptian Tales' by W.M. Flinders Petrie in a recent Dover Publications collection we learn the following about the brothers in shortened version of a free translation:

"The older brother name was Anpu and the younger was Bata. Anpu had a house and a pretty wife. He loved his good hearted younger brother as if he was his own son. Bata was an excellent worker who ploughed the land with his brother's oxen. (Here we can find the two Egyptian brothers closely tied to Taurus and the Compass in the form of the 'oxen' and the 'plow' -Author). Bata was a good brother because the spirit of god resided in him. After a long day at work on the field he brought the harvest to his older brother and he went to the stable and slept alongside the cattle. They had fertile farmland that produced them everything they desired.

Life progressed well amongst those three until the wife of
Anpu, the older brother laid eyes on the youthful beauty of Bata.
She suggested to him that they make love while her husband is
away. Bata was innocent and righteous, thus this kind of talk
made him mad. Bata told his brother's wife that he thought of her
as his mother. He also warned her not to again try to talk to him
about any wicked ideas. When the older brother came home, the
wife – being afraid that Bata will tell on her – presented herself
with self-inflicted bruises on her face that she blamed on the
abuse of the younger brother. She weepingly told her husband
that Bata suggested to her to have a romantic relationship. Now,
hearing these evil words the elder brother became as a panther of
the south and hid himself in the barn waiting for his younger
brother to arrive home from the fields with the cows. He was
determined to kill Bata for his wicked thoughts. As Bata herded
the cattle inside the barn he heard the first cow warning him
about the older brother who stood behind the barn door with a
large knife in his hand. Bata looked under the door and seen the
feet of his older brother waiting there for him with the knife in
his hand. Bata threw his load down the ground and started
running away from the barn. His elder brother followed him in a
close pursue. At this point the younger brother cried out to Ra
Harakhti, the Sun God: -

> "My good Lord! Thou art he who divides the evil from
> the good." And Ra stood and heard all his cry; and Ra
> made a wide water between him and his elder brother,
> (dividing the Red Sea –author) and it was full of
> crocodiles (the role of the Dragon - author) and the one
> brother was on one bank, and the other on the other bank;
> and the elder brother smote twice on his hands at not
> slaying him. Thus did he. And the younger brother called
> to the elder on the bank, saying;
> 'Stand still until the dawn of the day; and then Ra ariseth,
> I shall judge with thee before Him, and He discerneth
> between the good and the evil. (Judgment comes by the
> rising Sun at dawn –author) For I shall not be with thee

any more for ever; I shall not be in the place in which thou art; I shall go to the valley of the acacia' (that is the 'perfect valley' between the two trees or as in the birth canal of the 'cosmic womb' – author) ... Then the youth took a knife, and cut off his flesh, and cast it into the water, and the fish swallowed it. (blood sacrifice by a knife at the water where the 'fish' / Orion lives - author) ... Now many days after these things, the younger brother was in the valley of the acacia; there was none with him; he spent his time in hunting the beasts of the desert, ... and he met the Nine Gods ... and they said unto him, 'Ho! Bata, bull of the Nine Gods, art thou remaining alone? ... And Ra Harakhti said to Khnumu, 'Behold, frame thou a woman for Bata, that he may not remain alive alone'. ... The essence of every god was in her. The seven Hathors came to see her; they said with one Mouth, 'She will die a sharp death.'

The story goes on. Needless to say that in this mythological tale we can again discover the crocodile , the river bank with a schism that is like the 'Red Sea' along with 'two brothers' who fight against each other. We can see that the Sun and the seven goddesses (Hathors, the harlots – first goddess of the Venus Transit pair followed by the Seven Years of Famine) play a significant part in this cosmic tragedy. Elements of some of the biblical stories also clearly shine through. The 'valley of the acacia' is the same cosmic birthplace that is occupied by the 'crocodile'. It is the perfect valley that sits in between the Magnetic North and the Polar North that is thought by some as the sacred birth canal.

There is not a mention of a 'hawk' per se, but we know that Ra or Ra-Harakhti is depicted as the falcon headed or the hawk headed god with the Sun on top surrounded by a serpent. The story repeats the basic elements of earth change scenario.

Not only the Egyptian main gods were tied to these magnificent birds of prey, but both the Roman and Greek main gods were closely associated with the Eagle, which carried through into most European and American cultures. To this day these birds are kept in high regards as a messenger of the gods by the original Native Americans and the newly arrived Europeans.

Attila the Hun - who is considered the founding father of Hungary by the Hungarians - was the ruler who was given the 'Sword of God'. Similarly, the English legends mention King Arthur as the favorite of god, who is able to pull the 'sword' out of the 'rock' as a prerequisite for divine ruling over a nation. Except, the rock is the 'core' of the Earth and the 'rod of iron' or the magic 'sword' can be thought of as the imaginary iron rod sticking out from the core toward the Magnetic North. When the sword is pulled out of the core-rock of the earth, then it can roll and have the axis shift and thereby, start the rulership of the new Prince. Only the gods can grant these sort of ultimate magic cosmic powers. Attila, the 'Scourge of God' died at the age of about 50. This happened on the night he married his fifth wife a blond German Princess, who apparently poisoned him on the wedding night. He was buried in three coffins that were placed one into the other. The inner coffin was made of iron, the middle one was silver and the outer coffin was made out of gold. These are commonly mentioned metals in the biblical and mythological tales and these may be references to the Earth's core, the New Moon and the Sun as a reminder of that ancient cosmic tragedy, which destroyed the Earth nearly 12,000years ago. Attila was not only 50 years of age, but also there were 50 people who carried him to his last voyage. It was a numerical reminder for the Jubilee. After he was buried under the river Tisza in south central Hungary – that required a new path for the river to be made for a detour – then the water of the river was let back over Attila's coffin to forever hide that secret place. (Unless there was never a secret place, but only an astronomical legend for reminders!)

The fifty people who buried Attila were slain on their return to the camp by fifty bowyers to keep the place a secret for eternity for everybody involved. The twice fifty may well refer to the 'hundred' league and the 100 Venus Transit pairs or even adding the sacred couple to the fifty and coming up with 52 - may be the 52year length of merging the Lunar and Solar calendar cycles and with the 104 adding Venus to it.

The main legend of the Hungarians that seems to be tied to their need find a permanent homeland in the 8th Century Europe is the Legend of Emese (pronounced Emeshe). Here I would like to interject that the 'crocodile' hieroglyphic symbol is spelled 'meseh'. The Hungarian word for 'bedtime story' is 'mese'. Although the origin of the name 'Emese', is thought to be derived from the word 'emo', meaning something like 'breast or teats'. This 'breasted' ancient Queen of the Hungarians, who at that time resided in the land of the Khazars - in present day Ukraine - was praying to God to find a permanent country for the nomadic Hungarians. When she fell asleep one night she dreamt that a 'Hawk' flew above in the sky and impregnated her with an embryo of a male child who would be the country-founding king of the Hungarians. Emese - told by the 'divine hawk' – knew that the son would be the founder of the country of the Hungarians, but He would never be allowed to actually see the new land. (That is the Old King / Sun has to die first before the axis shift occurs. – author). Queen Emese named her son 'Almos' (very close to the biblical Amos), which meant the one who was 'dreamt' or simply the 'sleepy one'.. When King Almos became old and wise he ordered his soldiers to explore the rich land of Hungary as a possible new territory for their country.   Seven tribes met at the eastern out skirts of the Carpathian Mountains of Transylvania and made a 'blood' pact. They cut the veins on their wrists and poured the blood into a grail, mixed it and all of them drank from it, thereby becoming 'blood brothers'.

Each of the tribal leaders swore allegiance to Almos who was the head of the leading Magyar tribe, noble remnants of an ancient Priesthood. Almos, the King asked the rest of them to sacrifice Him before the new land is reached to assure that the prophecy of the Hawk in Emese's dream is full-filled. He elevated his son, Arpad to be the leader of the Magyar tribe and made the other tribal leaders swear that until the Hungarian-Magyar people existed, the country leaders would be chosen from the off-springs of the Arpad family of the noble leading Magyar tribe. (the name Arpad is also found in the Bible). This blood sealed pact was agreed around 895 AD and as history tells us all the kings of Hungary were elected from the House of Arpad until the lineage died out by the year 1301. Now, back to the task of King Almos who needed to find a new land for his people whose faith was decided by the sacred hawk. Therefore, after careful military preparation - the Hungarian troops in 896 A.D. swarmed into the Carpathian basin through a narrow mountain pass. Reportedly, a 'hawk' was flying above them ahead to show the way to the Hungarians through the pass. Speeding up the journey the hawk was credited with saving most of them from a certain slaughter from the enemy that was following them closely behind.

This is how the Hungarian legends preserved the cosmic sacredness of the hawk for our generation.

This was in essence similar to Egyptian and even Native American legends as far as the seven tribes and the hawk is concerned. Also, the ritual of sacrificing the old king (sun) so the new prince king (sunspot) can lead us into the 'new land' (axis shift) is also a familiar mythological theme. The name Amos and Arpad are both found in the Bible and furthermore the 'two brothers' Hunor and Magor who chased the Golden Elk and founded the Hungarian nation with fifty warriors, were the favorite sons of Nimrod (Orion) the legendary biblical hunter.

Now, since we are on the subject of Hungarian legends, let me share one with you that is somewhat more personal, but it is also mysterious for a number of reasons. The legend goes as follows:

"In the year of 997 AD the nomadic pagan Hungarians - who already resided in Hungary for over one hundred years - were surrounded by civilized European Christian nations. They had no choice, but to slowly give in to the increasing demands of the neighbors who called for the Christianizing of the barbarian herds of the Nature loving pagans. The leading ruler of the pagans, named Koppany opposed the young Christian Stephen (who later became St. Stephen for his effort of very effectively converting the Hungarians to the Catholic Christian faith). Even Attila, the Hun was promised a 'holy crown' by the Pope around 450 AD when He spared Rome after He talked to His Holiness at the city gates. In the late 990's when the wise old king Geza – Stephen father's - died the ancient pagan laws called for his brother Koppany to inherit the throne by marrying Geza's widow. The pagan Koppany already had four wives and that did not fit well with Geza's widowed wife who believed in the new morals. German priests in the art of the Christian moral values educated the widow queen, along with her son Stephen. A war erupted amongst the largely pagan Hungarians against the smaller Christian fraction who were supported by the invading German army. With the help of the Germans, the Christian Hungarians won and the body of the pagan Koppany was cut into four pieces and each part was displayed in the four corners of the country. There was only one more prominent druid priest who was still standing in the way of Christianizing the rest of the Hungarian pagans. His name was Bal Aton (Baal Aton?). The name likely sound familiar to a number of you as the largest fresh water lake of Europe that is in Hungary is still named after this pagan druid priest Bal Aton. This is known as Lake Balaton. Before I start into this personally important story, let me remind you that according to the biblical tales, the 'heathen' believers in the Holy Bible prayed to a god named Baal.

The druid pagan priest first name was Aton, that is not only the famous name of the Egyptian God Aton, but it is also the origin for the name of the Hebrew Adon and the Greek Adonis. These are not coincidences!

Now, the advancing Christian troops reached the Northeastern bank of Lake Balaton in 997 AD, where the last stand of this pagan priest was positioned on top of a volcanic mountain. The Christian soldiers caught up with the druid priest and his faith was sealed. With his last breath the pagan priest cursed the pious Hungarians that they should not have nature-based spirituality for exactly a thousand year to come.

Now, I heard this ancient legend from Zoltan Nagy Solyomfi (nicknamed 'Hawk'). He was one of the two Hungarian Sun Dancers participating in a sacred Lakota Sioux Indian ceremony in South Park, Colorado. There were the four of us participating, two guys from Hungary and my wife and I. The year was 1996, exactly 1,000years after the curse was issued. All four of us were convinced that our participation in the sacred Native American Sundance ritual broke the thousand-year old curse of the druid priest, Bal Aton. I do not know whether the curse actually had to do with anyone of us, but one thing I know. The next summer I 'sundanced' again and in a break I proceeded to the Sun Dance Tree and I prayed there to God. I told the Almighty that I was ready to receive some wisdom if He wanted to share some with me His undeserving subject. The next six months was magical and I learned a lot. Within a year I had my book 'The Celestial Clock' completed. This, I achieved after working my ten hour workdays as a primary care doctor with a family and my spiritual growth to attend to. I honestly felt that the knowledge for my book was spiritually inspired. Four years later Zoltan 'Hawk' led the first Sun Dance on Hungarian soil. The curse of the pagan medicine man Aton was now completely lifted.

My initial encounter with Zoltan 'Hawk' happened in 1995 when my family visited Hungary. We were guests at the 'Indian' Camp. About two hundred Hungarians spent two weeks in the mountains of Bakony in loincloths pretending to be Native American Indians. Strict rules kept the experience authentically native. Then 'Hawk' heard that I was visiting from the States, thus he came over to introduce himself to us in the Lakota camp. We played our parts honorably as Native American warriors of differing tribes. Was it a co-incidence or spiritual design?

It is difficult to know whether there is any spiritual basis or karma to the actions we choose in our current life. For years I struggled with the fact that may be I should consider a past life regression seminar. I was weary of the fact that may be my over acting mind would generate scenarios that my truth seeking spiritual soul would not accept as facts. Finally, through some sequence of coincidences my wife and I ended up in one of those 'past life regression' seminars given by A.R.E., the Edgar Cayce spiritual organization. Without comparing notes, both my wife and I ended up re-living a previous existence in the early 1500's. I was a Spanish nobleman, such as Cortez, ready to ship out to the Americas. My wife lived a life of a Medicine woman who was killed by the religious zealots of the Inquisition. Apparently, we were positioned on opposite isles of the spiritual-religious fence. May be it was our over active imagination, but regardless it would explain to me our love for the Lakota Native American Spirituality and our choice to move to a predominantly Hispanic community. The Hispanics in our area originate from Spain. They arrived a few hundred years ago as part of the Castilian immigrants displaced by the bulging forces of the Spanish Inquisition. I am still not certain that the lessons of past lives play a role in our current decisions, but it is a worthy endeavor to consider in our spiritual growths.

Chapter Six
Set, Seth, Sethos, Seti, Sata, and Satan

As much as the concept of Satan is strongly embedded in the traditional thinking of people, it might not have the historical background some preachers would like to believe. As matter of fact, most of my research leads back to the actual earth change event where heat, lava may have come out of the belly of the globe. The intense heat from an erupting sunspot or several coronal mass ejections reaching the earth, followed by the lava flow and related catastrophic events could depict a hellish state. On the spiritual plane it would not make sense to build a big fire under the kettle and let the soul be burn there for eternity. Spirits don't have pain receptors. But if it is thought of as a spiritual suffering, then the Bad Spirit who is condemned to Hell, should undergo viewing footage of his silly mistakes in life, thus be ashamed spiritually - without the physical aspects of building a huge fire. Just by examining the mythical stories with the related names attached to the evil ones, a person can easily trace back the origin for the names of Satan. Not only we will learn that there is no Hell in a religious sense - other than on Earth - but we will also decipher the reason why this name is attached to the hot burning fire. In Figure 6-1 we can study the parts of the hieroglyphic picture named Sata, or the Serpent Spirit of Sata. Attaching an 'n' to the name Sata would make it plural in Spanish and we will explore that angle also to see if there are any writings in the Egyptian stories where 'multiple fiery serpents' from the sky are attached to our sunspot eruption theory. First, let's look at Figure 6-1 to dissect the meaning of the word Sa-Ta. The hieroglyphic word for the 'evil Satan' begins with the same cosmic 'Goose' as the name for the purifier 'Son of the Sun'. The evil 'serpent' and devil 'goat' will be obvious by bookend.

SA-TA = Serpent Spirit Sata or Satan

(The letter 'N' is the 'serpent' ∧∧∧∧∧∧)

The Egyptian name 'Sa-Ta' or 'SATAN' is the originator of the biblical Satan.

FIGURE 6-1. Sata May Be The Originator Of Satan.
(Modified from Schumann-Antelme/Rossini's IHH)

Although, we read this name as Sa-ta from the hieroglyphic symbol of the Goose (Sa) and the Belt (Ta) there is one more figure there, which is the Serpent. If we equate the Serpent with the wavy line of resonation (N), which the Serpent actually stands for, then the full name of this picture would read 'Satan'. The disturbing idea for the religious conservatives may be that the Goose, Orion, and the Serpent are all integral parts of the cosmic concept of the 'coming of the Son of the Sun who is the Purifier of sins'. Is it possible that the 'Satanic' cults and their opposing fundamentalist religious groups actually keeping alive the legend of the same cosmic tragedy without knowing?

Thus, let's review what we know. The Goose navigates North to South using the electromagnetic field of the Earth. The Galactic Plane is lined up North to South to the Magnetic North and the Polar North. The belt represents Orion. Below that is the 'serpent', which we discovered to be the increased 'resonation' from the sky. Thus, 'Satan' is not an evil person or an animal or any combination of, but <u>our reading of that hieroglyphic picture is - *that the negative* events *are tied to the electromagnetic force from the Galactic Center, which creates an increased resonation when the three* cosmic planes meet in Orion.</u> The Sun's role is not mentioned in that hieroglyphic picture. And as we remarked earlier, it may be more than one fiery serpent that hit earth in a short period of time. The Judeo-Christian Satan is usually shown as a 'Goat-like' figure. Chapter 8 will shed some light on that!

A quote from Erik Hornung's magnificent book titled 'The Ancient Egyptian Books Of The Afterlife', mentions snakes in plural in association with a Sun eruption. It is when talking about the fourth hour of the Amduat:

> " This **well-watered** abundant
> landscape **ends at the fourth hour. ...**
> Here lies the **desert** of Rosetau, the 'Land of Sokar,
> who is on his sand,' a desolate, sandy realm
> **teeming with snakes** whose uncanny movement
> is emphasized by the legs and **wings on their
> bodies**. A **zigzag route filled with fire** and
> repeatedly blocked by doors leads through the region
> of this hour. For the first time, the **solar barque**
> needs to be towed for it to make progress, and the
> barque itself turns into **a serpent whose fiery
> breath pierces a pathway** through the otherwise
> impenetrable gloom. In the very middle of this
> darkly menacing hour, **Horus** and Sokar look after
> the **solar Eye**, protecting and renewing it, ... "
>
> (Author's heavyset)

Thus, the fourth hour ends the abundance of water for the last twelve hours of the Amduat. It would be the year 2007 today. What would allow a 'Fiery Lake' to develop here on Earth?

Fire spirits from the fifth 'hour' of the Book of That Which is in the Underworld.

FIGURE 6-2A. The Lake Of Fire
(Modified from Wilkinson's Reading Egyptian Art)

The Lake of Fire is tied to the Sacred Door as the 'Sleigh' that is sliding down unforgivingly into a hellish state. Classical Greek mythology writes about Vulcan, the god of fire in the book of 'The Myths of Greece and Rome' by H.A.Guerber:

"**Vulcan**, or Hephaestus, son of Jupiter and Juno, **god of fire and the forge**, seldom joined the general council of the gods. His aversion to Olympus was of old standing. ... The intervening space between heaven and earth was so great, that Vulcan's fall lasted during one whole day and night, ... **he injured one of his legs**, ...**left him lame ...** Vulcan ... withdrew to the solitudes of **Mount Aetna**, where he established a great forge in the **heart of the mountain**, in partnership with the Cyclopes, who helped him manufacture ... objects from the **metals** found in ... **the bosom of the earth**." (Author's heavyset)

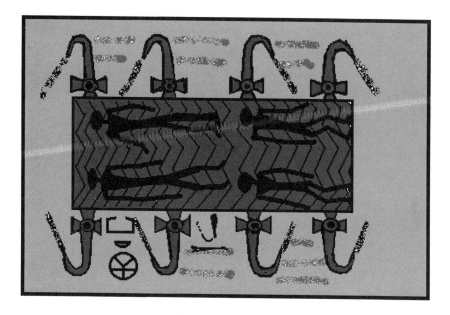

FIGURE 6-2B. Lake Of Fire With Bodies Of The Damned
(Modified from Wilkinson's Reading Egyptian Art)

The 'opening of the gate' of the house of Heaven is shown next
to the half cycle symbol and the Venus symbol in the left lower
corner of Figure 6-2B. This provides us with an exact timing of
the Lake of Fire in between the Two Venus Transits. The eight
'fire' symbols may refer to the last eight years and the seven
years of famine. These are connected to the 'pool' of fire. Dead
bodies or evil spirits are floating on the bottom of the pool. The
fire is puffing out fumes that may represent the plumes of the
erupting volcanoes. How interestingly the Egyptians were able to
tie this fiery hell to the innocent appearing 'sleigh'. Fire and ice.
These extreme temperatures during the upheaval of Earth were so
unbelievably dramatic to the few survivals that nothing short of
talking about total destruction of mankind sufficed. It generated
stories about fire stealing heroes and old horny Greek gods, shape
shifting Native American heroes and an angry pyromaniac Judeo-
Christian God. This was a lasting soap opera at its fiery best.

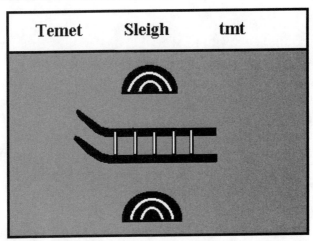

Temet   Sleigh   tmt

**The 'sleigh' hieroglyphic symbol is in the name 'Atum'.
Now 'temet' means 'sleigh' but what's sliding in Egypt?**

FIGURE 6-2 C: The Sleigh Divides The Two Half Cycles
(Modified from Illustrated Hieroglyphic Handbook by
Schumann-Antelme & Rossini)

Let me begin with a Bible quote, which probably relate to
Figures 6-2A and 6-2B about the Lake of Fire:

> "9 … And **fire came down from God out of
> heaven** and devoured them.
> 10 The **devil**, who **deceived them**, was cast into
> the **lake of fire** …"
> (Bible, Revelation, Chapter 20, Vs. 9-10)

There is a big problem here! The 'fire' everybody associated
only with Hell is coming straight from God and right out of
Heaven! We know scientifically that it is how things happen in
our earth change scenario. It foils the idea of an idyllic and serene
Heaven one can descend to after a well-deserved death.

There are no safe places anymore. Heaven is as fiery as Hell should be. The 'Devil' or 'Satan' with his fire from Hell seems to have a trick all the way up to Heaven. May be the Day of the Lord is not different from the hellish fire and brimstone - whether it comes from above or from below. May be it is all the same. Purification can only proceed with almost total destruction.

Now, one can say that this 'boiling heat' has nothing to do with the shift of the 'Magnetic North', but our accurate Holy Bible states differently:

> "12 Then the Lord said to me, "You have seen well, for I am ready **to perform My word**."
> 13 And the **word of the Lord came to me** the second time, saying, "What do you see?" And I said, "I see a **boiling pot**, and it is **facing away from the north**."

(Bible, Jeremiah, Chapter 1, Vs.12-13)

The 'boiling pot' that is 'facing away from the north' is the Magnetic North shifting toward the south direction where the Polar North is. He will 'perform his 'word', thus it is a serious act rather than casual conversation! So, this 'boiling pot' leaning away from the north will be caused by the 'word' of God that comes as a strong resonation out of His mouth. How good it is to understand the Scripture scientifically for the first time.

The Figure 6-2A labeled the Lake of Fire is from the Tomb of Seti I, Thebes. Nineteenth Dynasty. Besides the Dynasty being the one following Akhenaten's rule, even the grammatical or spelling similarities alone make me think that Seti I is ideologically related to the negative concept of the canine God Set and also the 'bad brother' Seth. The 'door-shaped' sled is trying to imply two concepts in one; first, the opening of the 'door or gate', and the secondly a 'sled', which begins a 'sliding down' into trouble.

This is from the Book of the Amduat. But there are several different books, such as the Book of the Night, Book of Caverns, Book of Nut, Book of the Afterlife, Book of the Heavenly Cow and others. Figure 6-2 C confirms that. The 'sleigh' that they commonly show in the pictures of the 4th, 5th, or 6th 'hour of the last twelve hours here implies a 'division point' between the two half cycles. Thus, it defines the point of 'down sliding' which happens between the two half cycles of the 12,000year periods. Interestingly, this word 'temet' that defines the Egyptian sleigh – in Hungarian 'temet' means 'buries' as in someone would bury the dead. The word 'temeto' in Hungarian means 'cemetery'. Likely, the Egyptian 'sleigh' began the process toward a mass extinction of the human race 12,000years ago.

Another tool of the Egyptians come to mind, that is the **'whip'**, which is pronounced **'kurbash'** and it is very similar to the Hungarian whip called **'korbach'**. But I still state that not one ethnic group can claim a sole divine origin from the Egyptian Priesthood - who were the remnants of the Atlantean inhabitants - as we all are derived from them.

The significance of the **'sleigh'** in a country like Egypt - whose climate is mainly Saharan Africa that is hot and dry and probably never seen real snow and they should not know about sleighs – cannot refer to just an actual winter time theme. It is almost like having the Eskimos drawing 'palm trees and coconuts' on their animal skins in their ancient legends.

If the 'palm tree' sounds absurd in Alaska, then we should be just as shocked to see a 'sleigh' in northern Africa. Unless, Santa Claus had to make an emergency landing during an equipment malfunction. This is probably as good and likely explanation as the Egyptologist would provide to explain the presence of the sleigh in Africa.

A stroke of an ingenious, the **'sleigh'** - that is obviously alien to the Egyptian hot desert culture - **was used by the priesthood to indicate a sudden earth change.** Since showing any form of 'heat' that was associated with the sunspot eruption could have been easily misinterpreted as 'another very hot summer in the desert'. It would have not given the desired shock effect. In this spelling we have the two half cycles below and above the 'sleigh' to show that its action happens at the end of a half period. These half cycle shapes spell out the name of King 'Tut', except in place of the 'quail chick' we find the 'sleigh'.

The golden colored 'Easter' chick signifies the birth of the golden colored Prince of the Sun. It can bring disaster first then the New Sun may be a few years later. The sliding down action of the 'sleigh' represents that catastrophic action, but even this downhill slide is broken up by a few zigzag 'jumpers' as Earth staggered through some back and forth drunken steps. Amazingly original!

Returning back to the previous Figure 6-2 B 'The Lake of Fire' seems to be related to the same 'fifth hour'. This period today would correspond to the year of 2008. That is because in our own Mayan Calendar ending of 2012 and also in the Babylonian Epic of Gilgamesh the first year seems to be the year prior to the first Venus Transit, that is 2003. It is difficult to guess exactly when the 'warning' barks happened. Interestingly, the Chinese Year 4074 of the Fire Dog starts in January 2006. The Egyptian Lake of Fire is found in the Papyrus of Bakenmut. Was the 'Lake of Fire' designation described an event such as the eruption of the huge volcano of the Yellowstone Park or was the boiling inferno associated with the 'Ring of Fire' of the Pacific Rim? We may soon witness it again as we are nearing the end of an 11,600year old era when these ancient tragedies can repeat themselves. Will we be witnesses to incredible powers moving and shaking of our resilient Mother Earth? Nobody knows for sure.

FIGURE 6-2 D. Ramesses I and the Jackal-Headed God
(Modified from Wilkinson's Reading Egyptian Art)

The **'Golden-haired' pharaoh Ramesses I** has very similar hair as any of the main Egyptian or Greek gods would do. This **golden hair** is as much of the **representation of the Sun's power as the 'golden fleece'** of the Greco-Roman Ram. Casually hanging around with a human who has dog head or a dog who grew a human body is not a commonly noble thing to do. This display is reinforcing the fact that the pharaohs were not meant to represent human kings. The Sun reference in conjunction with the dog is the timing of the Sunspot eruption soon after Sirius the **Dog Star** reaches its highest position in the sky, **end of July to mid-August**. His barking might warn us of the coming tragedy.

Anubis appears with his brother Horus around the deceased mummy of their father, Osiris, to help with his resurrection.

Set, the canine god often shown carrying the emblem for the Union of the Two Lands. Anubis is part of the Judgment Hall of Osiris. As the Egyptian Dog/Jackal he is shown to be involved forming the meaning of the word 'Meri', that is 'to love' in Figure 3-8. Then further on in Figure 4-4 he reappears under the alias Upuaut, the Opener of the Roads. Certainly, all of these dogs and jackals are supportive of the theory, but the question naturally arises; - Is this Jackal/Dog god named Set, or Upuaut, or Anubis and the others, are they all and one in the same, that is the Dog Star, Sirius? Astronomically that would make perfect sense. Ramesses I with golden hair and a serpent uraeus headdress may be a representation of the erupting Sun.

In the Songs of Isis, the following are being said about Horus and Isis according to Professor Barbara S. Lesko in her fabulous book titled 'The Great Goddesses of Egypt':
"Isis continues:
… Your sacred image, Orion in heaven,
Rises and sets;
I am Sothis following him,
I will not depart from him! …"

Then a few stanzas later Isis continues:
"Isis comes to you, Oh Lord of the Horizon, according as
she **begat the Unique One, the leader of the gods**;

She will protect you,
she will protect your face,
She will protect the face of Horus,
Even the woman who created a male for her father,
Mistress of the Universe, who came forth from the **Eye of
Horus, Noble Serpent, which flamed forth from Re,**
and which came forth from the pupil in **the eye of Atum
When Re arose on the First Occasion."**

(Author's heavyset)

219

How much clearer can the Ra Priests spell this out? The birth of the 'Unique One' who is the new leader of the gods is from Isis (Venus), Mistress of the Universe. The initial stanza ties this to Orion and Sothis, the Dog Star. The birth of this unique 'Prince' is also connected to the 'Eye' of the Sun God Re and 'He' erupts as a 'Noble Serpent' flaming out of the Sun. This is emphasized to be on a 'First Occasion' that means to me that there will be another 'rising' that day, thus the prophecy of 'two rising' or re-birth of the Egyptian ruler will be full-filled.

The 'eye' of Re is the Sunspot on the Sun, the 'third eye of Shiva'. A larger 'eye' of God is that of the Galactic Center. The same 'spiral pair' that makes up the center of the Galaxy is what one may call the 'pair of opposing energies' or the 'male and female union of the creator force'. Those two spirals that radiate to the left or the right are the forces which control the two half cycles of any of the orbital paths.

Figure 5-3 shows the map of the Milky Way Galaxy. The galactic bulge or the larger part of the Galaxy is fashioned in the form of a sacred 'eye'. This is most likely what the ancients referred to as the 'Eye of God'. This galactic eye or even 'embryo' form of the 'spiral pairs' could explain a lot of the complexity of the astrophysics governing our Universe from the smallest to the largest creations. There are two spirals that make up the eye, which can be equated to the two horns of the Ram or the Lamb that are the creative forces of the Milky Way Galaxy. Even our Sun has two axes that can be thought of as another set of horns on another sheep. Then the third set of 'Lambly' horns of a spiral pair belongs to the Earth. So the Celtic Druids were right about the fact that three pairs of spirals were governing everything in Life. But how did they know it? Was there a more advanced civilization before us or did aliens come to Earth to teach us a higher science?

FIGURE 6-3: The Sacred 'EYE of God' is the Galactic Center

    Anybody who scientifically desires to understand our Universe and the creations that live in it must consider the 'spiral' or the 'spiral pair' as the creative forces. Any straight linear or circular equations about the creative forces need to be specified and reexamined in view of the spiral pairs creating half cycle endings. And this is only the simplistic 'two-dimensional' representation of the forces. A three-dimensional approach would be a more accurate scientific model. Utilizing our 2-D paper even with a 3-D idea is difficult enough to present. Multiple realities or the complexity of several universes folding on themselves are certainly not something I am willing to tackle. In my next Figure I will show that the secret power of the **Ark of the Covenant** lies in the **Spiral Fibonacci's numbers of the Galactic Center.**

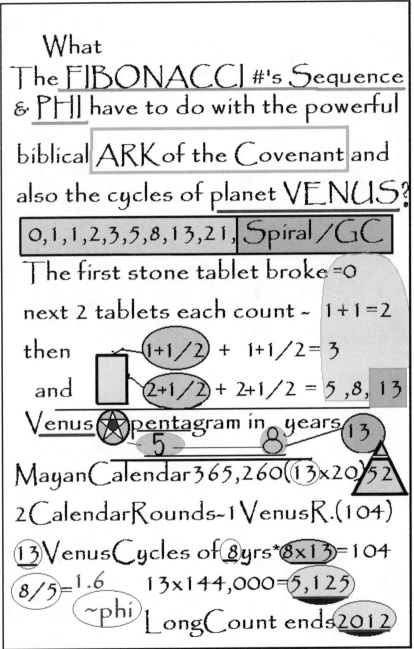

What
The FIBONACCI #'s Sequence
& PHI have to do with the powerful

biblical ARK of the Covenant and

also the cycles of planet VENUS?

0,1,1,2,3,5,8,13,21, Spiral /GC

The first stone tablet broke =0

next 2 tablets each count ~ 1+1=2

then $(1+1/2)$ + 1+1/2= 3

and $(2+1/2)$ + 2+1/2 = 5 ,8, 13

Venus pentagram in years 13
5   8

MayanCalendar 365,260 (13x20) 52

2CalendarRounds~1VenusR.(104)

(13)VenusCycles of (8)yrs* (8x13)=104

(8/5)=1.6   13x144,000= (5,125)

(~phi) LongCount ends (2012)

FIGURE 6-4: The Spiral Secrets of the Ark of the Covenant

222

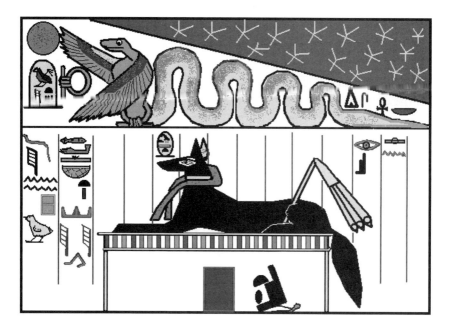

FIGURE 6-5: The Winged Serpent and the Jackal Deities
(Modified from T.G.H. James' Ramesses II)

Figure 6-5 depicts the Winged Serpent and Anubis the jackal god in the burial chamber of the Tomb of Nefertari protecting the cartouche of Nefertari over his nose. The jackal posses the whip of rulers. He lays on a bed that has a brick shaped 'hearth' in the middle below representing the core of the earth. To the right of the 'hearth' is a black throne that stands for the pole of the earth. More importantly, a 'creature' is under the 'W' shaped throne tilting it out of balance. To me it is very symbolically revealing. Above the jackal is the Serpent touching the sun with a wing and whose serpentine shape is increasing in height. This evil serpent has wings – not due to an ancient DNA experiment gone wrong – but because the old bards needed to tell us that this fiery serpent flew toward us from the Sun traveling through the sky.

Another hieroglyphic symbol in this picture, which captures my imagination is to the left and below the front paws of Anubis. The hieroglyph is between the two feathers that usually associated with strong wind. The symbol is a pair of legs cut off below the waist. The reason for that is to place the emphasis only on the action of 'walking' without tying it to a human or a deity. The 'walking pair of legs' to me symbolizes the moving away of the Magnetic North axis from its original position. We will see the 'walking legs' again in the last chapter when we analyze the Last Eight Gods before the Judgment Day in Figure 8-1

Further in Figure 6-5 above the tail of the Serpent there are four symbols. The first one from the left is the 'delta' or 'tent' symbol of 'male eruption'. The second sign is the 'cane' representing 'axis shift'. The third sign is the 'ankh' that is the symbol of the goddess, the transit of the planet 'Venus'. The last sign is the 'grail' that not only emphasizes the known fact that the Lord likes 'fire oblation' for an offering, but it also implies a 'pot', which can tilt and if it is turned upside down it would resemble a Sun coming up or even a half cycle. Very simple symbols hiding very complex cosmic ideas!

Now, I would not even want to guess on the official explanation of that picture's meaning from the Egyptologists. Would it be something like: - ' *Flying Serpents and Lazy Dogs ruled the quiet households of the Egyptians?* '

Chapter Seven
Evil Serpents

The evil serpent is well known in mythology and religious lore. It was the serpent at the beginning of biblical creation that tempted Eve. If we substitute Eve for Venus, Adam for Atum, the Lord for Aton the Sun eruption and the Serpent for 'Resonation' we might begin understanding the hidden Egyptian teachings.

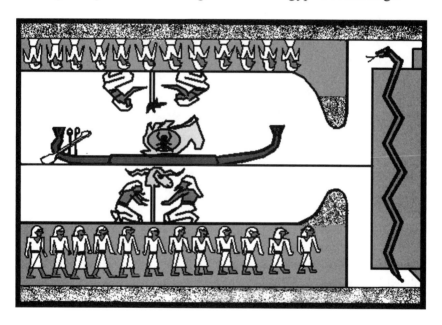

FIGURE 7-1. The Serpent Guards the Door of Heaven (Modified from Erik Hornung's The Ancient Egyptian Books of the Afterlife, Book of Gates, First Hour.)

In Figure 7-1, we see the 12 gods on either side of the boat, representing the 12,000year half cycles, which end with the opening of the gate of heaven. The evil serpent is the one who lurks by the celestial door. The Lamb and the Dog is adored.

FIGURE 7-2. Solar Barque in the Netherworld
(Modified from Wilkinson's Reading Egyptian Art.
Solar Barque in the Underworld, Papyrus of Herytwebkhet
Twenty-first Dynasty)

In Figure 7-2 the Dog Deity is harpooning the Serpent, which is shown as the water in the Underworld. The water snake brings the astronomical constellation Hydra to mind. In the next and final chapter we will decipher the relationship of the hawk to the dog and the water snake. There are four dogs and four serpents towing the solar barque. The number four may again mean the four movements of the earth out of its path. Four knocks on the celestial door. Even the Hungarians have a saying, which may relate to that, which goes something like that; - 'Three is the Hungarian Truth and One is added to it.' It sounds like three knocks at equal division followed by the fourth one a little bit delayed.

Not only there is a serpent underneath the barque, but also the Hawk-headed god wears the symbol of the Sun with a serpent wrapped around it. The hawk also has a 'was' scepter in his hand, which to me represents the iron core – Magnetic North.

As one might recall, the sunspot eruption causes the Magnetic North to shift. Since, the Magnetic North is represented by Vega, whose Arabic name means 'the swooping eagle / hawk', it might not be a great surprise that it is mentioned in the Book of Job.

> "25 'Now my **days are swifter than a runner**;
> they flee away, they see no good.
> 26 They pass by like **swift** ships, like an **eagle swooping** on its prey.' "
> (Bible, Book of Job, Ch. 9,

Another well-known and mythologically interesting bird is the Ibis or 'stork' that brings the 'baby' is standing in the back of the boat second behind the hawk in Figure 7-2.

FIGURE 7-3. The Lynx-Cat is Killing the Serpent
(Modified from Wilkinson's Reading Egyptian Art)

In the next chapter when we talk about and depict the eight gods who stand before the end section, the **lynx** on that row of gods is placed as the second god. For those who are not well versed in the art of astronomy, the 'lynx' constellation is not too far from the Polar North region. More importantly it is straight **above the Cancer constellation** that spreads across the Ecliptic. In Figure 8-5 of the next Chapter we will finally discover the method and the reason for this brutal act. In the Tomb of Inherkhau, Thebes, a very similar depiction is shown, except the animal that is cutting off the head of the serpent under the solar tree is the hare or rabbit. May be the example of the Easter Bunny carries the remnants of this ancient symbolic tradition meaning a sudden jump?

FIGURE 7-4. Fire Spirits, Serpents, and the Sphinx
(Modified from Erik Hornung's The Ancient Egyptian Books of the Afterlife)

The fourth hour (2006) seems to be bringing the first Sunspot eruption, then in the **fifth hour** of the Amduat (the parallel of 2007 today) the obvious message is that there was a **'sliding'** action. **The sled is shaped as the heavenly door.** The four fiery heads may represent the four insults against the earth resulting in the drunken movements of the globe accompanied by underwater volcanic eruptions. The **serpent** is shown with the **Ankh**, followed by four heads that may be tying the event within four years of the **Venus Transit**, which still would be 2007 today.

The Sphinx is facing the serpent. The leonine connection for the serpent stands for August, the Leo sign in astrology. As matter of fact, the rising of the Dog Star is in the first week of the Leo sign that is during the last week of July. The second week of Leo brings us to the Sacred Cosmic Marriage celebration of Hathor and Horus, the 5 Evil Days of the Mayan Calendar and the 5 Epagomenal Days of the birth of the Egyptian gods.

The other significance is that the Flood of Noah happened about 11,600years ago when we were in the Age of Leo. Thus, there is a double meaning for the age and the month during the last Deluge. This time the Leo sign will only stand for the month. The Age is that of the Aquarius, who will pour the water out its vase. So who said that we would have 'no more floods'? The flood will come about seven years after the fire from the Sun. Below in Figure 7-5 we can see the Serpent sitting in the middle of the Sun disk ready to strike.

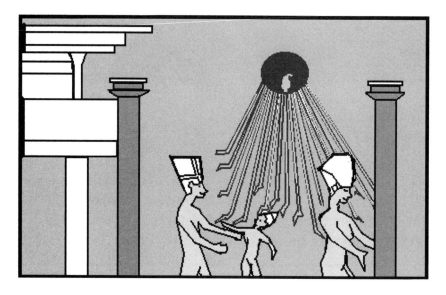

FIGURE 7-5. The Serpent is The Erupting Resonation of the Sun (Modified from Wilkinson's Reading Egyptian Art)

In the book 'Legends & Lore' written mainly about Chinese wisdom and the mythology of the Dragon, the following has been stated: "The Dragons of Hidden Treasure are also said to be responsible for volcanoes and produce gaping, lava-filled fissures in the ground when they leave their lairs to visit Heaven."

"... the Red Dragon of the South, Qiantang, who caused such devastating floods with his wild temper that Shangdi, supreme ruler of Heaven, sentenced him to be shackled to a pillar..."

Volcanism, lava flow, possibly earthquakes along with the Flood and the pillar is tied together into the Red Dragon. In Chinese astrology the Year of the Dragon is in 2000 and 2012.

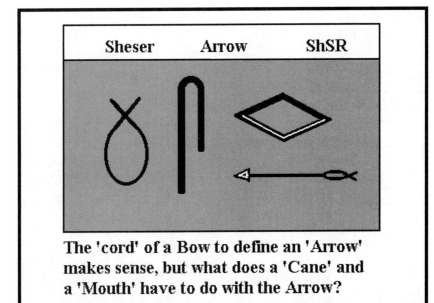

Sheser   Arrow   ShSR

The 'cord' of a Bow to define an 'Arrow' makes sense, but what does a 'Cane' and a 'Mouth' have to do with the Arrow?

FIGURE 7-6: The Arrow With The Mouth
(Modified from IHH by Schumann-Antelme & Rossini)

The hieroglyphic spelling of the 'Arrow' only makes sense in the cosmic interpretation where the opening of the 'mouth of god' causes the arrow to be shut at Earth. Even the end of the arrow shows a 'fish' symbol (Orion) and the arrow point is shown as a pyramid with a smaller pyramid (tent) inside of it. It is another attempt to define Earth changes.

FIGURE 7-7: Ra in the Boat with a Strange Foot and a Swallow (Modified from Wilkinson's Reading Egyptian Art, from the tomb of Sennedjem, Thebes, Nineteenth Dynasty)

The picture in Figure 7-7 is from the Nineteenth Dynasty. That is a 'dynasty' (year?) after Aton, the Sun God ruled Egypt. Ra is in the boat on water, but there is a large column of water erupting from the subterranean area. In the Bible it is commonly mentioned as 'the underwater fountains erupting'. Interestingly, this 'river' is starting at the 'foot'.

Those of you who are familiar with astronomy know that the longest constellation in the sky called **'river' Eridanus begins at the foot of Orion.** The main star of the foot is the star **'Rigel'.** Anytime a foot is mentioned in mythology, especially if it is tied to the river or the riverbank, the answer is Rigel! For my pious religious Christian students here I have to mention Christ teaching about 'washing one's foot'. Yes, it is a humble spiritual service to perform, but Christ's concern was as much about cosmic teaching as it was about service and hygiene.

Remaining with Figure 7-7, the 'foot of Orion' is being pushed down by a 'weight' which has 'seven divisions' that is attached to a 'pillar / cane'. The 'seven weights' likely signify the Polar North, Ursa Minor the Bear that consists of seven stars, but it might even refer to the seven stars of Pleiades pointing to the East as the Sun God, Ra is sitting in the solar bark. Remember how we began the first chapter with the quote from the Book of Job? Well, it was about the 'Bear, Orion, and the Pleiades'. Naturally, that is what I am relating to above when we analyze the picture in Figure 7-7.

The 'weight' in that same figure is attached to a 'cane' that is most likely symbolizing the Magnetic North. The 'two-edged sword' on top of the weight is derived from the hands of Perseus or Mithra, the Bull-killing hero above Taurus, or may even have a reference to the 'scissors' of Cancer. Thus, we connect even the 'two brothers' Mithra and Orion to the concept of the Bear and the Pleiades in this figure. Naturally, the Sun disc with the wrapped around serpent on top of the hawk-headed Ra is about the Sunspot eruption. Such a silly picture with so much cosmic knowledge incorporated.

The **'swallow'** that innocently perches on top of the erupting river is the **swift flying bird**, which represents the **fast flying disaster** from air.

Several pages ago I quoted from the Book of Job in Chapter 9 where his days are passing by as 'swift' ships or like an eagle 'swooping' on its prey. This ties the 'swift flying' to the star Vega, the 'swooping eagle'. The Lakota Indians have an oral legend about a 'swift flying one'. I heard the story several times from my adopted Lakota Mom, Marie Two-Charger, who made sure over and over again that I could pronounce this magical and difficult name 'hwuyenkiya?', but surely I should not try to spell it. It seemed to be somehow related to the revered 'Iktomi', the Spider, who is identified with the star constellation Orion amongst South and Central American Natives. Was this ancient oral legend of the Lakota Sioux Indians about a tragedy that happened almost 12,000years ago?

In the Babylonian The Epic of Gilgamesh by Kovacs the year when the 'violent wind' passed by is in Tablet IV (the Fourth Year of the Egyptian Amduat, which today would fall on 2006). This Tablet IV is labeled 'The Journey To The Cedar Forest' and the First Stage begins as such:

> "At twenty leagues they broke for some food, at thirty leagues they stopped for the night, **walking fifty leagues in a whole day, a walk of a month and a half**.
> On the third day they drew near to the Lebanon. They **dug a well facing Shamash (the setting sun)**, …
> … **a violent wind passed through** so he attached a covering. …
> … Why am I so disturbed? Did a god pass by? Why are my muscles trembling? ….
> … In the mountain gorges … **the mountain fell down on me** …"

The walk of fifty leagues in a day that would usually take a month and a half sounds to me as a partial axis shift.

Then some of the animals which line up in the next chapter are mentioned in Tablet VI that would correspond to today's 2008. This is how Kovacs writes about those astronomical animals in The Epic of Gilgamesh:

> "I will have harnessed for you a **chariot of lapis lazuli and gold**, ... It will be harnessed with great storming mountain mules! ...
>
> Your **she-goats** will bear triplets, your **ewes** twins, your **donkey** under burden will overtake the mule, your **steed at the chariot** will be bristling to gallop, your **ox at the yoke** will have no match.
>
> Gilgamesh addressed **Princess Ishtar** saying:
>
> "What would I have to give you **if I married you**?"

Most of these astronomical animals will line up in our next and last chapter. The she-goat Capella is part of the Charioteer constellation. The most likely year for the emergence of the Chariot of the Sun was two years after the first Venus Transit that would be the year 2006 today. The next year must had started the seven years of famine to complete the last fourteen years, consisting of the seven years of bounty and the next seven years of tragedy. The donkey would be a very important piece of the astronomical puzzle as part of the famous Cancer constellation. We will tie these animals into a cohesive secret of the Ancients in the next chapter.

Chapter Eight
The Last Eight Gods

Both in the Egyptian Enigmatic Book of the Afterlife and in the Bible, there is a **sacred EIGHT**, which leads up to a major evil human disaster. Usually in the Bible it is the Flood of Noah. In the Book of the Afterlife, it is the Judgment Hall of Osiris that is the gateway to the Netherworld.

From the **biblical Adam** it takes exactly **eight 'generations'** to get **to the time of Noah** and there are **eight people on the Ark.** Then we can also detect the number eight as Plutarch describes the old romance of Cleopatra of Egypt to the Cesar of the Greco-Roman Empire. This was certainly an attempt to tie the Egyptian rulers to the Roman Emperors. In it we observe Julius Cesar and Octavius – who later declares that He is the 'Son of the Divine' and changes his name to Augustus Cesar, the 'eight' month of the year, the month of Leo! Both of these Roman rulers are falling in love with Queen Cleopatra, whose early demise comes by the bite of an evil snake. Is it real history or also cosmic mythology? Interestingly, after this powerful and likely symbolic 'marriage' of the Roman Emperor to the Egyptian Queen over 2,000years ago we could observe the emergence of the collection of books today we call the Bible. It is not only very likely, but anymore a scholarly certainty that the ancient's myths from the Egyptians, Greco-Romans, Hindus and Babylonians were collected into one Holy Book. Thus, the Bible is mainly a translated astronomical Egyptian Mystery School Teaching wisdom presented to the then uneducated masses of Europe and the Middle East as magic and a history of ethnic strife of that region. It is not any different then the earlier Egyptian, Hindu and Greek.attempts to bring these same stories alive - EXCEPT one major fatal change happened! The half human half animal gods became fully human and real!

This magical human transformation of the lovely Ram-headed gods made the divine tales much more popular with most people – thus, we were able to preserve them as history over the long millennia - but at the same time these stories became so humanly historical that it was almost impossible to revert them back to their original life saving cosmic knowledge. Sure, a number of valuable animal and astronomical clues remained in the sacred tales, but not enough to clearly translate them back to the vital intended meanings. Secret societies – likely the remnants and the natural outgrowths of the order of the Egyptian Ra Priesthood – tried their best to develop a number of valuable keys that would allow the reversal of false history back to astronomical science. As you clearly can observe by now – they utterly and miserably failed. Their attempts to increase the membership roll and spread the illumination to a larger number of participants only resulted in quantity, but badly suffered in quality. Mostly it was the regular churchgoers who joined and they had nothing new to add and most importantly, very little spiritual openness to receive. The 'secret' remains a big elusive secret even from the members of the secret societies. Now, that is how one can keep secrets even from themselves in this permissive age of information gathering and pointed news leaking.

Now, let us get back to the important number eight. Thus, from the Egyptian Teachings, then we need to identify those crucial 'eight' gods or generations leading up to the punitive Judgment of God. Erik Hornung shows in his book 'The Ancient Egyptian Books of the Afterlife' that within that collection of writings there is an Enigmatic Book of the Afterlife. This work contains symbols that are not translated into regular picture hieroglyphics. Figure 8-1A shows the **Eight Gods lining up to be judged.** The two goddesses likely represent the two Venuses as they are shown both at the upper and lower level of the scene. On the upper level the Ram headed Amun, the Galactic Spiral Force, is shown again in between the Venus Transit pair.

Another idea for the spiral ram horns is the Magnetic North and the Polar North, which not only controlled and rotated by the Galactic Center and the Spiral Solar Dynamo, but it also wobbles out slowly in a spiral fashion. That spiral wobble of the Polar North axis of the Earth was seven meters in diameter in the 1960'o, and it is now a fifth of a mile yearly. The scientific proof for that spiral wobble is the **Chandler Wobble** of the polar axis, which was theorized by the Mr. Chandler in the 1890's and proven by governmental agencies in the 1970's by measuring and plotting of the path of the wandering North Pole yearly.

Returning to Fig. 8-1A, the middle section shows the Hawk headed Horus radiating dark rays to the canine Anubis. Horus represents the Sun, but there is an old Horus and a young Horus. Those are likely designations for the Son and the Sun concept.

FIGURE 8-1A. The Last Eight Gods Before Judgment
(Slightly modified from Hornung's The Ancient Egyptian
Books of the Afterlife)

237

The eight 'gods' on the upper level are shown from left to right beginning with the 1.goat, and then progressing on with the 2.lynx cat 3.lion, 4.bald head/face – turned 90 degrees, 5.human head with hair, 6.snake /vulture? 7.bull/cow and 8.male god.

The 'donkey' is not only the animal symbol of the American Democratic Party, but even it is grouped together in the Book of Job with several other creatures. In the next quote the 'goat' is mentioned - it is the first of the eight figures - and the 'donkey' is part of the 'Crab' below the astronomical 'lynx' in the sky as we learn later: " Do you know the time when the **wild mountain goats** bear young? Or can you mark when the **deer** gives birth?' ...

5 'Who set the **wild donkey** free? Who loosed the bonds of the onager ...?' ...

9 'Will the **wild ox** be willing to serve you?' ...

12 ' The wings of the **ostrich** wave proudly, but are her wings and pinions like the kindly **stork**'s?'

19 'Have you given the **horse** strength? Have you clothed his neck with thunder?'

20 Can you frighten him like a **locust**? ...

26 'Does the **hawk fly** by your wisdom, and spread its wings **toward the south**?'..." (Au. - Heavyset) (Bible, Book of Job, Chapter 39, Vs. 1-26.)

The wide variety of these animals herded into only one chapter of the Book of Job suggests to me that Job knew more about the symbolic nature of the creatures than one could easily decipher from between the lines. The horse - we did not spend much time discussing earlier, but enough to say that it - is Sagittarius, which stands for the Center of our Milky Way Galaxy. By current scientific estimates it takes 200 million years for our Galaxy to take a full turn. The Ancients were well aware of that. Their knowledge is reflected in the statements about the 'two hundred million horsemen' who are ready to do battle.

The 'goat' appears as one of the corner stars of the 'Charioteer' constellation. The 'chariot of fire' is connected to the 'goat' and the 'birth' of the kids in the hot summer of June or July.

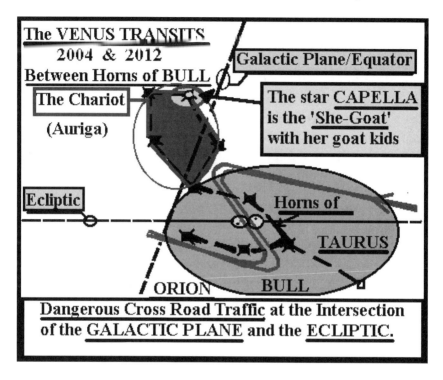

FIGURE 8-1B: Capella is the She-Goat

A star named **'goat' is Capella**, which is **part of the fiery Charioteer**. Of the high magnitude stars it is one of the few that lies almost on the Galactic Plane. The Magnetic North's axis shift from North to South presumably happens parallel along side the powerful Galactic Plane. **The Chariot of Fire** is very obviously related to our solar eruption theory. The story of Ben-Hur or the tale of Phaeton and a number of Sun and fire related myths start from this constellation. Thus, eight years prior to the Flood the main disaster began by an overactive Sun in the summer.

This fiery summer happened around 2 or 3 years after the first Venus Transit of 96 to a 100 pairs ago, or about 11,600years prior to now. **So our first animal of the last eight ties the 'Goat' to the 'Chariot of Fire' and to that faithful tragic year.** The goat star Capella is not only very important for the conclusion of our cosmic story, but it was essential for the survival of the baby Greek god Zeus. The 'She-goat' was called Amaltheia by the ancient Greeks and earned her fame as the 'wet nurse of Zeus' while he was hidden as a baby in a cave on Mount Ida. Capella in Latin refers to 'Little Nanny' for her role of feeding the baby god. Later Zeus used her hide to make the famous thunder-shield (aigis) and her horns provided the 'cornucopia', the horn of plenty (keras amaltheias).

In 'The Sibylline Oracles' of the Jewish Pseudoepigraphra from Barnstone's The Other Bible the following quote is on pg. 504:

> "Then mortals in desperation, in the **last stages of famine**, will devour their own parents, will consume them greedily as food. ... As a result of grievous wars the **bloodstained ocean** will be filled with flesh and blood of insensate men. ... I saw the **threatening of the gleaming sun** among the stars and the moon's grievous wrath among the lightning flashes. The stars travailed with war and God suffered them to fight. **In place of the sun, long flames rose** in revolt, and the two-horned revolution of the moon was changed. **Mounted on Leo's back Lucifer waged battle**. **Capricorn smote the heel of the young Taurus**, and Taurus snatched the day of return from Capricorn. **Orion** removed the scales so they disappeared. Virgo changed her sphere with the Twins in Aries. The **Pleiades** no longer appeared and the **Dragon** disowned the belt. Pisces entered into Leo's girdle. **Cancer** did not stay for he **feared Orion**. Scorpio drew up his tail, because of savage **Leo**, and the **dogstar** perished from the **sun's flame**."

(Author's heavyset)

Even the Hindu Myths tie the fire destruction to the goat:

> "Then the triple **world was totally destroyed by the fire** of Siva's anger, ... And even when everything had been destroyed, the **noble lord** who is an ocean of pity granted them safety, and **gave the head of a goat** to the man Daksa and revived him " (Hindu Myths, pg. 251)

> "Then the **mightiest of the mighty** saw his father Agni approaching, and he honored Agni, who remained there together with the group of Mothers, who was born of anger; she held her trident in her hand and protected him as if he were her own son. The cruel daughter of the **ocean of blood**, the drinker of blood, embraced the great general and cared for him as if he were her own son. And **Agni** transformed himself into a **goat-headed** merchant with many children, " (Hindu Myths, Penguin, pg.114)

As we learned earlier Siva is the Sun and Agni is the Hindu Fire God and both of those are tied to the head of the goat.

We noted the goat in the Egyptians, Jewish, and the Hindu Myths, so now we can take a look at to see if the goat or the other animals in Figure 8-1A appear in the Bible and are tied to the number 'eight' and fire. This is how the Bible writes about the animals: " 26 And the Lord spoke to Moses saying:

> 27 When a **bull** or a **sheep** or a **goat is born**, it shall be **seven days** with its mother; and from the **eighth day** and thereafter it shall be accepted as **an offering made by fire to the Lord.**" (Author's heavyset)
> (Leviticus, Chapter 22, Vs. 26-27)

Not only the 'Goat is born' in the above quote from the Bible, but it is tied to the number 'eight' and to the offering made by 'fire' to the Lord. Is it only a coincidence or may be our theory is correct and even the Bible contains mainly astronomical clues?

241

> "12 Then he shall take a censer full of **burning coals of fire** from the altar before the Lord, …
> 14 He shall take some of the **blood of the bull** and sprinkle it with his finger on the mercy seat **on the east side**; and before the mercy seat he shall sprinkle some of the blood with his finger **seven times**.
> 15 Then he shall kill the **goat of the sin offering**, " (Author's heavyset)
> (Leviticus, Ch.16. Verses 12-15)

There are seven days after the birth and the eighth day seems to end it. Afterwards the blood of the bull is tied to the burning fire and matched with the east side that is unmistakably a clear astronomical marker for the seven star sisters of the Pleiades. All of this is tied to a burning fire at the altar of the Lord.

When we glance back to Figure 8-1 we can see the bull, goat and ram in the top row. We also run into the biblical lion and the serpent. It becomes clear that the Semitic science Priests of Ra brought us the Egyptian Mystery School Teachings through the Old Testament of the Bible. The degraded morals of the declining Greco-Roman Empire along with the mixing together of several ethnic groups with differing values within the immense borders necessitated the combined emergence of human appearing gods, saints and a law that preached morality, but forgot science and astronomy. This uneducated agricultural population base shoved the doors wide open for the Dark Ages to march into Europe. Not until the emergence of science and enlightenment about 300years ago the darkness of ignorance slowly started to dissipate.

Returning back to Figure 8-1, it is important to realize that the top row figures are 'mummified' and have no arms, which is to show that the 'king' lost the right arm, that is the 90degree angle solar stabilization of the earth.

Sacred Cosmic Marriage

The lower register shows the same four 'gods', the jackal, hawk, ram, and male gods for the first four years 'mummified' then the next four years with small upper extremities. The first four are wearing white outfit and the next four mainly dark, which may be alluding to the fact that during the eight years of Venus cycle we have the planet four years as a Morning Star and four year as an Evening Star. Reviewing some of the biblical quotes one can find the frequent mentioning of the Morning Star. Consistent with my theory - that the lack of arms on those gods may be significant - in the middle section after the initial four group of markings, the depiction of the arms reappear in a 90degree angle above the leg markings.

The important question is whether the upper, middle, and lower registers are symbolic representations of the upper, middle, and inner part of the Earth's geo-dynamo? A few more quotes will bring the fire, harlot, jackal and even the bald man (the fourth god in the row) from the Bible to our Egyptian round table.

> "7 All her carved images shall be beaten to pieces, and all her pay as a **harlot shall be burned with the fire;** ...
> 8 Therefore I will wail and **howl**, I will go stripped and **naked**; I will make a wailing like the **jackals** and a mourning like the **ostriches,** ...
> 16 **Make yourself bald** and cut off your hair, ..."
> (Author's heavyset) (Bible, Micah, Ch.1, Vs.7-16)

I do not desire to be repetitious about the combined wisdom of the harlot, fire, owl, jackal, and ostrich and making oneself bald. I would just like to know if any of your preachers in the churches thoroughly explained the meanings of these interrelated subjects?

The **nakedness** is tied to the Sunspot eruption because the intense heat made burns and boils on people's body and they were not able to stand the clothing on themselves.

Therefore, 'revealing or uncovering ones nakedness' in the Bible is not the action of a pervert human, but it is about the intense heat of this ancient cosmic event. The **ostrich** feather was a symbol worn by Ma'at Goddess of Truth and Justice, and she was closely tied to the judgment scene of this Egyptian disaster. The ostrich is a bird that cannot fly anymore and puts its head into the sand ('dunes'?) when in fear! Another intended meaning of this 'feather of truth' was that if the feather (the unseen and lightweight cosmic force) were heavier and more forceful than the heart of the 'witch' (the Core of Mother Earth), then Judgment would follow. This was not, by any means, only meant judging of an individual soul, rather judgment would fall upon the 'sinners' of the entire Earth. Well, it was not morally driven as you know, but it was the timely rhythmic arrival of the Cosmic Wind that needed to reverse the failing magnetic field of the Geo-Dynamo.

Returning back to the related ancient Classical Greco-Roman mythology, I shall outline the labors of Hercules to see if there is a close correlation to the astronomical animal symbols of the Egyptians.

0   Before the 12 Labors began Hercules became 'wild' and in a fit of madness he killed his wife and threw his three children into the **FIRE**. (Goat? / Chariot of Fire)
1. In his first labor Hercules slew the Nemean **LION**. (Both the month of August and the Age of Leo!)
2. During the second labor our Hero killed the seven-headed **serpent, the HYDRA** of Lerna. During this act he **crushed CANCER, the CRAB**. (DONKEYS!)
3. In the third labor he captured the **Golden STAG** of Cerynea in the cold winter snowfall up in the North. (The astronomical 'three skips of the antelope in the sky and the severe cold winter that followed the Sunspot eruption)

4. Overcoming the wild **BOAR** of Erymanthus in Arcadia happened during the fourth labor. During this task Hercules mortally wounded his beloved tutor Chiron, who became the constellation **Sagittarius**.
5. In his fifth task Hercules was appointed to clean the filthy stables of King Augeas of Elis. The Giant had to **DIVERT the** fast running **RIVER** Alpheus to flush the barn then he guided the stream back to its old course.
6. The sixth labor brought the capture of the **mad BULL** of Crete that was given to King Minos, ruler of the island, by **Neptune, God of the Sea**.
7. The task of the seventh labor of Hercules involved feeding King Diomedes of Thrace to his own **cannibalistic HORSES**, who were then taken captive.
8. In the eighth labor Hercules was sent to the Land of the **AMAZONS** to retrieve a girdle worn by Queen Hippolyte. On the way home the hero saved the Trojan **VIRGIN**, Hesione from the jaws of the **sea monster**.
9. The ninth task seen the slaying of the **metallic birds** of Stymphalia from the depth of the Earth causing 3 years of **DARKNESS** over the stagnant waters of the lake.
10. In this labor He captured the **CATTLE** of Geryones and slew a thief **Giant** named Cacus in a dark **CAVE**.
11. This task was to find the **Golden Apples of Hesperus**, god of the West, also known as **EVENING STAR**. A fierce **DRAGON** was guarding the apples. Hercules **set free Prometheus** also who was still bound by chains.
12. In the last and most difficult labor Hercules needed to carry the **TRIPLE-HEADED DOG** back into his cage **to end the time of bondage**.
    In his other pursuits Hercules also helped Jason and the Argonauts and was part of the first siege of Troy.

Instead of analyzing the labors I encourage my readers to come up with their own discoveries about the sequence of events of this ancient tragedy.

Now, I will explore the first few letters of our cosmic Alphabet. The first letter is the Greek 'alpha' and it is called 'aleph' in Hebrew, which very revealingly means 'ox'. It is named the 'OX' as it is representing the astronomical 'bull horns' where the Venus Transit occurs. You may recall, the cow horn hieroglyphic symbol that translates to 'oopet' or the opening, it is 'A' here.

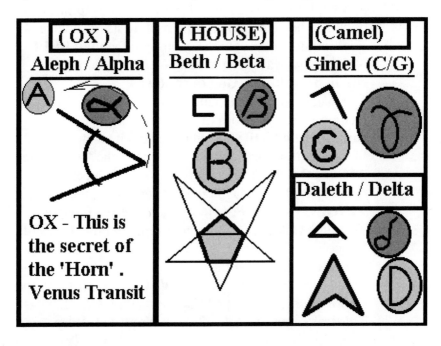

FIGURE 8-2 A: The Initial Phoenician and Hebrew ABC

Tying the Hebrew Alphabet to these last eight years might seem like a long stretch for some, but with the first letter 'Aleph' (Alpha) we have a reasonable start. It would be the first Venus Transit of the pair. In today's calendar it would correspond to the year 2004. The second letter is 'beta' in Greek and it is the Hebrew 'beth' that literally means 'house'. The biblical town names, such as 'Beth-el' and 'Beth-le-hem' sure provide us a special meaning to this second letter of the alphabet.

So, let us see how the Phoenicians, Hebrews, and Greeks brought us the foundation for our current alphabets. The third letter 'c/g' is less obvious initially, but it is definitely connected to a spiral force. Following that, the 'delta / daleth' is the 'door' that is naturally the 'male force' of eruption in the Universe. It would correspond to 2007 in today's Venus Transit Calendar. The Ra Priesthood was keen in their design of every aspects of future learning.

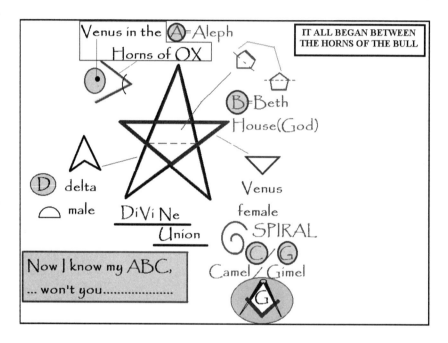

FIGURE 8-2 B: Now I Know My ABC

The letter 'A' is obviously both an astronomical and geometric symbol. The 'bull horn' is the place where the Transit of Venus occurs, which is 'Oopet' the Opening and the compass. Knowing that the Venus Transit is the main secret of the ages, it makes sense that it would symbolize the first letter of the Alphabet.

247

The Venus Transit occurs eight years apart, and in the middle of that period is when the purifying Lord of the fiery evil earth changes appeared from the erupting Sun. Cleverly, the graphic nature of the number '8' represents a simple never ending 'eternity' that includes 'two halves to the whole'.

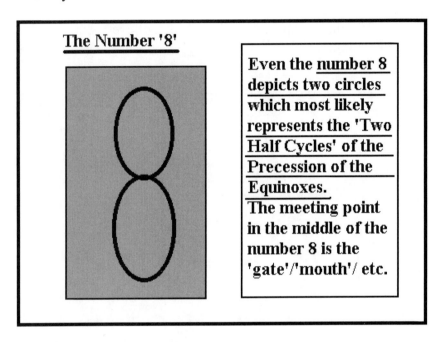

The Number '8'

Even the <u>number 8</u> depicts <u>two circles</u> which most likely represents the 'Two Half Cycles' of the Precession of the Equinoxes.
The meeting point in the middle of the number 8 is the 'gate'/'mouth'/ etc.

FIGURE 8-3: The Number Eight

Another important hieroglyphic clue is the '**winepress**' sign. It is clearly a very similar shape to the 'Little Dipper' or the 'Big Dipper'. A 'dipper' contains water that can be poured out all over the Earth, but also if it is turned upside down it will take the shape of the 'winepress'. This was an important discovery for me for a while - until I found out that there is better candidate for this elusive 'winepress'. Thus, as obvious as it seems, shockingly the Little Dipper is not the final answer for the symbolism of the 'winepress'. Our answer will be forthcoming in Figure 8-5.

How is then this winepress relates to our earth change scenario? During those turbulent times the axis shifted and the pressure on the geo-dynamo caused the under water volcanism to erupt and turn the ocean blood red. This increased pressure, which caused the 'water to turn to wine', is an old trick, but only cosmic divine forces can master it – nobody else!

In preparation for the next few figures, let me remind you that our Lord and Satan are on 'talking' terms. This ties the 'donkey' to a 'shining light' from the Old and the New Testament:

> "12 And the **Lord said to Satan,** …
>
> … 14 And a messenger came to Job and said,
> 'The **oxen** were plowing and the **donkeys** feeding
> beside them. …
>
> …16 And a messenger came to Job and said,
> **'The fire of God fell from heaven and burned
> up the sheep,** " (Bible, Job, Chapter 1, Vs 12-16)

> " Then Moses took his wife and his sons and set
> them on a **donkey** and he returned to the land of
> Egypt. And **Moses took the rod of God** in his
> hand."   (Bible, Exodus, Chapter 4, Vs. 20)

> "24 When he was gone, a **lion** met him on the road
> and **killed him.** And his **corpse** was thrown on the
> road, and the **donkey stood by it. The lion also
> stood by the corpse.**"
>   (Bible, Kings I, Chapter 13, Vs. 24)

> "24 A **wild donkey** used to the wilderness, that
> sniffs at the **wind** in her **desire**; in her **time of
> mating**, who can **turn** her away?"
>   (Bible, Jeremiah, Chapter 2, Vs. 24)

The 'cosmic' sex act is connected to the biblical wild donkey.

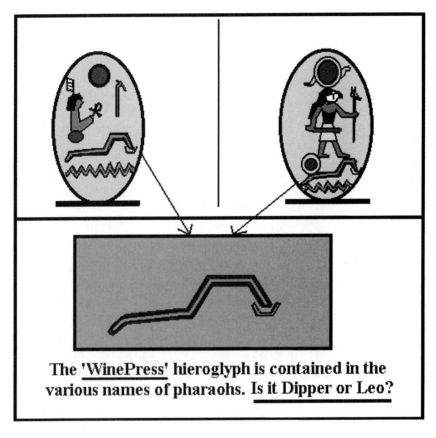

The 'WinePress' hieroglyph is contained in the various names of pharaohs. Is it Dipper or Leo?

FIGURE 8-4: The Wine Press is The Dipper or Is It?

Thus, the wine press was tied the geo-dynamo by the grape colored Red Sea effect. In Hindu mythology it was the 'bloody' menstruation of Mother Earth that caused this red color.

Since a person from let's say the city of Denver in Colorado could not see the Magnetic North tilting to the Polar North, thus the astronomer priests shifted their focus down further toward the South amongst the constellations. The distance between Magnetic North and Polar North is the same length as the distance between the Lynx and the head of Hydra.

Thus, the axis shift was recorded as the Lynx cutting off the head of Hydra. The Water Serpent 'raising' from the ocean was symbolic of the waves of the sea emerging and being poured out on the surface of the Earth. The water turned red not from the blood of Hydra, but from the erupting underwater volcanisms.

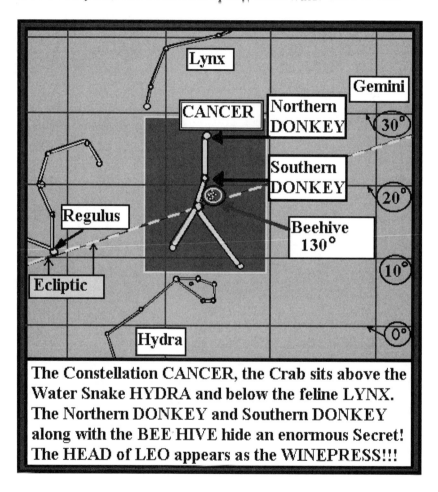

The Constellation CANCER, the Crab sits above the Water Snake HYDRA and below the feline LYNX. The Northern DONKEY and Southern DONKEY along with the BEE HIVE hide an enormous Secret! The HEAD of LEO appears as the WINEPRESS!!!

FIGURE 8-5: The Secret of The Crab, Donkey, Winepress, Hydra, Beehive and Biblical Numbers
(Modified from David H. Levy's Skywatching)

The water to blood or to wine is immortalized in countless ancient tales. The orgies of the God of Wine, Bacchus celebrated this past tragedy of the 'drunken Earth'. The crown – Corona Australis, found in the Galactic Center – symbolically worn by the Roman Ceasars was another reminder of this ancient 'orgy'. The priestly Catholic tradition of drinking wine during Mass or consuming the grape juice of the Fundamentalist Christians and the Orthodox Jews secretly carries this same ancient cosmic knowledge. We can pay 'salute' to the old bards who made this awful memory of earth destruction into a holy celebration or even much worse, a medieval pictorial depiction of drunken orgies of fat and balding, plump Greek gods.

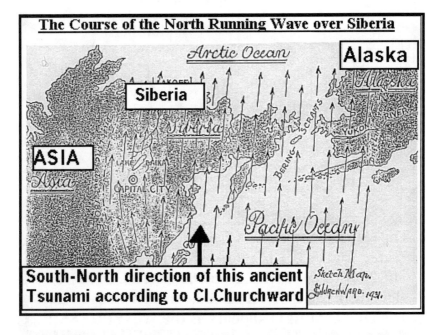

FIGURE 8-6A: The Large Tsunami During The Axis Shift (Slightly modified from the book of Col. James Churchward titled 'The Children of Mu', Courtesy of BE Books, Alb. NM)

Col. James Churchward a century ago showed the direction of a northwardly tsunami in the Pacific Ocean, which likely happened alongside Noah's Flood. Figure 8-6A shows that large tsunami.

Then Professor Andrews, a 1800th century American geologist quoted in the book Cataclysm! - mentions an 800 feet high tidal wave that deposited ocean sand only one side of the mountains and caused the extinction of the hairy mammoth. A tidal wave this high would bulldoze things flat for hundreds of miles inland and the salty sand would make the land sterile for harvest for several years. The volcanic ashes from the sky would block out the Sun for three years making any harvest impossible, thus setting up the land for the lethal seven years of famine. Both of these events fit the same timeline in our theory. If there were a North to South axis shift – as we demonstrated in Figure 8-5 - then it would certainly create a huge tidal wave toward the opposite direction from the fast axis shift. The simultaneous earthquakes could also be responsible for this unimaginable ancient tragedy. The most likely dates for these astronomical markers would be 11,600years ago. Today, the corresponding years would be 2006 or 2007 of the Venus Transit calendar. If 2006 or 2007 is the year of the birth of the Son of the Sun, then the 'She-goat / Capella' of the Charioteer lines up with the Sun around June 21st of the Summer Solstice. The second astronomical marker of the last eight would be in 2006 or 2007 that are the 'Donkeys' of the Crab. This alignment - of Cancer to the Sun - is during the July 26th to the mid-August period of the summer. This was the famed biblical 'early Harvest'. This time period coincides with the Day of the Lord, the Atonement, the Sacred Cosmic Marriage of the Egyptian Gods, and the 'five epagomenal days representing the birth of the Egyptian and Mayan Gods'. From the Hindu Myths we even have the Day:

> "On the sixth lunar day in the bright half of the month, when the moon is in the constellation Deer's Head, the son of Siva appeared on the surface of the earth."

"The day preceding the new moon, the day after the full moon, the day of the new moon and the day of the full moon – these auspicious days…the chariots shone …"
(Hindu Myths, Penguin Classics, pgs. 168 & 132)

The Hindu Deer Head constellation is apparently the top part of Orion. The crescent Moon would be in that position toward the end of September. So by different accounts the dates go from June 21st until the end of summer. The most prominent date still remains the early part of August for the beginning of this ancient tragedy. I am hoping that our inquiry into the exact date and the sequence of events surrounding the Deluge would make Noah have a smile with joy while he is watching over us from the Happy Hunting Grounds.

The most amazing astronomical story that ties this ancient enigma together is contained in Figure 8-5. If what we allege is true about this ancient axis shift then the North to South movement has to be documented in the sky with a number of important mythical animal constellations along with the winepress. And it is!

Let us start out slow with the celestial mythologies of these constellations in the sky to see if they match our assumptions. For a starter it is worth looking back to the previous chapter to study Figure 7-3 in which picture the spotted 'Lynx' cat is shown cutting off the head of Hydra, the Water Snake. It all happens next to the Sacred Tree 'axis', which will shift. The Cancer constellation with the claws that represents the 'scissors' to cut, also brilliantly shaped as an upside down 'delta' symbol, thus bringing the 'male' force back into a different depiction of the same earth change scenario. The Ra Priest carefully tailored and tied this ancient tragedy into a complex mythology. They labored very hard to give multiple examples and several interconnected meanings to each pictures.

Beginning with the tale of the Crab it is curious to learn that in Classical Greek mythology Hercules was closely involved with the Cancer. Hercules proved to be a natural born hero as early as a baby when with his chubby little hands he choked the life out of the two serpents Juno sent against him. Being a giant with enormous strength and bulging muscles Hercules still turned out to be a very studious pupil. Cherishing wisdom, he was educated by Chiron, the wise Centaur in preparation for his future Labors.

After his divine training he eagerly set out to save the world and to seek fortunes. He has not gotten too far in his journey before he ran into two beautiful ladies. One of them was called Virtue and the other maiden was named Vice. The latter one promised love, luck and riches to Hercules if he followed her. While the more modest and less fun loving Virtue warned him that if he followed her, poverty and a lot of hardship would ensue his noble heroic fights. This righteous giant desired nothing else, but to defeat evil in the world. In line with Chiron's teachings it did not take long for Hercules to come up with the right answer. After a brief, but thorough consideration of these two prospects offered to him Hercules naturally chose the difficult road ahead. He despised the easy travel on Pleasure's harlot train. After the successful completion of several good heroic deeds Hercules was allowed to marry the beautiful Princess Megara of Thebes. They had three gorgeous children and would have lived happily ever after, if Juno again had gotten jealous of his blissful fortune. This previously sane hero – if there is such a thing in a steroid laden and muscle bound world - was driven into a mad fit and killed his beloved wife and threw his three children into the fire. Does that remind some of you of the little 'Gipsy' kid who was mistakenly thrown into the fire in the Italian Opera of the Troubadour? Well, when Hercules came to his senses the intense remorse he felt drove him into a mountain escape. Not until Mercury came by with the decisions of the gods to have Hercules serve Eurystheus, King of Argon was he ready to take on his world saving tasks.

For his first labor he killed the Nemean Lion and on the second labor Hercules was sent out on an urgent service call to repair the 'marshes' of Lerna that was guarded by Hydra, the seven-headed water snake. The treacherous serpent was mindlessly killing off animals and innocent people, if there ever was such thing. With a sharp double-edged sword in his hands, Hercules begin chopping off the seven heads of Hydra, but as soon as the heads rolled off the beast's neck, seven more grew out of the severed stumps. Hercules' friend Iolaus started to cauterize the bleeding necks with a burning rod of iron in his hand. Finally, the two of them succeeded. Although, Hercules still had one more thing to do before it was all over. By stepping on the Crab he crushed the evil crustacean who was sent by Juno to bite at his feet. For his attempt the gods honored the Crab and placed him into the starry sky as the constellation Cancer. As an act of acknowledging victory Hercules dipped his arrow into the venom of Hydra for future use.

Now, before we continue with our heroic journey in fighting evil, let us look back at the Figure 8-5. Can you imagine that when the Northern Kingdom of the Magnetic North's iron rod 'swooped down' from the direction of the constellation 'Lynx' through the body of the 'Crab' - which consists of the notable Northern Donkey and the Southern Donkey – there was an action of squeezing out some fine pressed 'red wine' from the oceans. The 'sickle-shaped' head of Leo on the left side of the Figure is the likely 'winepress' that was pushed down toward the ecliptic for this visual imagery to take place. These and other symbols are widely displayed in our society.

Remember the Egyptian 'Lynx Cat' in earlier in Figure 7-3 and in Figure 8-1? In Chapter 7 she was cutting off the head of the snake by the sacred tree. In Chapter 8 in the first picture she stands as the second one in the row of the eight gods. See how all of this is carefully tied together by the Ra Priests?

The southern shift made the head of the Hydra – this monster of Loch Ness - bob in and out of the fiery oceans. The open 'claw-like-scissors' of the Crab reached toward the head of the water snake. An animal character that likely made the **Crab** a choice of the mythmakers was its peculiar habit of **'walking sideways'**, a movement mimicking the Earth's axis shift. This late summer period is when the Sun crosses in front of the Crab in the first few days of August. It is also the time when the five 'epagomenal' days were celebrated by the Mayans and the Egyptians. This is the same period when Hathor, the Goddess of Love traveled to meet her husband for the Sacred Cosmic Marriage Ceremony. This is the Day of the Lord, the 'early Harvest' when the Lord brought fire from Heaven. Thus, these Northern and Southern Donkeys marked the direction of the path of the axis shift and timed it to the early August day of the summer.

The **'Donkeys'** representing **'stubbornness in travel'** had to secretly signify that the Earth became stagnant after these Bachus-like drunken movements of our globe. Before we do any more arduous and heroic labors, let me draw your attention to the M 44 open star clusters named **Beehive**. Do you remember the inside contour of the Star of David? It had a 'beehive' shaped inner core. This important piece of Hebrew Wisdom means several things on multiple levels, but for us it represents the 'marrying together of the cosmic female and male pyramids'. This celestial sex act creates the Son of the Sun and in this instance the symbolic sacred geometry shape of the obvious 'Beehive'. The secret connotations of the golden colored viscous honey drop to the 'rapture' of the yellow Sun King needs not to be explained in details. Several depictions amongst the Egyptian wall paintings immortalize the swarm of bees attacking humans. At times these **bees have even been shown without heads**. **This headless state must be related to the concept of beheading of the water snake Hydra.**

The vicious attack of the venomous bees is a painful reminder to reenact the swarming of the sunrays burning the human skin during the enormous solar eruptions about 11,600years ago. See Figure 8-7. Now, let us examine the symbols of the Zodiac. The SCALE of Libra in the picture of Figure 8-6 will tilt exactly in a 90degree angle on the HORIZONTAL PLANE when the WINEPRESS is pushing down VERTICALLY!

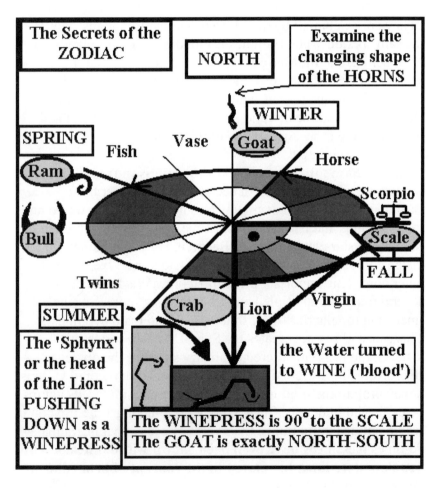

FIGURE 8-6B: The Secrets of the ZODIAC

Other than the She-Goat of Capella, we find another 'Goat' in the month of the Capricorn exactly to the North. Thus, the lesson is repeated where the 'Goat' pushes down from North to South (Galactic Plane) and the 'Scale' tilts along the East to West (Horizon / Ecliptic /Sun path) to cause the 'Winepress' to 'turn the waters of the oceans into wine.' As we can observe, there was no fault in the design of the ancient astronomer priests.

They perfectly matched their scientific messages on multiple levels. It was our understanding that was lacking. If the zealous corrupt priests of the Dark Ages had their ways we would not have most of these information to work with. The lesson is that religious tolerance in all ages should be the norm. History teaches us that most of the time in the past our blind folded religious tendency was not to realize the significant secrets that were carefully woven into the sacred books. Always we are so eager to burn any holy books that different from our own or have the 'godly' calling to stump out the remnants of ancient rituals of any old belief systems that are different from our own dogma. Only wisdom based careful inspection of these seemingly differing religious practices will yield the mainly elusive 'illuminative' understanding that in the 'core' all of these sacred teachings lye the same cosmic message whether it is from Africa or Europe.

Returning to the picture of Figure 8-6, another interesting observation is that the SPIRAL horns of Aries representing the beginning of the ancient year and the spiral Galactic Forces are followed by the BULL HORNS of Taurus, which stands for the 'Two axes' of Earth. It makes perfect sense, since the two spirals are controlling the axis of the Magnetic North and Polar North. Further up 'north' in our Figure we can see the 'Horns of the Goat' being still spiral in nature, but it is 'stretched out' in the North South direction. Is it only a coincidence or an incredibly marvelous design? We will never know.

The 'goat' imagery brings back childhood memories about the 'two stubborn goats' fighting on a fallen log of tree across a deep trench. One of the goats succeeded in his attempt to 'ram' its way across that deep fissure. The mountain goat combines the wisdom of the Ram and the Goat along with the fallen axis of the Earth.

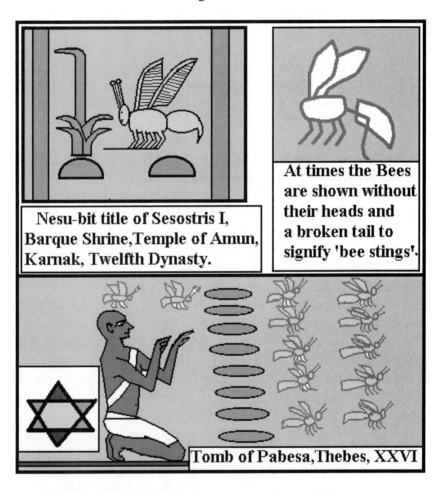

Nesu-bit title of Sesostris I, Barque Shrine, Temple of Amun, Karnak, Twelfth Dynasty.

At times the Bees are shown without their heads and a broken tail to signify 'bee stings'.

Tomb of Pabesa, Thebes, XXVI

FIGURE 8-7: The Meaning of Bees and the Beehive
(Modified from Wilkinson's Reading Egyptian Art)

In Figure 8-7 at the left upper hand corner the picture shows what looks like two pillars and a dry plant along with the two half cycle hieroglyphs. It is not just about an annoying little insect! The 'bee' is positioned in between the 'Two Pillars' of the Earth and between the 'Two Half Cycles' - each representing the end of a 12,000year period. Now we know what the 'buzz' is about.

The Star of David is my addition into the picture. The inside of it clearly depicts the 'beehive' shape. One may even associate the six sides with six illuminated beams coming out of an overheated Sun. On top is a small 'pyramid' representing the 'male force' and the bottom portion displays the 'feminine force' of an upside down pyramid. I guess, having a golden sun-colored drop of honey or a 'swarm of buzzing bees' in between this sensuous pyramid couple ready to perform the cosmic sex act is initially a strange concept. On either side of the beehive is a 'sand clock' indicating that the center is dividing two important time cycles. How much sacred information can we derive from geometry? This is simple brilliance of the Ancients! The upper right hand corner depicts a headless bee that fits our theory. The bottom portion is actually originally titled as an - 'agricultural scene showing hives and the collection of honey'. I have some strong disagreement about that with the scholars. First of all the man is holding both hands in the typical Egyptian posture of 'adoration'. He adores the incredible force of Nature that moves and shakes things that have not been real active in 12,000years. The fact that he is half naked around a swarm of bees puts a little doubt in my mind about his true intentions in collecting honey.

Returning back to Figure 8-5 I can share another hunch with my readers. The 130degrees on the horizontally placed ecliptic reminds me that some sacred tales talk about the 130 shekels it takes to buy a bride. Is it related to celestial coordinates? What about the number 30 or even the 10 percent in the Bible? Is it a distance in the vertical measure of shift? Surely, I do not know.

With the importance of the 'bee hive' one more vital clue is revealed to us. The 'bear' is not only chosen because it can get on top of the 'sacred tree' and it is a 'polar' animal', but also the fact that it climbs the 'axis tree' to steal some 'honey'. Big Trouble!

In conclusion of my research, I would like to thank my readers who stayed with me through out this book. I covered a number of areas of astronomical secrets explaining an ancient disaster that happened almost 12,000years ago and is connected to the Flood of Noah. May be by better understanding our tragic past, we will be able to avoid needless sufferings in the future. I have to say that there are still a whole lot more secrets left for anybody who is genuinely interested to discover. These secrets came to me through – not by being PhD flashing academia, not by joining Bible study groups or elite research organizations – but by my own personal study, dreams, visions and prayers. Only by believing in a Perfect Righteous Common Creator Force for all humans - while ignoring the dangerous and vicious dogmas of most religions - I was able to come this far with my own theory. Only a spiritual universal scientific approach will reveal cosmic truths about the rhythm of endless creation. No need to worry, the Creator will not be mad at you for respectfully looking at its other creations. His name is the Almighty for a good reason. 'He/She' has created and continues to govern everything in this Universe. Although, we sometimes might believe it happened by mistake - He even formed all your strange neighbors and funky relatives. Thus, the moral teaching to 'love thy neighbor' is still valid even though he or she may not only act, but also believe different from your own. Within the confines of some loose and innocent basic moral tenets, let us celebrate our colorful and vivid spontaneous creative differences. Anybody who is willing to follow simply the 'Golden Rule' will be able to be a member of our Global Village. Let us learn from each other.

Glossary of terms and the name of gods.

Ahat   -   A Cow Goddess.

Aker   - The 'twin lion' deity. Incidentally 'Iker' means 'twins'
   In Hungarian and also 'two' is similar in Mongolian.

Akert-khentet-auset-s - One of the seven deities mentioned in
   The Book of the Dead. These seven provided food for
   the Deceased in the Underworld and commonly
   depicted as wearing horns on their head with the solar
   disk in between.

Akhet - Goddess of the Nile, seasons and the sunset.

Ament – Goddess who lived in a tree by the edge of the desert.
   Protector of the West, guardian of the gate to the
   Afterworld.

Amenti – The western gate to the abode of the dead.

Amun   - **(Amen, Amon, Ammon, Amoun)** A main Ram-
   Headed God, commonly shown with two consorts.
   Several related or identical deities are Amun-Ra, or
   also spelled Amen-Ra, and Amon-Re (The Great Sun).
   Amen also means 'Hidden'.

Amset - **(Ameshet)** One of the Four Sons of Horus. The others
   were Hapi, Duamutef, and Qebhsenuef.

Anatha - A mountain goddess.

Anatis - The goddess of the moon.

Anka   - A creator goddess, Khnum's wife.

Anpu / Anubis - Canine Son of Osiris. Came from his affair with
   the harlot goddess Nephthys. He was also worshipped
   under the name 'Upuaut' (Opener of the Road).

Anuket - The companion or daughter of Khnum and Sati. Her
   sacred animal was the gazelle.

Apep -   The great Snake Deity of Darkness.
Apis -   The Sacred Bull usually crowned with the solar disk and the uraeus serpent.
Apophis – The Serpent.
Ashtoreth - Lion-headed Goddess of War and Goddess of the Moon, but also associated with the planet Venus. Linguistically related to the Syrian Astarte or the Babylonian Ishtar, who stood for Venus.
Aton / Aten - The Sun itself. The heretic young Pharaoh Akhen-Aton declared Aton to be the only true 'God', in His attempt to establish a monotheistic religion in the XVIII. Dynasty.
Atum – A primordial god. His name is spelled by a sleigh and an owl. The meaning of the sleigh the 'tem / tum' in words both mean 'complete and incomplete', the eternal, the opposites in union therefore symbolizes the endless cosmic cycle. This Egyptian god was likely the originator for the biblical name of Adam.
Bahet - Goddess of wealth and abundance.
Bakha – The incarnation of Menthu as the Sacred Bull, a personification of the heat of the sun.
Bastet – A lion or a feline goddess symbolizing the fertilizing force of the Sun's rays. She is also associated with the eye of the sun god, Ra.
Baht   - Emblem of the goddess Bat / Hathor.
Bes   - The patron deity for pregnant women, children, music. Commonly depicted full facing as a bearded dwarf.
Bubastis-Goddess of childbirth.
Busiris – A king of Egypt, who sacrificed strangers to the gods during a period of famine. He even captured Hercules, who escaped and returned to slay the king.
Buto - Serpent goddess of Lower Egypt who spits poison and fire on the enemies of the Pharaoh.
Cartouche – An elliptical seal encircling the Pharaoh's names.
Cheops – A royal name of a Pharaoh. Khufu is another version.

Chem - The god of increase. Also pronounced or spelled Ham.
Crocodilopolis – The home of the Crocodile deity.
Dendera – A sacred city in Egypt associated with Hathor.
Djed pillar – A symbolic act of the 'raising of the Djed
    pillar' by the pharaoh, such as Seti I, was a ceremonial
    re enactment for the resurrection of Osiris.
Duamutef – One of the four sons of Horus. Shown as a
    Mummified man with Jackal head.
Geb   - Masculine god representation of the Earth
Hagar - A desert goddess of Lower Egypt.
Hak - A frog-headed goddess of resurrection.
Hapi - One of the four sons of Horus. Protector god of the
    River Nile. Represented as a mummified man with a
    Head of a Baboon.
Harpocrates – (Hor-pa-kraat) "Horus the Child", the son of Isis
    and Osiris. God of silence. Likely originator of the
    biblical Old Testamental 'Child' concept.
Hast - One of the goddesses of the Underworld.
Hathor –(Het-Heru, Het-Hert) "The House of Horus" She is
    the goddess of femininity, fertility, dance and song.
    Her headdress includes the sun disk in between the
    horns worn by her.
Heqet - A primordial frog-headed goddess.
Horus - (Hor, Heru) The falcon-headed son of Osiris and Isis.
    One of the most important deities of Egypt. Upon
    reaching adulthood he avenges his father's death. He
    defeats and castrates Set, his evil uncle. As *Heru-Ur*,
    "Horus the Elder" he is considered as the patron deity of
    Upper Egypt (Southern Kingdom or 'Polar North'?).
Ihy - The god who plays the sistrum.
Imhotep – The god of science and medicine.
Isis – **(Auset)** The goddess of marriage, love, motherhood.
    She is the Mother of Horus. She has learned the Secret
    Name of Ra and became the most powerful healer.

Ka – Thought of as a kind of Spirit, Vital Force of Life or the metaphysical 'double' of a person. In the hieroglyphic form it is depicted as two connected and raised arms.

Khepri / Kheper - The scarab-headed creator god symbolic of the Sun and is associated with 'create & transform'.

Khnemu / Khnum – A ram-headed god similar to Amun who fashioned humans on the potter's wheel.

Khonsu- God of the Moon. Amen and Mut are his parents.

Khufu – See Cheops.

Maat - The daughter of Ra and the wife of Thoth. Goddess of Truth and Justice, implying "Cosmic Order". She wears the ostrich feather in her hair as an Indian would. Her feather used to weigh the heart of the deceased on the Scale at the Judgment scene of the Dead.

Mentu – A falcon-headed war god of Thebes.

Min (Menu) – A form of Amen with an erect penis holding a flail of the pharaoh. His full name means 'Min, Bull of his Mother'. Worshiped as the God of Virility.

Mut - Mother Goddess. The wife of Amen in Thebes and the mother of Khonsu, the moon god.

Nefertari – (Aahmes) Protector / punisher goddess of humans.

Nefertiti – Queen Nefertiti.

Nefertem – The young son of Ptah and Sekhmet, associated with the rising sun. Associated with the Lotus. The spelling of his name consists of a Harp (trachea and heart), Worm, Mouth, Sled, and an Owl.

Neith – Ancient goddess of war.

Netcher (Neter)– Means 'God'. Similar sounding to Nature.

Netcheret – Means 'Goddess'.

Nekhbet – Patron Goddess of Upper Egypt.

Nephthys (Nebt-het) The youngest child of Geb (Male Earth) and Nut (Female Sky). The sister and wife of evil Set and invariably the mother of Anubis by Osiris (or Set). After Set murdered his brother Osiris, Nephthys abandoned him and she helped her sister Isis to resurrect Osiris and to care for Horus. She is Goddess of the West and protector of the dead. In my theory she is the equivalent of the biblical Harlot.

Nut – (Nuit) Daughter of Shu and Tefnut, sister and wife of Geb, mother of Osiris, Set, Isis, and Nephthys. She is the Goddess of the Sky depicted arching over her husband with blue skin covered with stars.

Osiris (Ausar, Woseer, "Vizier/Vezir") – He is the God of Resurrection. The first-born child of Geb and Nut. He is the Judge of the Dead in the Underworld and ruler of the Afterlife. Osiris was killed by his jealous brother Set. His name is written as a Feather, Quail Chick, Eye, Square, Horizon or Half Circle and a Candy Cane. According to legends, Osiris ruled the world of men in the beginning, after the Sun God, Ra had abandoned it to rule the sky.

Pakhet – Lion-goddess.

Pharaoh – Deified God King 'the Son of the Sun God, Ra'.

Ptah - Creator God of the Universe. Worshipped in Memphis. Husband of Sekhmet and the father of Nefertem. He is commonly depicted as a bearded man wearing a skullcap and holding in his hands the Scepter, Djed and the Ankh signs.

Qebhsenuef- One of the Four Sons of Horus. Shown as a mummified man with the head of a Falcon.

Qetesh – Goddess of Love and Beauty, who is shown naked, standing or riding upon a lion. Considered a consort of Min, god of virility.

Ra – (Re / Rah) The Sun God. He is connected to or identified with Horus. Considered as a Creative Principle. In the Fifth Dynasty, Userkaf, a High Priest of Ra added the term 'Sa-Ra' (Sah-Rah / Shah-Ra) meaning 'Son of the Sun' to the titles of the pharaohs. Ra was the father of Shu and Tefnut, grandfather of Geb (Earth) and Nut (Sky) and great-grandfather to Osiris, Set, Isis and Nephthys. By this he became the great-great-grandfather of Horus, who he was also identified with.

Ramses II- (Ra-Mes-SS /Ramsess) An apparent Pharaoh. Even mentioned in the Old Testament of the Bible. "Wesir-Maat-Ra" was his crowning name of his reign, which consist of a Sun symbol, a Jackal-headed staff and the goddess Maat. The crowning cartouche of Ramses II is also translated as "Powerful is the balance of Ra.", that is understood in a cosmic sense.

Ra-Horakhty (Ra-Hoor-Khuit) - "Ra, who is Horus of the Horizon."

Sata – Serpent Spirit, Sata. Along with Set, likely the originator of the biblical concept of Satan. Shown amongst the hieroglyphics as a Goose, Belt with Three Circles and a Serpent.

Sati (Satis / Satet) – Archer goddess who personified the waterfalls of the Nile.

Sebek (Seb, Sobek) – The Crocodile Deity. Corresponds to the Dragon in Nordic or Judeo-Christian mythology. In the Middle Kingdom, as 'Sebek-Ra' it was worshipped as a primordial deity.

Seker – The god of death.

Sekhet – The wife of Ptah in the ennead of Memphis.

Sekhmet – A powerful Lion Goddess associated with the Sun. When the Sun God Ra grew angry at the people, he ripped out one of his eyes and threw it to the Earth where it became Sekhmet, a ravaging lion goddess.

Selket – A scorpion goddess.

Serapis – In Greco-Roman version is an alternative designation of Osiris and it referred to the Underworld.

Seshat – Goddess of books and writing.

Set (Seth) – God of the desert. The son of Geb and Nut. The evil brother and killer of Osiris.

Setekh – Means hound.

Seti I – Thought to be an apparent historical pharaoh.

Shu – Child of Ra. Husband of Tefnut and the father of Geb and Nut. Shu holds up the sky as God of Air and his wife Tefnut is the Goddess of Dew, Rain, and Daybreak, thus associated with the eastern mountain of sunrises.

Sothis – Egyptian feminine name for the dog-star Sirius, whose rise heralded the Egyptian New Year. The Egyptians kept a Sothic Calendar, which lasted 1460years.

Smotef – One of the Four Lesser Gods of the Dead.

Snouf – Hawk headed god. His name means 'bleeder'. He is one of the Four Lesser Gods of the Dead.

Sottef / Smotef – One of the Four Lesser Gods of the Dead.

Tauret – A hippopotamus goddess, an animal form of the Goddess Mut. At times depicted as a pregnant hippo.

Tefnut – The Goddess of Dew and Rain, associated with the daybreak.

Thoth – The 'scribe', that is the Ibis-headed God of Learning.

Ua – One of the Goddesses of the Underworld.

Uat – Goddess of Water.

Udjat – It is the Eye of Ra or the Eye of Horus. In another version it is Atum, the creator god who only has one eye, the Udjat eye.

Wadjeet – The Cobra Goddess

Sacred Cosmic Marriage

ALPHABETIC MEANINGS
OF HIEROGLYPHIC SINGS
(After Wilkinson's Reading Egyptian Art)

	A (Aleph) **Alpha**		**C** (Gimel) **Gamma**
	Á (AA/Ah) **A accent**		**H/E** Ⓔ (Heh)
	B (Beth) **Beta**		**H**
	D (Daleth) **Delta**		**KH** (Khet)
	DJ		**KH**
	F (Feh)		**I** (Ee)

271

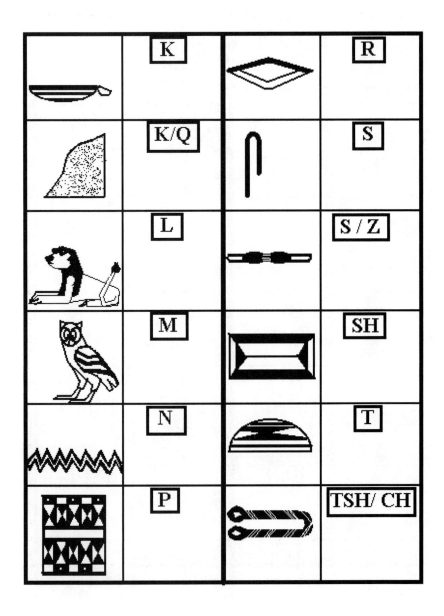

	K		R
	K/Q		S
	L		S / Z
	M		SH
	N		T
	P		TSH/ CH

	W / U 'OO'		AH-OO
	W / U 'OO'		AH-A
	Y		AHDJ
	Y		AHK
	AB		BAH
	AKH		BEH/Hoo

273

	DJA		HEDJ
	DJED		HEM
	DJER		HEM
	DJOO		HEN
	GEM		HER
	HA		HES

	KHA		KHEN
	KHÁH		KHER
	KHET		EEN
	KHOO		EER
	KHA		EES
	KHEN		YOO

	KA		MEE
	KEM		MEN
	KED		MER (?)
	KES		MER
	MA		MES
	MEH		MET

	MOO (MU)		NEN
	NEB		NES
	NEB		NET
	NEDJ		NOO (NU)
	NEH		PA
	NEM		PEH

	PER		**SEN**
	ROO		**SET**
	SA / ZA		**SOO (SU)**
	ZA / SA		**SHA**
	SAH		**SHED**
	SEK		**SHEN**

	SHES		TSHA (CHA)
	SHOO (SHU)		TSHEZ (CHEZ)
	TA		WA
	TA		WAH
	TEE (TI)		OODJ (UDJ)
	TEM		OON (UN)

	OON (UN)		HOT
	OOP OP ? (UP)		HEKA
	OOR (UR)		HETEP
	AH-HAH		KHEPER
	ANKH		KHEROO (KHERU)
	AHSHA		KHENEM

	YOON (YUN)		**ROODJ (RUDJ)**
	MENEKH		**SEBA (SHEBA?)**
	MOOT (MUT)		**SEE-AH**
	NEDJEM		**SEKHEM**
	NEFER		**SEMA**
	NETCHER		**SENEDJ**

	SHEMAH		WAS
	SHEMES		OOHEM (UHEM)
	SHESEP		OOSER (WESIR)
	TYOO (TYU)		
	WADJ		
	WAH		

BIBLIOGRAPHY

1. Agnese, Giorgio and Re, Maurizio, *Ancient Egypt,* Barnes & Noble, New York, 2001.
2. Allan, D. S., and Delair, J.B., *Cataclysm!* Bear & Co., Santa Fe, 1997.
3. Barnstone, Willis, The Other Bible, Harper, San Francisco, 1984.
4. Bauval, Robert and Gilbert, Adrian, *The Orion Mystery,* Crown Publishers, New York, 1994.
5. Bell, Art and Strieber, Whitley, *The Coming Global Superstorm,* Pocket Books, New York, 1999.
6. Blavatsky, H.P., *Isis Unveiled I & II,* Theosophical University Press, Pasadena, 1988.
7. Boyle, Ed and Weaver, Andrew, *Conveying Past Climates,* Nature, 3 November 1994.
8. Broecker, Wallace S., *Massive Iceberg Discharges As Triggers For Global Climate Change,* Nature, 1 December 1994.
9. Budge, E. A. Wallis, *An Egyptian Hieroglyphic Dictionary,* Dover Publications, Inc., New York, 1978.
10. Budge, E. A. Wallis, *Legends of the Egyptian Gods,* Dover Publications, Inc., New York, 1994.
11. Budge, E. A. Wallis, *The Egyptian Book Of The Dead,* Dover Publications, Inc., New York, 1967.
12. Campbell, Joseph, *The Hero With A Thousand Faces,* Bollingen Foundation, New York, 1949.
13. Childress, David Hatcher, *Lost Cities series,* AUP, Kempton
14. Churchward, James, *The Sacred Symbols of Mu,* BE Books/ Brotherhood of Life, Inc., Albuquerque, 1995.
15. Clark, Rosemary, Sacred Tradition in Ancient Egypt, Llewellyn, St.Paul, MN., 2000.

16. Cotterell, Arthur, *Classical Mythology,* Lorenz Books, New York, 1999.
17. Cotterell, Arthur and Storm, Rachel, *The Ultimate Encyclopedia Of Mythology,* Hermes House, London, 2003.
18. Cotterell, Maurice, *The Tutankhamon Prophecies,* Headline Book Publishing, London, 1999.
19. Covey, Curt, *The Earth's Orbit And The Ice Ages,* Scientific American,
20. Ducz, Laszlo, *The Hawk That Lives Amongst Us,* Antologia Publishing, Lakitelek, 1993.
21. Ekruff, Joachim, *Stars and Planets,* Barron's Nature Guide.
22. Eliade, Mircea, *Patterns In Comparative Religion,* Meridian Books, Cleveland, 1966.
23. Erikson, Jon, *Ice Ages,* TAB Books, Blue Ridge Summit, 1990.
24. Farrington, Karen, *The History Of Religion,* Barnes & Noble, New York, 2001.
25. Folger, Tim, *Waves Of Destruction,* Discover, May 1994.
26. Gaer, Joseph, *How The Great Religions Began,* Dodd, Mead & Company, New York, 1957.
27. Gadalla, Moustafa, Tut-Ankh-Amen. The Living Image Of The Lord, Bastet Publishing, Erie, Pa., 1997.
28. Gaspar, William A., *The Celestial Clock,* Adam & Eva Publishing, Inc., Clovis, N.M., 2002.
29. Gideons International, *The Holy Bible,* Thomas Nelson, Inc., 1985.
30. Gilbert, Adrian G. and Cotterell, M.M., *The Mayan Prophecies,* Element, Boston, 1995.
31. Guerber, H. A., *The Myths Of Greece And Rome,* Dover Publications, Inc., Mineola, 1993.
32. Halevi, Z'ev ben Shimon, *The Work Of The Kabbalist,* Samuel Weiser, Inc., Maine, 1986.
33. Hancock, Graham, *Fingerprints Of The Gods,* Crown Trade Paperbacks, New York, 1995.
34. Heidel, Alexander, *Gilgamesh Epic And Old Testament Parallels,* University Of Chicago Press, Chicago, 1971.
35. Hoppal, Mihaly, *Shamans,* Helikon Publishers, Budapest, 1994.

36. Horgan, John, *Antarctic Meltdown,* Scientific American, March, 1993.
37. Hornung, Erik, *The Ancient Egyptian Books Of The Afterlife,* Cornell University Press, Ithaca and London, 1999.
38. Jackson, Joseph H., and Baumert, John, *Pictorial Guide To The Planets,* Harper & Row Publishers, New York, 1981.
39. Jenkins, John Major, *Maya Cosmogenesis 2012,* Bear & Co. Publishing, Santa Fe, N.M., 1998.
40. Jenkins, John Major, *Galactic Alignment,* Bear & Co. / Inner Traditions Publishing, Rochester, Vermont, 2002.
41. James, T.G.H. and De Luca, A., *Tutankhamun,* White Star / Metro Books, Vercelli, Italy /New York, 2000.
42. James, T.G.H., *Ramesses II,* White Star / Friedman & Fairfax, Vercelli, Italy / New York, 2002.
43. Kerr, Richard A. *Even Warmer Climates Get The Shivers,* Science, 16 July 1993.
44. Kerr, Richard A., *No Way To Cool The Ultimate Greenhouse,* Science, 29 October 1993.
45. Kerr, Richard A., *The Whole World Had A Case Of The Ice Age Shivers,* Science, 24 December 1993.
46. Kersey, Graves, *The World's Sixteen Crucified Saviors,* Adventures Unlimited Press, Kempton, 2001.
47. Kiszely, Istvan, *The Ancient History Of The Hungarians,* ELTE University Publishing, Budapest, 1996.
48. Kortvelyessy, Laszlo, *The Electric Universe,* Edition EFO, Budapest, 1998.
49. Kovacs, Maureen Gallery, *The Epic Of Gilgamesh,* Stanford University Press, Stanford, 1989.
50. LaViolette, Paul, *Earth Under Fire,* Starlane Publications, Schenectady, 1997.
51. Lesko, Barbara, S. *The Great Goddesses of Egypt,* University of Oklahoma Press, Norman, 1999.
52. Levy, David H., *Skywatching,* Time Life Books, San Francisco, 1995.
53. Mariner, Rodney, Rabbi, *The Torah*, Henry Holt and Company, Inc. New York, 1996.

54. Maspero, Gaston Sir, *Popular Stories of Ancient Egypt,* Oxford University Press, New York, 2004.
55. Moncrieff, Hope, A.R., *A Treasury Of Classical Mythology,* Barnes & Noble, New York, 1992.
56. Muller, W. Max, *Egyptian Mythology,* Dover Publications, Inc. Mineola, N.Y., 2004.
57. O'Flaherty, Doniger Wendy, *Hindu Myths,* Penguin Books, London, 1975.
58. Oakes, Lorna and Gahlin, Lucia, *Ancient Egypt,* Hermes House, London, 2002.
59. Ovid, *Ovid's Metamorphoses,* P.W. Suttaby and B. Crosby & Co., London, 1807.
60. Patrick, Richard, *Greek Mythology,* Chartwell Books, Inc., Secaucus, 1989.
61. Patrick, Richard and Croft, Peter, *Classic Ancient Mythology,* Crescent Books, New York, 1988.
62. Petrie, Flinders W.M., *Egyptian Tales,* Dover Publications, Inc., Mineola, N.Y., 1999.
63. Pike, Albert, *Morals And Dogma,* AASR / TSCOTTSJ, Charleston, 1871.
64. Plato, *Timaeus,* Liberal Arts Press, New York, 1959.
65. Potok, Chaim, *Wanderings: History Of The Jews,* Fawcett Crest, New York, 1980.
66. Raymo, Chet, *365 Starry Nights,* Fireside / Simon & Schuster, Inc., New York, 1982.
67. Roberts, T.R., Roberts, M.J. and Katz, B.P., *Mythology,* Metro Books, New York, 1997.
68. Ruddiman, W. F. and McIntire, A., *Oceanic Mechanisms For Amplification Of The 23,000 Year Ice Volume Cycle,* Science, Vol. 212, #4495, 8 May 1981.
69. Rukl, A., *The Encyclopedia Of Stars & Planets,* Ivy Leaf Publishing, London, 1982.
70. Santillana, Giorgio De, and Von Dechend, Hertha, *Hamlet's Mill,* Gambit, Boston, 1969.
71. Schumann-Antelme & Stephane Rossini, *Illustrated Hieroglyphics Handbook,* Sterling Publishing Co., Inc., New York, 2002.

72. Schwaller de Lubicz, R. A. *The Temple Of Man,* Inner Traditions International, Rochester, Vermont, 1998.
73. Seredy, Kate, *The White Stag,* Viking Press, New York, 1969.
74. Silverman, David P. *Ancient Egypt,* Oxford University Press, New York, 2003.
75. Ulansey, David, *The Origins Of The Mithraic Mysteries,* Oxford University Press, New York, 1989.
76. West, John Anthony, *Serpent In The Sky,* Versa Press / Theosophical Publishing House, Wheaton, 1993.
77. White, Robert M., *The Great Climate Debate,* Scientific American, Vol. 263, Number 1, Pg. 36, July 1990.
78. Wilkinson, Richard, H. *Reading Egyptian Art,* Thames and Hudson, London, 1992.

PERMISSIONS

We are grateful to the following institutions; individuals and authors for allowing us to quote, modify and use their material. Thanks to:

- BE Books Publishing, Albuquerque, and N.M.
- The Trustees of the British Museum, London
- The Trustees of the University Museum, Philadelphia
- Dover Publications, Inc., New York
- Adventures Unlimited Press, Kempton, IL
- Stanford University Press, Stanford
- Sterling Publishing Co., Inc., New York
- Thames and Hudson, London
- Oxford University Press, New York
- To the independent authors and progressive scientists
- Inga Szekely and her parents Laszlo & Erzsi Szekely for the use of their Egyptian photographs
- My wife, Eva and our children for discussing ideas
- My friend Ben Garcia for discussing some of these ideas
- To the Australian Aboriginal, Nordic Nomadic, Chinese, Hun and Ugorian, Phoenician, Sumerian, Native African, Hawaiian, Polynesian, Arab, Persian, Hindu, Siberian, Tibetan, Hebrew and Native American cultures that maintained customs and rituals even before writing and civilization permeated our lives.
- To the unknowing religious masses who for thousands of years carried the knowledge of written wisdom to this time of possible scientific interpretation.

About The Author

William A. Gaspar, MD is a full time Internal Medicine doctor in New Mexico. He was born in Pittsburgh in 1957, and by 1961 his family relocated back to Europe, first to Germany and very shortly afterwards they ended up in Hungary. William grew up in poverty in the Communist country, but he has good memories of his childhood and glad that he received an excellent education in Europe. In 1976 he met Eva and they have been together for almost 30years now. They have two adult children; Rubina Xenia and Austin Keane.

William became interested in Earth changes, Ice Age cycles and Astronomy in the form of Comparative Mythology in 1981, the year he came back to the US after escaping from Hungary with his family. He had strong unexplained spiritual push to study those various subjects. Initially, he had difficulty finding the time, because relearning the English language, starting College first then Medical School along with taking care of his family was more than a full time obligation. Although, he could hardly find the time, William had to spend more and more time researching the issues that were keeping his spiritual fire burning. The last 25years he is researching the meanings of the scientific and astronomical secrets hidden in various sacred books. He writes his books part time. His first book 'The Celestial Clock' was published a few years ago. This 'Sacred Cosmic Marriage' is his second work. A third one is currently being edited and expected to be out by the late summer of 2006. It is titled 'The Harlot' and it will be a fictional novel.

About the Publisher

Adam & Eva Publishing, Inc. is located in North Central New Mexico, about 45 minutes away from Taos. It is a self-publishing company founded by William A. Gaspar, MD and Eva Gaspar. Its purpose is not to put out money making best selling books that have to compromise the quality and profoundness of its message to meet the needs of a larger segment of the population. These scholarly books are written for those who are searching for the Universal Cosmic Truth amongst the pages of the ancient Holy Books of any culture. Finally, today's science has caught up with the astronomical and cosmic sciences of the Ancients, who knew and wrote about an ancient disaster. We will only dispense extremely well researched and clearly documented, albeit rebellious, ideas that can be found in the Holy Books and rituals of major cultures.

You may purchase any of these books either in your bookstore, on Amazon.com or by sending a $24.00 or a $18.00 personal check or Money order for either books:

1., 'The Celestial Clock' by Wm. Gaspar ($24)
2., 'Sacred Cosmic Marriage' by Gaspar ($24)
3., "The Harlot' by Wm. Gaspar ($18)
   this includes the $4 S+H fee and the price of the book. Discounts on multiple books can be discussed by calling 1-505-387-5816
   On 2-5 books only one S+H is charged!
   Allow 2-3 weeks to receive book.
Address: **Adam & Eva Publishing, Inc., P.O. Box 241, Holman, N.M. 87723**
(please, indicate which title!)